INSIDE INDONESIAN SOCIETY

Other Niels Mulder titles published by The Pepin Press:

Inside Thai Society
Interpretations of Everyday Life

Inside Southeast Asia
Religion • Everyday Life • Cultural Change

For a complete list of Pepin Press publications, write or fax to the address overleaf.

Niels Mulder

INSIDE INDONESIAN SOCIETY

Cultural Change in Java

THE PEPIN PRESS

Amsterdam • Kuala Lumpur

First published by The Pepin Press in 1996

Second edition of *Inside Indonesian Society. An Interpretation of Cultural Change in Java.*
Editions Duang Kamol, Bangkok (1994).

© 1996, Niels Mulder
© for this edition, The Pepin Press BV

ISBN 90 5496 026 4

This book is edited, designed and produced by The Pepin Press
Editor: Dorine van den Beukel
Cover photos: Luca Invernizzi Tettoni

The Pepin Press
POB 10349
1001 EH Amsterdam
TEL 31 20 4202021
FAX 31 20 4201152

Printed in Singapore

Contents

Preface

Historically, it may be argued that my connexion with Java begins in the late 16th century when the first traders from Amsterdam arrived on the shores of what is now known as Indonesia. Ever since then, the archipelago has attracted Dutchmen by the droves, although not always for academic reasons. Yet even that first expedition already yielded a method for the study of Malay,[1] then as now the *lingua franca* of a far-flung trading territory in which the various nations of Southeast Asia met each other and the merchants of the world.

Whether the intrusion of the Europeans into this commerce was an auspicious or ominous occurrence should be left to others to judge. It seems to be the fortune and the fate of Southeast Asia to be a crossroads where Indians, Chinese, and Arabs met before they were joined by the forerunners of what is now called the era of European expansion. From early exchanges and discovery, this led to trading empires, colonization and subjugation, then to political independence and the spread of western cultural forms known as globalization.

Be that as it may, being born in the later days of empire, Indonesia was naturally on my mental map. Presented as an exotic string of emerald islands stretching along the equator, it exercised a powerful spell and stirred my fantasies. Later, at university, my interest was disciplined by all those scholars who had worked in the colony and come back to Holland to teach. As they focussed my interests on matters of culture and society, a potential career centring on Southeast Asia gradually came to seem a possibility.

Because of historical circumstances, it was not immediately possible to go to Indonesia when I graduated in 1964. By way of Thailand and the South-East Asia studies programme of Northern Illinois University, I finally reached the country early in 1969. My aim was to do research in Java, a project that evolved into a fascination with contemporary culture: how do they understand and conceptualize; how do they look at life; how do they evaluate their experiences?

Over the years that I have been coming to Yogyakarta, it has

---

1 Denys Lombard (ed), *Le "Spraeck-ende Woord-boek" de Frederick de Houtman, première methode de Malais parlé (fin du XVIe siècle)*, PEFEO 74. Paris: Maisonneuve, 1970.

always been these questions that have preoccupied me and that have given direction to my activities, such as questioning, interviewing, discussing, reading, looking around, then interpreting. But making statements about 'them', the anonymous others, 'the Javanese', is hazardous and demands caution. I know some people in town, urban educated folk, who were and are kind enough to teach me and to engage in an exchange of opinions. It is because of these contacts that I have had the temerity to say something about a Javanese way of perceiving that I think can be identified in many aspects of Indonesian life as it is unfolding in modern Java.

Culturally conditioned perception is not static or unchangeable, although it normally alters more slowly than the pace of changing circumstance. As a mental guide through life, it needs to respond to the novel and the new, from fan to ventilator to air-conditioning, from horse-drawn *andong* to pedicab to passenger van to urban bus, from sultanate to republic to global affairs, from poverty to development to progress. Such evolutions all took place during the relatively short period that I have been associated with the people and the town of Yogyakarta; this process is reflected in my writings.

My dissertation, *Mysticism and Everyday Life in Contemporary Java*, has definitely lost its contemporaneity now. It reflects life in the early days of the present political order when the town was relatively isolated and still untouched by Development. The observations date from my first field work in 1969-70, with a follow-up in 1973. When I came back on three occasions around 1980, so much had changed that I needed to do a new book to explain the dynamics of culture in Yogya. In *Individual and Society in Java*, I analyzed the evolving trends, many of which — but not all — continued into the early 1990s when I had another chance to visit for almost three months. The results are recorded in this present work.

Over all these years, many people have helped me to learn to see and understand, to observe and interpret, and the list of those to whom I am indebted for sharing their knowledge with me, for guidance, discussion, criticism, and advice, or for hospitality, comfort, and interest, is too long to recount. The most relevant persons have been acknowledged in my previous writings, and it was a pleasure to meet quite a few of them again earlier this year. Most people who contributed to my new insights, however, were of a younger generation. Generally, I met them during and after seminars where we discussed gender ideology and feminism, interreligious relationships, the concept of power, indigenous psychology, human rights, and other topics that were in the forefront of their, or our, minds. Often they came to me to seek advice about academic assignments or how to realize hopes and plans for the future.

In Yogyakarta, I had the pleasure and the privilege of enjoying Martin van Bruinessen's wit and hospitality. I profited from his extensive network of local contacts, so smoothing the way to gathering all sorts of information, while his experience of the 1980s proved to be a most valuable resource after an absence of ten years. For commentary on earlier versions of this text I am again grateful to Martin, and also to Anton Lucas and Budi Susanto; for its present format I should compliment my editor, Geoffrey Walton, typesetter Edward Stauffer, and publisher Suk Soongswang.

Niels Mulder
Bangkok, December 1992

Preface to the present edition

This reissue of the original edition appearing with Editions Duang Kamol in Bangkok was made possible by the generosity of its chairman, Suk Soonswang, the venturesomeness of Pepin van Roojen and the good care of Dorine van den Beukel, both of The Pepin Press in Amsterdam. It offered me the opportunity to make some minor revisions.

Niels Mulder
Amsterdam, October 1995

Note on spelling of words and names

Indonesian words have been written according to the convention of 1972 that unified the spelling of the national language and Malaysian Malay. The rules concerned have also been applied to the transcription of Javanese. If, however, reference is made to older titles, they have been given in their original orthography.

The Dutch spelling of personal names is preferred by many and calls for the caution of the non-initiate. A name such as Tjiek Soemardjan should nowadays be written as Cik Sumarjan, and pronounced as Tyik Soomarjan, the value of the **c** being **ty**, and the **u** an **oo**, while there are no long-sounding vowels, so that **ie** equates with **i**.

It is improper to pluralize Indonesian words other than by doubling them; generally it will be clear whether one or more are meant. From the context also follows whether terms are Indonesian or Javanese. In the cases that need clarification, (I) has been added to indicate that the word belongs to the national language.

In Javanese the consonants **d** and **t** may be aspirated or plosive, which is spelled accordingly, a single **t** standing for the plosive pronunciation of the French, such as in Toulouse, the **th** sounding as the **t** in time — and certainly not as the **th** in *thigh*. It is also usual to distinguish **e** from **è** and **é**; it is a pity that this is not done in Indonesian. A further peculiarity of Javanese is that the open **a** is often sounded as an **o**, for instance, **Martana** equates with **Martono**.

Note on indexing and references

When appropriate, the index refers only to the pages that best explain certain terms. The most relevant titles have been listed in the bibliography; others in footnotes only. All names of authors occur in the Index of names. The short glossary explains terms of address.

Introduction

This book has been written to explain the evolution of culture in Indonesia as it can be observed and experienced on Java, the most populous island of the nation, and home to the Javanese who constitute half the country's population and form by far the largest single ethnic group in Southeast Asia. In the analysis, material is brought together that is illustrative of the civilization of the South-Central Javanese sultanates in the present century, because this background explains much of the current development of a Javanese-Indonesian culture in the capital, Jakarta. This culture has meanwhile also strongly influenced other urban areas, which means, of course, also the town of Yogyakarta.

I imagine my readership will be composed of three, not necessarily exclusive, groups. The largest one will probably be those educated laymen who are interested in the country and who want to understand it better, because of their intellectual interest or professional activities. In developing a rather sophisticated interpretation of the Javanese-Indonesian cultural process, the book is also written for the experts on the country and academic colleagues. Although they will often disagree with my expositions, they are sure to recognize a lot, and I am certain that many will be amused. In order that students may also profit from my efforts, I have larded the text with explanatory footnotes and references to the currently most useful literature that, if consulted, will refer back to older, and eventually original, source material.

My observations in Indonesia cluster in three research periods, each separated from the other by a ten year interval. Most of my work I did in Yogyakarta, although Jakarta could never be avoided. Meanwhile, the interplay between the national and the local cultures has grown so intensive that Javanese life in the sultanate can no longer be considered in relative isolation from its wider environment. Of course, the greater context in which a society evolves should never be neglected, but the rapid opening up of local life to outside influences is one of the most striking phenomena of modern times, particularly in third world countries where their own high-cultural heritages are eroding rapidly under the onslaught of foreign-produced fashions and examples that seem to offer the irresistible enlurements of high status and contemporary chic.

The old upper class, as the main carrier of high culture, has lost its former exemplary prestige and their influence is approaching a nadir. The emergence of middle classes, whose ambitions are gathering steam, is largely fueled by modern education and a changing economy. Carrying little cultural luggage from the past, its members eagerly search for examples to admire and imitate. These new people are putting their stamp on current social development, giving rise to a Javanese-Indonesian culture whose evolution is at present dominated by Development, Money, New Order Government, Modern Schooling, Technology, Javaneseness, Consumer Culture, Islam, and Globalization. As they are the main players on the cultural scene, this book is largely concerned with describing their roles.

The ensuing analysis pays close attention to the evaluation of the moral content of social arrangements. The ethical component of relationships stands in marked contrast to those of technical, political, and businesslike expediency. It makes bonds binding, tying the individual to others in a personal way; he feels involved and important. It touches on more than psychological functioning, as it also evokes the values of authenticity, or the genuine. The experience of these latter seems to suffer in a 'modernizing' society that appears to have cut loose from its time-honoured moral moorings in the interests of accelerating the progression into the beckoning future.

I am apprehensive about this evolution, and it is certainly not Indonesia alone that is now reaping the dire consequences of its resolve to run off after progress, leaving behind its cultural baggage, including the sense of nationalism that once brought it to birth. As a result, the morally binding areas of life seem to be contracting, at the same time that the sense of sharing in a common weal and of public responsibility have so far failed to evolve. This absence of transcendency, of overarching commitments, gives life a sterile quality in many countries of the third world, where a new type of global 'great tradition' seems to be coming about, a new type of urban culture that is lacking in urbanity, where imitation passes for genuine and instant symbols for authenticity.

Naturally, though, people also remain to some extent prisoners to their past and, however exciting the race into the future may be, old ways and patterns of thought retain something of their abiding influence. Things remain, therefore, quite recognizable, and I had much fun in mining the newspapers, government statements and speeches, schoolbooks, magazine articles, seminar papers, and similar publications, for their significance. These documents — in which I tried to read between the lines and to evaluate in the context of modern Indonesia — provided the direct inspiration for writing this book in its present format.

As always, my main sources of information, interpretation, and commentary were members of the educated middle classes, such as teachers and professors, journalists, columnists, artists and authors, *budayawan*,[1] clergy, professionals and businessmen, besides many advanced students and budding intellectuals, so, basically, potential and actual opinion-makers. When I sometimes refer to other informants, it has been specified in the text.

An acute complication in writing a study of cultural change is that such a process is drastically uneven. When I note, for instance, that the command of High Javanese is rapidly fading in urban Yogyakarta, this does not mean that all young people are suddenly ignorant of the polite language. I am acquainted with an intellectual Muhammadiyah family engrossed in *kejawèn* civilization in which communication between the relatively young parents and their children is conducted entirely in good Javanese. Yet these people are also eminently modern and well travelled.

Besides this, one meets members of different generations who have grown up in dramatically dissimilar historical circumstances, who now participate in divergent cultural worlds, but who still interact, and thus mutually influence each other. This interlacing does not result in homogeneity, though, and to attempt to grasp the variety, the process, and the shape of the present, it is imperative to have a good understanding of the cultural background. So it will be demonstrated throughout this study that although *kebatinan* as a practice is declining, its salient patterns of thought resurface in many areas of life, from the ideology of leadership to lottery prediction, from the crafting of a biography to speculative development planning. Yet how the patterns of the past are going to affect new practices and procedures is simply not pre-

1 *Budayawan*, well-known partners in the on-going discourse about the cultural evolution of Indonesian society, such as many of the participants of the national Cultural Congress (1991) and those participants in *Kompas*'s seminar Towards a New Indonesian Society (Sularto, 1990).

dictable; they erode, lose value, and even acquire new meanings, which makes, for instance, the idea of the 'Javanization' of Indonesian culture distasteful to many Javanese, who are unwilling to acknowledge the parentage of the Jakartan mongrel. However the case may be, I hope that my endeavour will contribute to the reader's ability to decipher contemporary Indonesian materials.

Organization of the study

The first chapter contains a description of my experiences and observations in Yogyakarta over the 24 years in which the city changed from a dignified, yet impoverished, seat of indigenous Javanese government to a bustling Indonesian town. It is also the account of my changing views as Money, Consumer Culture, and Development have gained their grip on urban life.

The second chapter looks at this evolution in a more theoretical perspective, explaining the decapitation of the culture of the Javanese heart land and the loss of its *kejawèn* civilization. Now lacking in great-traditional points of orientation, wider society appears emptied of moral content, while being filled by the vague attributes of Indonesianization. Both result in a new importance of the ethical content of popular, little-traditional arrangements, and an upsurge of religious enthusiasms that have to compete, however, with the monetarization of life and the mass-cultural dulling of the senses.

Chapter 3 discusses the Javanization of culture in Indonesia by demonstrating the continuity of South-Central Javanese patterns of thought and behaviour in the ruling circles of the nation. In ensuring their ideological hegemony, Javanese ideas are actively propagated and used to explain the official conceptualization of leadership and power that is analyzed in chapter 4. In an intricate way, the dominant establishment connected their legitimation with basic assumptions about family and gender, ideas that are again officially promoted. As basic principles of everyday life, these and their meaning for wider social organization are brought into full focus in chapter 5.

Much attention is given to the relative roles of men and women, and the prevailing gender ideology. My hope in doing so is also to open the eyes of Indonesian feminists to the deeper dimensions of male-female relationships that need to be reflected upon, and further researched, before accurate action programmes can be formulated. In these chapters about leadership, power, family, and gender I seemingly deviate from my intention of writing a study of cultural change by introducing a set of rather old-fashioned ideas. To do so is warranted, not just by the fact that they are constantly revitalized by government and school, but also because they provide a very useful point of reference against which to assess changes in the ideas and style of life of, especially, the new, urban-raised generations.

Chapter 6, about psychology, women, and conflict, has been written with similar aims, in mind; namely, to draw a base line from which to develop a culturally relevant psychology. Because of the paucity of data and reflection, I have had to construct my perspectives on the ground of anthropological observation, prevailing gender ideology, some established insights, and the relatively advanced thinking of Filipino psychologists. The result is therefore no better than an open-minded, speculative exploration that may hopefully draw attention away from western textbooks, while opening Indonesian eyes to their own situation. Just as in the previous chapter, women and gender relationships stand at the centre of this argument about the psychology of family life.

In chapter 7, I grasp the opportunity to summarize some of the patterns of thought that were discussed in the earlier chapters; it gives me occasion to tie up some loose ends, connecting morality with unity, or oneness, then also relating it to refinement, mastery, and aesthetics. By focusing here on religious preoccupations, it becomes clear that the often used notion of syncretism to describe Javanese religion is not very precise, and even misleading, because the term basically belongs to a different discourse that objectifies religion, that separates it from subjective experience. Javanese reasoning is not so much syncretizing as a matter of synthetizing, looking for the undifferentiated oneness that has overcome diversity. The chapter also contains an appraisal of just why an objectifying, analytical approach to problems can hardly be expected to spread soon.

With the above ideational and psychological material in position, chapter 8 can then proceed with a probably controversial and critical interpretation of the evolution of culture under the present dispensation. To put the process in perspective, recourse is taken to the thinking of the generation of 1928, their nationalism and ethical ideas. It provides a stark contrast to what, in fact, eventuated once political independence was achieved. In following the penchant for zestfully dangerous living of the first president, his successor wanted order, by any means, which for him has meant stability and development. Despite occasional protests, politics were neutralized, and schools sterilized, while society became cynical, and nationalism spontaneously aborted. The end product of all this is an amoral money-dominated public life that is culturally barren and given to imitative consumer culture.

This sad evolution evokes political criticism and the call for democracy and popular participation, but these will be very hard for any Indonesian government to foster. In their absence, however, religion and regionalism seem to be flourishing as identity-markers, with Islam trying to fill the moral void. Yet this is no one-way street, since the New Order is also embracing, and compromising, Islam.

The last chapter summarizes some of the findings, reflecting on what Indonesia has and has not become. It tries to establish the current mode of production that dominates the way the country is run, that weakens its solidarity, and that is hostile to national cultural development. Yet this set-up also shows some continuities with the (colonial) past, and the hierarchical order of Javanese society. The greatest originality the present social concourse displays, though, is probably its ethical vacuity.

The appendices have been excerpted from previous works that are out of print or difficult to obtain, and from newspapers. They demonstrate ways of thinking, both Javanese and mine, while serving as background to and illustrating the process of change in Yogyakarta. As observed before, change occurs unevenly, and the inhibited interpersonal communication that is the subject of APPENDIX A can often still be observed, although it has become far less common among the young. The description of lottery prediction in B is more than just fun, it also furnishes a characteristic example of the data and the way I looked at it in 1970; it adumbrates my present analysis in terms of *kebeneran*. In C we are reminded that the abuse of status, corruption, and cynicism are nothing new, and probably endemic to a strongly hierarchicizing environment in which relationships are always characterized by dominance versus subordination, and in which, behind the façade of harmony, respect for human dignity seems to be squelched. In a most up-to-date discussion, this problem is again presented in APPENDIX I.

The review of the evolution of social relationships in Yogyakarta presents a good deal of the interview material, largely seen from the perspective of informants, that I collected around 1980. The next appendix, E, provides the social background in which the changing of interpersonal ties makes sense, while also drawing attention to the silting up of the former cultural vitality of the Yogyanese environment. In F, the individual reaction to life in less than inspiring social surroundings is discussed; it seems to me that the evaluation is also largely valid for the present, since political participation and responsible citizenship are still discouraged, although the retreat within the self may now easily be traded in for the indifferent individualism of the anonymous urban scene.

APPENDIX G has the Islamicization process as its subject, while discussing as well whether the analysis of Javanese society in terms of *abangan* and *santri* is still useful these days. This is followed in H by a short description of recent work by the great novelist Pramoedya A. Toer, while I highlights the discussion about basic versus special Indonesian human rights that was stimulated by the abrogation of the aid relationships with the Dutch uncle.

CHAPTER 1

Three *windu* in Yogyakarta[1]

Since I had arrived on my trip from Bangkok to Yogyakarta by motor-cycle in April 1969, my bike always attracted attention. The main reason certainly was that there were not many of them about. There was so little traffic in town that I was even unsure whether it was legal to park my bike on Jalan Sudirman, then the northern thoroughfare of the town, when I went on my first visit to the Gunung Agung book store there. The wide street was clear of parked vehicles and, already familiar with the eagerness of certain policemen for some on-the-job side earnings, my European-trained perceptions told me that parking could be a traffic violation.

When I came out of the shop again, the shining cap of my petrol tank had disappeared on its way to the thieves' market, and I could not elicit any sympathy in my agitated desire for a hot pursuit of the wrong-doer from the local street-dwelling population propped up against the wall. Motor-cycles were apparently attractive objects of plunder and easily removable parts kept vanishing throughout my stay. I was shrewd enough, though, to replace the cap with the cheapest and most uninter-esting one I could find, making it even less desirable by purposedly damaging its surface so that it would be left alone — which it was until the very end of my sojourn. I also marked my mirrors so that I could identify them again at the same market. When I did so, the fence con-cerned posed as an honourable businessman, and it took a long palaver at the police station before I emerged in triumph after refusing any form of compromise. In spite of that, by the end of my stay, I had long been deprived of the benefit of a rear view.

Sometimes, my curious Thai number-plate became the focus of attention. In a way it looked familiar, and since two of its characters looked rather like Javanese letters, I jokingly tried to convince people that I had obtained one of the first of the new plates being issued in the

1 In the same way that Thai and Chinese observe 12-year periods, and Westerners celebrate decades, 8-year cycles — *windu* — hold something special for Javanese.

sultanate, the Special Territory of Yogyakarta, as a sign of its continuous Javaneseness. I do not think that many people believed me, but many found it a good idea that has of late been realized on the rear of the town buses that proclaim the name of the municipal company in Javanese script. During my original days in Yogya, though, there were as yet no buses.

Nowadays, there is a lot of traffic and really nothing special about motor-cycles, unless you make your living from them. When streets were still deserted — we went to the window on the rare occasions that a car passed in the street where I came to live — there were no people making their money from motorists, or, as we have seen, only in an indirect way, but now parking has grown into a big business and wherever drivers try to leave the vehicle in a main street, they will be met by some eager concessionaire who is quick to claim his one or two hundred rupiahs. Being guarded that way keeps petrol caps in place; apart from that, the modern adaptation to poor countries is that these days they can be locked.

Three *windu* ago, the parking business was confined to guarding bicycles, then the most normal of privately owned vehicles, and already quite prestigious. The town was pretty full of them with throngs of cyclists waiting in front of the often closed barriers of the railway crossings, regularly tumbling over each other when trying to make their lazy start — the pace of life was still slow in those days. The son of my housekeeper also had a push-bike that he used on my errands at the post office, and that featured as a budget item in my account book: *rupiah* 10 for bicycle-watching.

Seen from the point of spending hard European currency, the old ten rupiahs equate with the hundred they currently demand, then and now worth exactly ten Dutch cents. It is an example of the normally around ten-fold increase in Indonesian prices for consumer goods. During my first stay, I regularly bought the filterless clove cigarettes *Gudang Garam*, a pack of twelve costing Rp. 65 on the side-walk after some haggling. Today one pays Rp. 750, without bargaining, that being the official price on the revenue stamp. Of course, late at night you will not find a single vendor willing to part with his merchandise at that price; an extra Rp. 100 at least will be needed.

These *kretek* cigarettes, now filter-tipped and in a more luxurious carton, are aggressively advertized as an aspect of the lifestyle of the young macho who likes his coffee strong and his music loud. In brief, they fit the man who has taste *(pria punya selera)* and naturally attracts women. It is remarkable that in such Indonesian campaigns too, women are not only portrayed as sex objects but as also being eager to demonstrate their feebleness in finding the stench and bad taste an allurement. I have stopped smoking the brand.

In 1969, there were hardly any caucasians in town, probably less than thirty, twenty of whom were Catholic priests, all seemingly motorized on scooters and bikes, spectacular in their white cassocks. Because they still wore uniform, I was never mistaken for a missionary, but was sometimes thought to be a 'hippy', as the then still rare rucksack-toting tourists were called. Since I was in the habit of protecting my hair from dust by wearing a bleached Egyptian skull cap, one day I was mistaken for a '*haji* hippy' in a village on the outskirts.[2]

When walking through town, a white man still drew attention, mothers lifting their children while pointing to the ambulant curiosity, but on the whole — leaving aside throngs of excited children in back alley neighbourhoods — encounters were polite, one being greeted by that then characteristic little nod of the head and the "Hello uncle" *(dag oom)* reminiscent of the colonial days.

These days Europeans have little curiosity value. As tourists their worth is in the money they carry, and if they are a spectacle still, it is mainly because of their odd ways and dress. Often they wander around in attire more fit for a day on the beach than a visit to town, but who cares as long as they spend their cash. Over the years, a whole industry has developed around their presence, from transportation services and hotels to *batik* paintings and coarsely made *wayang* puppets as the most appreciated souvenirs.[3]

Part of the industry is not so *bona fide* and consists of con men who approach the foreigners by addressing them in Dutch, in the hope that the Hollanders among them will feel flattered and easily agree to

---

2 A *haji* is a man who has performed the pilgrimage to Mecca *(haj)*; as a symbol of having fulfilled this religious obligation, he is thenceforth entitled to wear a white skull-cap.

3 *Wayang*, the shadow play employing flat cut-out leather puppets, often dramatizing themes from Indian mythological epics. The puppets are also offered in their flat wooden *(kerucil)* and doll-like *(golèk)* shapes.

be taken on a guided tour, to buy in particular shops, or to spend the night at certain places. Having lowered their defenses, because of their pleasure in finding their language still spoken here, and the memory of old bonds it conjures up, some find themselves really opening up, especially their purses.

In spite of the financial inducements of tourism, the development of communication skills lags behind, with only very few people yet capable of expressing themselves in English. If a visitor strayed into any local university, he would find that the situation is not very different there either, chances being that he will be 'hello-mistered' there as much as elsewhere. This ubiquitous habit of saying *Mister* to every white foreigner, quite often irrespective of sex and frequently abbreviated to *Mis*, is a sign of the necessity to place people — in this case outside the normal relations of the society. Where the *Oom*, *Tuan*, and *Meneer* [4] of colonial days placed and ranked people as parts of one social order, *Mister* labels them as outsiders.

The unity of social life was still apparent during my first days of research, Yogya conveying the impression that it functioned as a self-contained and well-ordered social universe. Of course, it was an Indonesian city too, with a national university that attracted students from all over the archipelago, but it also impressed me because of the relative isolation in which Javanese — *kejawèn* [5] — expressions could flourish. It was the unquestioned *kota budaya*, the city of culture, where fine dancing was still practised, and where the sonorous music of the *gamelan* [6] floated through the night's tranquillity. And if there was a disturbance, or when a breach of the peace occurred, people were quick to point to the many outer-island students as the culprits. [7]

It was a laid-back, sleepy town. The only public transportation available consisted of pedicabs and horse-drawn carriages. These were apparently sufficient for the needs of the population as people did not move around a lot. This came in handy given my often impromptu man-

---

4 *Oom* is Dutch for uncle, *Meneer* for Sir; as terms of address to European or westernized men, they are still in use. *Tuan* is the Indonesian or Javanese polite form of address, normally for non-Indonesians.

5 *Kejawèn*, pertaining to the area of the South-Central Javanese sultanates. See p. 40-43.

6 *Gamelan*, Javanese orchestra in which percussion instruments predominate.

7 Outer Islands, all islands other than densely settled Java, Bali, and Madura.

ner of contacting people for interviews: normally I would find them at home. The peacefulness of the town may have been related to its poverty, a condition I was little aware of then. I only became conscious that most people in my neighbourhood went bare-foot or wore rubber sandals cut from old car tyres when I tried to buy a tin of shoe polish at a local store, and for a long time I interpreted things from the perspective of my appreciation of a quiet style of life and a certain idealistic aversion to gross material matters, rather than from the more down-to-earth one offered by actual, mundane economic considerations.

My way of viewing Javanese life was strongly supported by my study of mystical movements. On arriving in Yogya, I had had a far more conventional piece of sociological research in mind, based on Geertz's idea of political-cum-religious streams as a dominant clustering principle in the organization of the wider society. To me, having grown up in the Netherlands, this concept was easily accessible because of its applicability to conditions in Dutch society. Geertz (1960) called these streams (or pillars as they are known in Holland), *aliran*, and their existence was still very visible on billboards and signs at the beginning of the New Order.[8] But because I used the word in the same sense as Geertz, people in Yogya failed to understand my purpose and directed me to a variety of informants who they thought knowledgeable. Soon, I was in intensive contact with representatives of mystical streams, or sects, known as *aliran kebatinan*, and I liked it, thereby entering a world of thought, speculation and interesting religious and psychical practices that I came to understand as being at the heart of things Javanese and a quest for meaning in face of the challenges of recent history.

The mystical scene was certainly flourishing at the end of the 1960s, people being attracted for a great variety of reasons, ranging from opposition to the pretensions of politicized Islam to lottery prediction, from their quest for health and invulnerability to the cultivation of the inner self. For me, its essence seemed to lie in the latter variety, which was confirmed during several congresses of *kebatinan* adepts who wanted to cleanse the practice of mundane motivations and its

---

8 New Order, or *Orde Baru* (also *Orba*), is the name of president Soeharto's dispensation; it contrasts with the *Orla*, the old socio-political arrangements of the Sukarno era.

popular magical dimensions, making it at least as respectable as the established, officially recognized religions.

This 'pure' exercise of *kebatinan* is strongly inward-directed, concentrating attention on elusive inner resources with which it wants to come to grips, training the secretive hidden being *(batin)* and intuition *(rasa)* to be attuned to the divine inspiration that will function as a guide through life. And so, the *kebatinan* I came to know drew attention away from the world, finding satisfaction in mystical reasoning to explain the functioning of the cosmos, while extolling the virtue and the wisdom of calmly and gratefully accepting *(nrima)* life as it comes, in the consciousness that it all has a meaning, that the experience of life itself is the fulfilment of some higher will.

When I spent time in Yogya on several occasions around 1980, many people were not accepting life as they had done before. Money had become available and was exerting a pull on their inward directions. With cash to enjoy life in the world, their preoccupations had changed, and so had my friend Mas Hardi. When we met again in 1979, his former wife had died and his children had left the parental abode, so it would have been eminently possible for him to satisfy his life's wish that, in 1969, had been formulated as retiring from active involvement in the world through turning to a meditational and ascetic existence. But his life had taken another turn. He had remarried, his new wife being a rather spectacular, though much younger, woman. He also commented that his life in Singapore and Jakarta, where he went on weekly trips — monkey business, he called it — provided ample scope for worldly pleasures.

He was not the only one who had changed direction, since I found that sectarian *kebatinan* had much changed. Of course, it was much as before for the better organized streams, such as Pangestu[9] and Sapta Darma, but the scene was much less lively than before. This was connected to a general opening up of society and greatly increased possibilities for individual mobility among members of the middle classes, but also to that great preoccupation of the New Order for regulating,

9 On Pangestu, see Sartono Kartodirdjo, Religious responses to social change in Indonesia: the case of Pangestu, in his *Modern Indonesia: Tradition and Transformation.* (Yogyakarta: Gadjah Mada University Press, 1988:263-86).

taming and controlling life in all its aspects. While main stream *kebatinan* had always aspired to respectability and recognition, it possibly got more than it wanted when, in 1978, it became officially acknowledged as a valid expression of faith, represented by a bureau in the Department of Education and Culture, at the same time presenting itself publicly by means of a weekly hour on television, just like the other religions.

For many of the adepts and adherents, one of the attractions of *kebatinan* has always been its existence at the chiaroscuro fringe of society, its esotericism and preoccupation with the hazy depths of the interior life. So, when it became 'golkarized', adopted by the state,[10] many Moslems may have been irked, yet it was also a blow to organized mysticism in causing it to lose one of its distinguishing characteristics. At the same time, official ideas penetrated its discourse; the woman leader of Sapta Darma, *Sri* Pawenang, suddenly began propagating the message that the practice of *kebatinan* is very beneficial to national development.

This surrender to bureaucratization, officialese, and the attractions of the world is also connected to the changes that have come about in the social order in which mysticism had once thrived. The cultural setting of the sultanate has rapidly eroded, the palace *(kraton)* no longer being the dominant point of orientation for a social life that had been bound up in the sense of hierarchy and forms of etiquette that are inevitable under monarchy. But even then, if people had wanted to escape from these impositions, they had been free in the past to explore their inner dimensions as long as they had outwardly conformed.

These days people move around, no longer confined to a prescribed social station in life, and the quiet orderliness, that I still found noticeable in the late 1960s, is a thing of the past. Ordinary people have become mobile, physically, economically, socially, and they are not

---

10 Golkar is the government's corporatist organization of 'functional groups' that aspires to bring together all and sundry in Indonesian society. Civil servants must be members, but there are also associations of peasants and ulema, of teachers and labourers, and so forth, within Golkar. The process of becoming adopted, or co-opted, by the state is known as *golkarisasi*, golkarization. Golkar functions as the official political party.

likely to submit to control by the reins of hierarchy. Now Yogya is full of stir and movement, housing a rather opaque society, in which people do their own thing, and where discipline has been relaxed. While such bustle may incline some people to retreating into themselves in their search for tranquillity, others may find that the demands of modern life form an impediment to self-centred mystical practice, and opt for the less subtly complex and more unambiguous moral solutions offered by the great religions.

In 1980, I was most struck by the vitality of much of the officially recognized religious life, with churches and mosques filled to overflowing, while at the same time *kraton*-oriented rituals were rapidly declining in support. Many of the people who had seemed uninterested in religious matters were now going to the Friday prayers, and interest in Moslem subjects had become commonplace. This is not to say that the on-going Islamicization is a sign of fundamentalism — which it is not — but that it is a response to changing times in which religious association is one of the few ways open for moral self-expression in the secular and state-dominated New Order. Besides this, participation in any of the congregational religions may be seen as matching the modern way of thinking that emphasizes scientific reasoning rather than intuition and inner experience. Protestantism, Catholicism, and Islam each possess a reasoned theology based on impeccable literary sources that serve as the fountainhead of 'objective' truth, in contrast to the self-centred subjectivism of the mystic quest (APPENDIX G).

As well as religion, the arts also appeared to be thriving. During the 1970s and early 1980s, Indonesian literature seemed to be subject to a remarkable Javanization at the hands of Javanese authors. Umar Kayam and Linus Suryadi projected the old values of acceptance and deference, modesty and acquiescence on their female characters.[11] Their protagonists' faithful fulfilment of their fate or acceptance of their station in life was shown to lead in itself to moral righteousness or happiness. Although it may be argued that this wisdom is not fully applicable to the present any longer, the interest of these books lies in the depiction of Javanese ideals in a period of rapid change, characterized by the

---

11 Reference is to Umar Kayam, *Sri Sumarah dan Bawuk* (1975) and Linus Suryadi AG, *Pengakuan Pariyem* (*Pariyem's Confession*, 1981). See also chapter 6:98.

state's and the economy's penetration of social life, both of which threaten the integrity of the cultural heritage.

At the same time, other authors also celebrated quintessentially Javanese values. Both Kuntowijoyo's *Sermon on the Mount* (1976) and Harijadi Hartowardojo's *Date with Death* (1976) deal with mystical adventures, from the reunification with the void to just plain ordinary death in the case of deviating from the path. Such scenes of fate, mystery, and mystical progression from origin to destination abound in Danarto's writings, for instance, *Godlob* (1974), but also surfaced in the more widely read pop novels that were especially addressed to Jakarta's 'golden youth', the children of the first generation of rich parvenus.[12]

Even the construction of certain novels was Javanized, Mangunwijaya's *Weaverbirds* (1981) being a good example of a book that follows the sequence of the shadow play. It is interesting to note that this book starts on an apparently realistic theme, namely, collaboration with the Dutch during the Indonesian revolution, but then, gradually, the motifs of inevitability and the fulfilment of destiny take over the plot.

This Javanization of Indonesian literature coincided with a period in which people began to grow tired of the New Order rhetoric. With the image of the Indonesian nation now becoming distant and vague, while offering little to identify with other than Development, government propaganda, and censorship, the reworking of Javanese cultural themes became attractive again. In the process, new forms were developed, a new idiom was coined, and so, around 1980, Yogya was offering a lively cultural spectacle.

This was expressed in the continuing popularity of the dance, but not necessarily of the court variety. Next to classical dancing, the more lively Balinese style had come to enjoy considerable popularity among the younger people, and at the academy of dance all kinds of experimentation took place, an endeavour in which Bagong Kussudiardjo became quite successful and famous. Also *gamelan* playing was rejuve-

---

12 For instance, Eddy D. Iskandar, *Sok Nyentrik* (*Pretence*, 1977). It narrates the story of the fashionable and extravagant Inge, come to Jakarta upon her peasant parents' winning the lottery. Confused by her own ostentatious lifestyle and by extravagant peers, she falls ill, returns to her grandmother and former boyfriend, there becoming rural Ichik again. So, finding peace, she dies.

nated through the inspiring innovations of *Ki* Nartosabdho.

In theatre, too, new ideas came to the fore, and were presented in the impressive performances of Rendra and the members of his Theatre Workshop. More popular still was the *kethoprak* stage, a Javanese innovation based on the *stambul* comic opera that had developed among the colonial Indo-European community. While *kethoprak* takes historical and legendary events as its themes, it offers great scope through this for commentary and satire on the current social scene. Gradually, this theatre form also became accepted among the middle classes, whose active interest greatly increased variety and experimentation while adding a well-off segment of the public to its audience (Hatley, 1985).

The promise of *batik* painting soon degenerated into glib picture-making for tourists, some of whom, however, also had money to spend on the works of the established artists, such as Affandi, the dean of modern painting in Indonesia, his daughter Kartika, and her ex-husband Saptohudojo. Not all painters had stayed in Yogya, though. The money and the lure of wider vistas in Jakarta had already drawn Harijadi there in the 1970s. Taken altogether, the artistic scene made an impression of vitality, a kind of a regeneration of Javanese culture after being freed from the embrace of the court that had become stifling. Interest in its history and literature was institutionalized in both an official and a private centre for the study of Javanology, at the same time that important 19th century texts were either being translated into Indonesian or romanized to improve accessibility.

Even then, though, I recognized that despite this, all was not well, and that more was happening than the filling of the cultural vacuum created by the New Order with religion and art. The bureaucratic and monetary penetration of society had become very visible, and the sustaining structures of older cultural forms, such as the *kraton*, the knowledge of High Javanese, and middle class interest in *kebatinan* were giving way to less circumscribed modes of life. Simultaneously, national schooling was altering the outlook of the new generation, orientating it to Jakarta rather than to their own cultural environment. Greatly increased mobility, along with the impact of the droves of foreigners, were changing ideas, and the first signs of consumer culture were now apparent in the spending habits of youth and the newly affluent. But I was optimistic; *wayang* still attracted crowds, the *gamelan* was still heard — although in competition with local and western pop music — and cultural life appeared to be fizzing with a great many new ideas. What was going on was a contest of sorts between rapid Indonesianization, and thus marginalization as a cultural centre, and a revitalized Javanese cultural production, often on the basis of an appeal to a more popular taste, resulting in works that showed an awareness of the commoners' concerns, rather than those of the aristocracy.

It was clear that a number of my earlier interpretations about the absence of interest in the material world would have to be revised, or qualified. What was plausible in 1970 was certainly not remotely applicable ten years later. People were now enjoying a higher standard of living, could buy useful new appliances, playthings, and above all status symbols, and could also improve their environment; they had the opportunity to travel, were in contact with Jakarta, with Indonesia, and even the world. Perhaps they had not developed a scientific and technological interest in the realm of matter, but they were certainly taking pleasure in its more trifling and practicable attractions.

In 1980, I interpreted what I saw as a process in which the ideal separation of the inner from the social life was greatly reduced, with people becoming more open to societal happenings, pressures, and enticements. That made them each more vulnerable and less able to retreat into the reticent self. It brought people closer to each other without necessarily improving the quality of communication. It was as if the increasing agitation of urban life had spilt over into the homes and their psychical inner refuges (APPENDIX F).

Sociologically, the integrity of the structure had been breached and society was diversifying. Mobility also was eroding the moral underpinnings, the ethics of place in which a person — socially, at least — identified with his position and its inherent duties. Everything seemed to be on the move, Jakarta appeared to be much nearer, and yet, culturally, Yogyakarta was coming to life again, as it had so often in the past by reacting creatively to the challenges of the times (APPENDIX E).

The trends of change that had become obvious by the end of the 1970s went on growing over the next decade. *Andong* horse-drawn carriages and bicycles were giving way to van-like buses and motorbikes that were then succeeded by an impressive network of buses, minibuses, taxis, more motor-cycles, and private cars. Gone were the throngs of cyclists, their harmless tumblings over each other being replaced by real bloody accidents, heavy traffic, and parking problems. The increase in the number of vehicles has not yet led to traffic jams because of the current building of over- and by-passes, the circular route around town even being known by the English phrase *Ring Road* in apparent reference to its prestigious modernity.

The first signs of consumer culture entailed the rapid development of new shops on Jalan Solo, that soon became an alternative shopping venue to Malioboro Avenue. Both centres remain crowded, but would-be buyers are now exposed to a new style of competitive selling in the form of the air-conditioned supermarkets that attract and manipulate their customers with all the commercial gimmicks that this form of peddling goods has given rise to. Overall, there has been an explosion in advertising, now that spending money is there for the catching. It all looks depressingly similar to elsewhere. Watches, fashions and furniture being promoted by lifestyle magazines; advertisements featuring instant noodles being served by radiant housewives to their smiling husbands and children; soaps, shampoos, and beauty creams are recommended by attractive models and movie stars, while monthlies for men popularize the uniforms of the times, such as safari suits and, more expensive, the executive look. Apparently, the long-sleeved *batik* shirt, that had at least a national character, is on its way out, while having become associated with the rank-and-file civil servants who have to wear it on the the 17th-of-every-month celebration as a demonstration of their solidarity and *Korpri's* esprit de corps.[13]

Yet national fashions also flourish, namely those that are Islam-inspired, promoting a modish Muslim look for men, while combining variation with orthodoxy for women. The most widespread expression of religious dress is the *jilbab*, the headgear that exposes only the face. While formerly this cover was part of the uniform of Muhammadiyah schoolgirls,[14] it has recently become popular among young women, so much so that it even inspired the title of Emha Ainun Najib's successful

13 *Korpri, Korps Pegawai Republik Indonesia*, official civil servants' association.

14 Muhammadiyah, a socially active Islamic association that propagates a modernist interpretation of the faith. See, for instance, James L. Peacock, *Purifying the Faith: The Muhammadiyah Movement in Indonesian Islam.* Menloe Park: Benjamin/Cummings, 1978; also, Nakamura (1983).

revivalist play, *Seas of Jilbab*. But even then, sporting a *jilbab* makes no difference to the other garments women choose to wear, which may range from blue jeans to orthodox long skirts and socks, or from Parisian-inspired shoulder-padded blouses to what I must confess to finding rather enticing variations of older styles.

In spite of initial opposition to the *jilbab* in state schools, the headpiece is now also admitted there, as a sign that Islam is moving ahead in its penetration of society, and peer pressure among girls is very likely considerable. This is not to say that they will stick to this outward sign of religion, as many later opt for the more relaxed *kerudung* or *tudung* veil as a Moslem identity marker. For the younger women, it is a fashion now, an assertion similar to the satisfaction their brothers get from pasting *We Are The Moslem* stickers on house windows.

The town scene keeps changing. Few and courageous were the women who cut their hair back during my early days; these days the long braid is a head-turner and, following the lead set by a young movie star, shortly cropped hair has become modish recently. It almost looks like a sign of protest, and this hair-do certainly does not allow for the pinning on of the Javanese chignon, the *kondhé* that is part of the traditional lady's outfit. In town, this way of dressing is now restricted to ceremonial occasions and has lost its appeal among younger women who, nowadays, may even be seen in shorts.

Also, Colonel Sanders has come marching in, with, in his wake, Wendy's hamburger, California fried chicken, McDonald's, and all the others who offer junk food and international soft drinks. The modern style of eating must take place in a plastic setting and the food has to be fast, fixed-formula, and greasy. Of course, Indonesian entrepreneurs have also climbed on the band wagon, offering standard meals of deep fried carp, known as goldfish, to the tunes of western music in open-air pavilions that target the Sunday family excursion trade. This luxury has spread from West Java; the more modest treat of the ubiquitous Padang restaurants is the West Sumatran contribution to indigenous fast food. Even Javanese eating places follow the trend: instead of being called, for example, Patiently Waiting *(Sabar Menanti)* — for the customer — they are now more likely to be named Depot Fast Food.

The invasion of modernity seems to have been accompanied by a lowering of defensive caution. My first servant had the nerve-wracking habit of squatting in a corner behind my back if he needed something from me, waiting there patiently until I chanced to notice and address him. Naturally, in upper-class households such habits have not yet disappeared, and one may also still be waited on by servants who crouch and kneel, yet the circumspection and diffidence vis-à-vis status superiors is markedly less, and younger house personnel may hum while working and approach their patrons in a direct manner, some even daring to ask questions.

Household staff, just like workers in shops or supermarkets, have a defined relationship with the people they serve, and thus a measure of politeness will flavour the interaction, but where bonds are unclear, manners tend to fade as well. The order of Yogyakarta, in which everybody had a place, is a thing of the past and in their newly won freedom many people have become so relaxed as to be impolite. Not only may a visitor be either exuberantly greeted or totally ignored while making his way around town, but also, even in the presumably more conservative environment of the university, a greying elder who, though a foreigner is still correctly dressed, may be met by a total absence of manners. At the Faculty of Literature, a seated door-keeper did not even find it necessary to rise when he yelled out, "Who are you looking for?" from a distance. The times of squatting deferentially have gone, but no alternative show of manners appears to have been devised in its place, the mask of indifference assumed by students often being the only thing that hides their insecurity. And, quite often, even staff members show a relaxation of manners that not so long ago would have been taken for insolence.

The circumspection of yester-years implied a high degree of self-consciousness that is on its way out now, and it is not only awareness of one's own bearing but also that of culture that seems to be fading rapidly among the young. I was amazed at hearing so much Indonesian spoken now in the streets, the train, and on the bus, while very few young people indeed still have a reasonable command of High Javanese, the polite *kromo* language.[15] Their ignorance of, and lack of

---

15 *Kromo*, or *krama* in Javanese spelling, also High Javanese, is the polite form of the language used in speaking to superiors and among upper-class people. It is juxtaposed with *ngoko* or Low Javanese, used in addressing inferiors and among ordinary people and intimates. See Siegel, 1986.

interest in, their cultural heritage threaten its transmission; future- and action-oriented, they gradually disconnect themselves from the parental past, their world filling up with foreign-produced articles and symbols.

In walking through town, there is nothing unusual nowadays in hearing Michael Jackson and it is becoming rare indeed to hear people listening to the formerly omnipresent sound of the *gamelan*. One may also meet with the *dangdut* style of Rhoma Irama, Islamic revival and pop songs that are all Jakarta-produced.[16] It seems that home production is giving way to the more commercial. I tried to buy some greeting cards with Javanese motives, such as *batik* patterns and *wayang* personalities that once were very common. At present, they are almost impossible to find and there is certainly little variety to choose from. What is available, and in great quantity and variety, are the cards that sport Arabian symbols, western romanticism, pop culture, and familiar figures from the international comic strips.

The art scene has lost its vibrance, and even once popular shows, such as the *wayang wong* dance theatre performances, can no longer be seen at the local recreation park that has evolved into a type of funfair cum Disney Land. *Kethoprak* has reached the dead end of *kethoprak plèsètan*, a slapstick comedy show reminiscent of the British style sitcoms in which every second sentence has to draw the compulsory laughter of the audience, or where words like 'before' must be obsessively countered by 'befive'. While granting that in this jumbling of language and tumbling of actors an occasional piece of satire or wisdom may still be hiding, the art is no longer convincing, although still very popular.

The promise of Javanology has not been fulfilled and the subject has failed to develop. The *Serat Centhini* has meanwhile been romanized but does not attract buyers.[17] An occasional perfunctory seminar is held, more as a ceremony than as a means of stimulating interest. The

---

16 *Dangdut* is a lively type of modern Indonesian mass music, inspired by a Malayan beat; its great protagonist is Rhoma Irama. See William H. Frederick, Rhoma Irama and the *dangdut* style: aspects of contemporary Indonesian popular culture. *Indonesia* 34 (1982):103-30.

17 This transliteration was done by the Yayasan Centhini of Yogyakarta, a private foundation under the auspices of H. Karkono Partukusumo's Institute for Javanology. For further information on the *Serat Centhini* and its various romanizations, see Anderson, 1990:271-90.

kraton of Yogya has become outward directed, the new sultan being a *haji* and a businessman. Maintaining the palace and a few ceremonies has become a purpose in itself, but there is little that emanates as cultural guidance. The local newspapers still send a photographer when the sultan opens an exhibition or a seminar, and on occasion royal ceremonial or *kraton* economics may be explained in their pages. Practically, though, the vestiges of regal rule have become folklorized, existing residually as a mere museum and tourist attraction.

What is more common in the newspapers now is violence, crime, and sports from over the whole wide world. These space fillers, that were formerly largely absent, have no message in themselves and are totally irrelevant to local life. They compete for room with self-censored editorials, and the exploits and wisdom of the high in the land. Careful reading can sometimes be very informative, and the news is somewhat less sterile than ten years ago, but, on the whole, newspapers are tasteless, somewhat reflecting the state restraints and the sterility of the New Order that repress creativity and socio-political awareness.

It is true, though, that students sometimes protest, but their efforts are nothing in comparison to those of 1974 or 1978.[18] In the early months of 1992, the students at Gadjah Mada University rallied against their rector who wanted to be a candidate for the government party, Golkar. They felt that the embrace of the state should not be strengthened by actively associating the campus with New Order politics. There was also some stir off campus, a protest by pedicab drivers who felt threatened in the security of their livelihood, and sometimes factory workers protest against intolerable conditions and unjust dismissals.

There is some movement visible in society; not everything can be repressed, and a lot of commentary slips through by jokes, gossip, cartoons, and social satire. But the New Order has been very successful in its repression of the spirit of the young generation that is no longer much interested in anything at all, let alone Javanese culture. Not accustomed to meeting intellectual challenges, they are catered for by fast food and comics, by an explosive growth in the number of cinemas and

---

18 Reference is to the anti-Japanese riots of 15 January 1974 in Jakarta that became known as *Malari, Malapetaka 15 Januari* (The 15th of January Disaster). In 1978, nation-wide student protest was quelled by the army. See p. 129.

the diet of romanticism and violence they offer, by American TV comedies, and the pleasures that money can buy, such as a night at the new 600 person disco. They have been trained to work, to earn money and to spend it: that is what Development is about. They should be outward oriented, away from their own world, or rather, they should experience this in the material terms that mass culture provides.

The break with the past, with the parental generation, seems striking. Often the young relish speaking Indonesian with the Jakarta accent to show their 'urbanity'. Our young servant was almost protesting against my listening to Javanese music. Many parents complain about their suffering from the demands of their children, who are no longer educated in the Javanese wisdom of self-restraint. An older informant, who has always worked as a teacher, described the young people as having lost their sense of purpose and Javaneseness — which is a grave way of putting it in Yogya. But, however outward and materially oriented, the young are undeniably also Javanese, carriers of a different consciousness that is probably rather vague and not fired by a great measure of imagination. Yogyakarta has become part of Indonesia, a provincial town in the culturally dependent periphery, feeding on foreign resources rather than home-grown ones.

The confrontation with this situation in the early 1990s forced me to adjust my interpretations again. The process of the gradual opening up of society seemed to have led to a vacuousness, which the Indonesian component failed to fill, at the same time that Javanese identity became elusive, for observer and participant alike. A new actor had arrived on the cultural scene: a foreign-oriented consumer culture that devalues the local heritage and relegates the past to irrelevance. In this way, Yogyakarta is losing its function of cultural centre in the sense of producing and reproducing things Javanese; it has grown provincial since becoming submissive towards Jakarta, from where the new Javanese-Indonesian culture now spreads out, impoverished perhaps, but inevitable (chapter 8). For the time being, it can only be optimists who anticipate a Javanese cultural revival.

CHAPTER 2

The cultural process in Yogyakarta

Discussing the subject, an old professor used the word secularization to describe what was happening to cultural life and the world view
of people in Yogyakarta these days. He contrasted developments in the
city with the outlying areas of Central and East Java where "people still
clung to Mataram", and 'traditional' ways and beliefs still held sway.[1] He
thought that the personality of the previous sultan, Hamengku Buwono
IX, and the historical process that unfolded during his reign, explained
to a large extent the opening up of the town to national life. With its
having become a national city — the capital of the revolution, the seat
of the first Indonesian university — all kinds of people had flocked to
Yogya, and many of the local notables subsequently left for Jakarta after
the recognition of independence by the Dutch.

The sultan set the example for Java. The times had changed, Java
had become part of Indonesia, and its people had better orient themselves to the new centre. In becoming a modern politician, actively
propagating the *Orde Baru* party of Golkar, and being selected for the
vice-presidency (1973-78), he emphasized his national orientation, while
the vestiges of the old regal order of Yogyakarta were rapidly giving
way to that of the state, especially when development, communications,
and capitalist penetration became intensive in the 1970s, the culmina-
tion of a process that had long been gathering strength.

The professor added that he worried about how Javanese civilization, as he saw it, was now crumbling; there being no market for printed Javanese; that a rapid simplification of the language was coming
about with High Javanese on the verge of disappearing; and that he perceived a general erosion of supporting institutions, along with a continuous penetration of orthodox Islam, which he called the *santrinisasi* of
culture, in which Moslem principles and ceremonies replace the older

---

1 Mataram, the last enduring Javanese kingdom, the vestiges of which still function in Yogyakarta.

ones. He also noted the incompatibility of the programming of the modern media — TV, video, commercial radio — with traditional styles, that strongly affected the taste and choices of the young who, as they grew up, lost touch with the culture of older generations.

The only signs of hope he saw was the persistence of the language as the ritual idiom of speeches, of traditional marriage ceremonies, of the Javanese dress at solemnities, of *wayang* performances and *kethoprak* plays, so that people were obviously not totally alienated from *kejawèn* forms, but he doubted whether *kejawèn* was still alive and observed beyond ceremonial occasions. Accordingly, he felt *kejawèn* had been usurped, and survived as a mere external decoration.

It is worth scrutinizing the above argument and reflecting on such words as 'secularization', 'civilization', '*kejawèn*', and 'outward decoration'. The combination of the latter two especially struck me as odd. Is it possible to see *kejawèn* merely as form? I had always understood it as a way of perceiving, of viewing the world, that informs certain externals, but certainly not the other way round. To me *kejawèn* is at the heart of Javanese civilization, and although it is not a religion by itself, it belongs to an 'enchanted' way of life that does not distinguish between the sacred and the profane (chapter 7).

In general, *kejawèn* refers to the culture of the Javanese heart land that centres on the courts of Surakarta and Yogyakarta. Often, it is especially understood as Javanism, such as the mysticism and religious practices associated with the philosophy of life, or Javanese knowledge *(ngèlmu)*, that normally also has esoteric qualities. It is essential Javaneseness, composed of elements that are held to originate from the Hindu-Buddhist period of the island's history, in combination with older animistic thought. As a system of knowledge, *kejawèn* is singularly elaborate, containing a cosmology, mythology, and mystical teachings that give rise to a particular anthropology, or ideas about the nature of man and society, that, in its turn, informs ethics and morality while permeating tradition and style of life. In the light of this interpretation, the mere performance of ceremonies in a 'traditional' manner should never be called *kejawèn*.

As the heart of a great tradition, Javanism needs its sustaining institutions if it is to flourish. Mysticism depends on adepts and practitioners, teachers and teachings, innovators, such as *Ki* Ageng Suryomentaram,[2] and active sects, such as Pangestu. Without all these, it is destined to become a historical curiosity. Yet, because of active interest and reinterpretation, it is still kept alive, especially among older people. Whether it can continue as a vital tradition may, because of its marginalization, be questioned. The interest in it expressed among the less educated and the younger generation seems to focus more on its practical and magical aspects than on seeking philosophical insight and 'the perfection of life'. Consequently, esoteric healing practices thrive at the same time that there is much interest evident in Chinese and Japanese therapies, while the mystically inspired art of self-defence *(pencak silat)* and physical invulnerability are also doing well.

Marginalization, downward mobility, or loss of meaning seem to characterize the institutions that support *kejawèn*. The *wayang*, that is essential to keeping the mythology alive, attracts smaller crowds than before, and has the image of being awfully old-fashioned in the eyes of youth. Interestingly, many good performances are staged in Jakarta now, but more in the sense of ceremonial decoration than as a living manifestation of the *kejawèn* philosophy of life. It is true that some people still write books about the connexion between the shadow play and human psychology, also that good puppeteers *(dhalang)* can command considerable sums for their performances, but the younger people, who formerly were enthralled by these arts, are now more interested in trashy movies and videos.

The youthful public still flocks to *kethoprak*, but the widespread experimentation and innovation going on in that branch of theatre already demonstrate that it is no longer a guardian of Javaneseness, but rather, at times, a partial commentary on current events, a satirical potential that it shares with newer forms of dramatic art. These latter are invariably staged in Indonesian, a language that is also taking over in Jakartan *kethoprak*.

The production of *belles-lettres* in Javanese has long ceased to

2 *Ki* Ageng Suryomentaram a was princely ascetic and influential Javanese philosopher in the period between the world wars. He is best known for his *Kawruh Beja, The Knowledge of Happiness*, a *kebatinan* doctrine that makes no reference to God or dependence on Him. His teachings have been translated into Indonesian and enjoy some popularity at present, e.g., *Wejangan Pokok Ilmu Bahagia (The Most Important Teachings of the Science of Happiness).* Jakarta: Yayasan Idayu, 1976.

exist in any commercial form: literature is written in Indonesian, and so are the newspapers. What's more, the production of entertainment pulp (comics, dime novels, magazines), that was sometimes printed in Javanese until about twenty years ago, is in the national language now, even the strips that are based on the *wayang* stories. The national school system has greatly contributed to Indonesian's spread, and among those who read and write, Javanese just remains — what it has always been for most — an oral language that is not important in school; only two hours a week are taught and it is no examination subject.

In the old days in Java, people listened to the *wayang*, the theatre, poetry readings, philosophical discourse, and each other, and there were few who wrote histories, moral commentary, and mystical treatises. Even at that time, much of such writing centred on the courts, but for a long time now this tradition has been fading away. Again, few youngsters have any interest at all in these old writings, and even if they were to be attracted to this great tradition — which it once was — they would find themselves unable to read the Javanese script. Consequently this expression of *kejawèn* — its moralistic, mystical and religious literature — is rapidly losing its social relevance. The tradition lingers on among the dwindling band of elders. It is dying by attrition.

It is not only that the courts have lost their function as living centres of *kejawèn* — the *kraton* of Surakarta being its last heavily defended bastion — but they have not felt compelled to adopt an alternate role, as modern patrons of high culture. The study of Javanese attracts hardly any students at the universities, the recent centres of Javanology appear still-born, the art schools experiment and innovate, old monuments remain for tourists only, the archives are in a mess, or access to them is difficult, and the museums are in a sorry state. Government is preoccupied with progress, with the future; the only relevant part of the past apparent to them is the heroism of the revolution and the coming to power of the present dispensation.

There is little to sustain *kejawèn* and its hold over the minds of the majority; as an encompassing civilization of the heart land of Javanese culture it seems to be destined to live on as an oral tradition in the countryside, still carried on by some puppeteers and mystics, but out of touch with life in the cities, the crucial centres of high culture. The towns of Java are opening up to Jakarta, a process that has already far advanced in the case of Yogyakarta, and exposes them to a capital-produced culture that is at best a new Javanese-Indonesian hodgepodge with a secular taste, free of moral, wise, or deep dimensions, in which elements of the past are clearly recognizable, but that lacks its orderly patterns (chapters 3 and 8).

Kejawèn, and the civilization shaped by it, constituted a moral order, with a profound religious element. For the individual mystic this meant being serious in his *laku (nglakoni)*, or the following of an ascetic regimen in order to be in step with cosmic rhythm and destiny; for others, the realization of a wise and aesthetic life conforming to morality and careful of decorum. For all, it meant self-mastery, restraint, and accommodation to a cultivated, preferably tranquil, style of life that culminated in the virtuosity of the literati and the wisdom of the king. Idealistic as all this may sound, nevertheless it provided orientation and direction.

The loss of this order is perhaps best illustrated in the rapid vanishing of the mastery of High Javanese, of *kromo*. That language imposes order, as it were. It sets the ego apart, regulating a person's station in life vis-à-vis others, attributing honour, governing expectations and obligations. As such it is a symbol of urbanity and the morality that goes with it; it expresses beauty and virtue. It contrasts with *ngoko*, the language of equality that ignores hierarchical order, that does not need 'God' or king, that can be spontaneous and unrestrained (Siegel, 1985:15-33).

The present generation in town is almost ignorant of *kromo*, or knows too little of it. Fearing loss of face because of clumsy use of language, they prefer to express themselves in Indonesian in situations of inequality, while speaking a mixture of Low Javanese and the national language among themselves. They are no longer interested in the trappings of hierarchical social order, and, together with the self-constraints and aestheticism of *kromo*, the mandatory good forms and etiquette *(tatakrama, unggah-ungguh)* are on their way out. What remains is a little tradition, popular and folkish, spontaneous and alive, syncretizing and open to the future. Freed of the cultural leadership of an exemplary centre, local traditions may proliferate, while the last vestiges of Javanese civilization are rapidly relegated to the museum — if they survive at all — and frozen into harmless folklore. Stripped of its past and the moral context to which it once belonged, life in Yogya, it is correct to say, has secularized and oriented itself to a new order with little or no moral content.

The situation brings to mind the precedent of Mexico. With the arrival of the Spaniards, the great tradition was decapitated, but five hundred years later the local styles are still remarkably 'Indian'. In the major urban centres, another civilization has replaced the earlier one, and a Hispano-American culture does exercise its influence on local life, but it does not drive out language and customs, while having to content itself with the Indianization of Catholicism and other 'great' ideas. The older Javanese culture also seems to exist at a remove from life, withering more slowly in the outlying areas than in the foci of modernization and progress, making place for local traditions that will henceforward orient themselves to a new, encompassing culture that is severely short on moral content. Moral life will remain local life, the language will live on, but whether that will be so in five hundred years must be doubted.

The Javanese countryside is now being rapidly penetrated by a money economy, and by the state administration, by an Indonesian school system, by the mass media, and by new fashions and commodities. The system of production has changed beyond imagination over the past twenty years, reinforcing class differences and social diversification (Booth, 1988; Hüsken, 1996). As a result, Indonesianization will be more rapid and disruptive in Java than Hispanicization once was in Mexico, cutting people loose from their local and moral moorings, creating an ethical vacuum that may or may not be filled by Islam in its struggle against religious indifference.

Morally, Indonesianization has little to offer (chapters 8 and 9). The ideas of duty to social place and obligation to elders and superiors have now been superseded by money, and the example of the parvenus who symbolize an amoral order of business in which corruption naturally ensconces itself. The exercise of power has also been freed from moral constraints and dominates the practice of justice. Superficially, it looks like the restoration of Javanese hierarchical relationships, but the impression is false, because they no longer have any moral authority. Secularization indeed!

The vanishing of a social order which was expressed in *kromo*, self-constraint, and cultivated manners, brings a style of life to the fore that uses *ngoko*, that is more spontaneous and less bound by etiquette. It fits the small people, the plain *wong cilik*, who were held to provide the great contrast with the cultivated and accomplished *priyayi*.[3] Liberated from the oppressive weight of hierarchy, these former apparently enjoy their new-found freedom and certainly do not complain about the loss of *kejawèn*. Their popular culture is not vertically oriented to the leadership of court or presidential palace, but finds its moral direction in parents, respected elders *(sepuh, wong tuwa)*, and religious leaders *(kiai, guru)*, all of them people who are near and known.

Yet, in general, the moral content of relationships is diminishing at present, and this is not because of the disappearance of the self-repressive feelings of *sungkan* in facing superiors, or an erosion of the gratefulness due to others *(utang budi)* for help received. People still feel obliged to each other, but now they can often choose to pay for services, thus evading the ethical burdens of reciprocity. At the same time, the circle of people with whom they interact is rapidly expanding. This is due to physical and job mobility, the ease of travel, and the broadening of their mental horizons by the mass media and modern education. This spreading out of contacts also means that these tend to become less intensive, that there is less time available for their cultivation, and that a fair measure of anonymity colours interactions in town.

All this is strongly supported by contemporary schooling that offers a stark contrast with Javanese ideas about the guidance of children. What is highlighted in the Taman Siswa ideas of the 1920s, for instance, are the moral exemplariness of the school environment and the stimulation of initiative by "encouraging the pupil from behind". These days, however, the guiding light provided by overworked and underpaid teachers is not shining brightly, as school schedules are directed to Development, its required technical and mathematical skills,

---

3 *Priyayi*, member of the Javanese upper class. Defined as a social type by Clifford Geertz (1960), it may now be questioned whether old style *priyayi* still exist. They differ from the high civil servants of today, whose command of secular knowledge and technology is more important than birthright, absolute loyalty, and cultural refinement. The notion of *priyayi* basically belongs to a two class perception of society, namely, the peasantry, or little people, and the servants of government, or administrators, from assistant schoolteacher upwards. In his fine, novelized study and ethnographic gold-mine *Para Priyayi* (*The Priyayi*, 1992), Umar Kayam traces the evolution of the notion of *priyayi* through a family history of three generations.

to the neglect of the human sciences. This situation is aggravated by the Indonesianization of the teaching of the humanities that focuses all the pupils' attention on national history and Jakarta to the exclusion of the students' own cultural environment. His home language is hardly a subject worthy of attention and he is trained in a second language; the teaching of history by-passes the growth and achievements of civilization, while dwelling at length on fighting and political events; religion perishes in dogma, Arabic, and legalities; morality is the glorification of and obedience to the Pancasila state; the reading of literature is not stimulated and local culture is not taught. Also, the cramming of the school schedule and competitive ways of work, still stressing rote learning more than comprehension, kill creativity, imagination, human and moral development, while producing bland *Orde Baru* babies who are not very curious about life, and tend to political indifference.

In spite of its Indonesian orientation, national school education does not seem to make students particularly eager to identify with it. Their world is becoming an open one, penetrated by the mass media and the entertainment industry, both stimulating an outward directedness but offering little focus. Attention diffuses and everybody begins to follow his own tastes and preferences in a confusing urban setting where people had better look out for themselves if they want to survive. The cultural symbols of the young are furnished by pop stars and life-style propagation, movies and disco, Donald Duck and Garfield,[4] rock music and soap opera.

In these youngsters' lives, their parents tend to become less important than they were for their elder generation, especially as mothers now often work outside, finding part of their satisfaction and necessary money there, and thus exercising less pressure on their children. This leaves room for the young to pursue a greater degree of moral and economic independence at the same time that the relative vagueness of existence in wider society stimulates the safety and identity function of family solidarity.

---

4 International comic strip characters adorn school diaries, badges, greeting cards and T-shirts; their adventures have not (yet) become popular. The vast comic strip literature in shops, stalls, and reading rooms *(taman bacaan)* consists, now as before, of *wayang* stories, legends of Javanese kingdoms, and *silat* and *kung fu* fighting adventures.

In contrast to the *kejawèn* ideals of social organization, modern life seems to lack a compelling ethical orientation. Its tendency to express relationships in terms of money results in a higher degree of individualization, other people becoming indifferent equals for whom one no longer stoops in passing. As a result, the practice of *tenggang rasa* (I), of being considerate of others, is suffering. While people, also the young, are most often still cautious of others, their way of acting is purposive and fast. They know what they want and do not waste time with beating around the bush and the demonstrations of shyness that were once characteristic.

In the ethical vacuity of modern urban life, religion appears to flourish. By actively joining in organized, congregational religion — primarily Islam, but Protestantism and Catholicism are also thriving — people, young and old alike, may restore parts of identity and the feeling of righteousness in a general social life that offers little to cling to other than the fleeting symbols of mainly western mass culture; the measure of religious enthusiasm is impressive. That Islamicization will maintain its momentum for a long time to come seems unlikely, though. School almost seems to do everything possible to deprive religion of its positive aspects, routinizing it to the point of insipidity. But the onslaught of mass and consumer culture may also dull the senses to what is often held to contain the deeper, more essential dimensions of existence. For the time being, religion is modish, with rapidly increasing numbers of people fulfilling the requirement of the *haj*, which demonstrates, at least, the success of Development, and the fact that it is fashionable to have been to Mecca.

So, when analyzing the dynamics of culture in Yogyakarta, we may note that the high-cultural component of Javanese civilization is swiftly on its way out. If that is the cause of the pessimism of the informant at the end of the first chapter when he observed that the young people had lost their Javaneseness, then he may be right, but is it correct to equate Javaneseness with *kejawèn*? Members of the younger generation still most often find themselves primarily Javanese and only then Indonesian — in contrast, sometimes, to an older generation that lived through the time of nationalism and revolution. Their identity is grounded in a little tradition of Javaneseness that is becoming mixed with national components and competence in Indonesian. Because of the mass media, they develop a taste for the plastic forms of the international consumer culture that is devoid of depth. This may make religion attractive for many, because life in a 'disenchanted' world that is devoid of meaning is not conducive to inculcating the sense of security that is provided by a grounded cultural identity. How this identity is going to evolve in the interplay between *ngoko* culture, Indonesianization, a weakened sense of nationalism, foreign-styled mass culture, monetarization, and Islam, is impossible to foresee, but that it will retain a distinct Javanese flavour is safe to predict.

CHAPTER 3

Javanization

On a long hot Sunday afternoon in Jakarta, my interlocutor, an associate professor of middle age, grew peevish when I broached the subject of Javanization. When I, as a foreigner, thought that there was such a thing as the Javanization of Jakarta, of government and lifestyles, it only demonstrated that I did not understand anything of Javanese culture. "Calling what is going on here Javanization is an insult to Java. I know what I am talking about, I am a Javanese."

He was not the only one to show irritation at a subject that is vexing indeed. Moreover, it is ambiguous. To some people it simply means the spreading of the rural population of densely settled Java to the less heavily populated parts of the archipelago, the Outer Islands.[1] To others the meaning is less simple, as they take it to mean the conscious or unconscious imposition of Javanese patterns of thought and behaviour throughout Indonesia, and then the sense is one of cultural imperialism. In the above-mentioned case, the sense is more narrowly focused on the thinking and practice of those in power.

With its coming to power in 1966, the conservative military became initially the most powerful organized force, which resulted in the political ascendency of those who had physically fought the revolution against the Dutch. Although overwhelmingly Javanese in origin, they were first of all freedom fighters, and convinced that the first priorities after liberation were consolidation of their grasp on power and the imposition of order.

They were confronted with the stark realities of disorder generat-

---

1 As was to be expected, the government's transmigration of especially poor Javanese, who are resettled in Outer Indonesia, has generally not been welcomed by the indigenous populations there. Often, this has turned into outright resentment when the newcomers threaten to become a majority in the areas concerned, or when they receive preferential treatment (credits, agricultural assistance, housing facilities), or because of conflicting land claims and unfair compensation (Drake, 1989:132).

ed by the previous regime's revolutionary, liberal democratic, and 'guided' policy in which permanent revolution — or turmoil — seemed to have become the leading principle. Consequently, order, in the sense of political, military, and economic consolidation, became the watchword of the day, and with the successful establishment of Jakarta as the one and only power centre to which all others must submit, some people observed that the *kraton*, the palace and centre of power of the Javanese kings, had been moved from Middle Java to the present national capital.

This has to be seen as no mere simile, since in the context of Javanese monarchy, the king and the palace are potent embodiments of power, due in large part to their sacrosanct nature. But then, can the present leadership be seen as in any way incorporating supernatural power *(kasektèn)* that radiates the royal grandeur *(kawibawan)* that makes its acceptance 'spontaneous', such as is in the expected nature of a king? Is the government so infused with sacred power that it does not need outside props *(sekti tanpa jimat)*, winning without victimizing *(menang tanpa tawur)*; is it really effective because of the depth of brotherhood of all *(daya ing lebetipun perseduluran)*;[2] or is it primarily a military-backed establishment characterized by heavy-handed authoritarianism, or, worse still, a set of very ordinary people who have bumbled into high office and who do not know their limits, such as in the play *Pétruk Dadi Ratu*, the *lakon* about the clown who became king?

The ideals of Javanese kingship clearly imply far more than concentrating, holding, and exercising power, thus some people are quick to point to the different backgrounds of the current powerholders and the generation of 1928, the intellectual fathers of the Republic.[3] These first organized nationalists[4] consisted of professionals who were familiar

2 These well-known expressions about the qualities that power *should* have — independence because of inner strength, consideration for others, union — are generally attributed to the corpus of Ronggawarsita.

3 See Robert van Niel, *The Emergence of the Modern Indonesian Elite*. The Hague (etc): W. van Hoeve Ltd., 1960.

4 The first time the country is thought about in its totality, and in the perspective of eventual independence, is expressed in the name of the Indonesian Students' Association of 1922 in the Netherlands, the *Perbimpoenan Mahasiswa Indonesia*. In Indonesia, the nationalist ideal was first publicly acclaimed at the Youth Congress convened in 1928.

with the ideas of European humanism, democracy and socialism, that are also reflected in the original formulations of the principles of the Indonesian state. The freedom-fighters of the Indonesian Revolution are different, often rooted in popular culture, while receiving part of their schooling and outlook from other masters. Trained as members of the *PETA* and *Heibo*,[5] they were drilled by Japanese militarists and fascists during the tumultuous time of war and transition, and most of them had never been exposed to either the accomplishment of advanced Dutch education or the sophistication of Javanese high culture.

Accordingly, many people feel uneasy about the idea of Javanization if applied to the current regime. As they have it, it is the worst elements of the Javanese heritage that have been promoted, such as hierarchical rigidity, authoritarianism and arbitrariness,[6] a development which they call 'Mataramization' and 'feudalization', which are accompanied by a fondness for status display and arrogance, for which the word *priyayiisme* is used: behaving like a member of the Javanese upper class.

From the choice of their words, Mataram and *priyayi*, it is already clear that the abuse of status is not a mere deviation from ideals about royal power, but a recognizable historical phenomenon. Does that make it Javanese, or is it just an attribute of power per se that, if left unchecked, by its nature leads to dictatorship, corruption and capriciousness? If the latter is the case, then it is unfair to speak about Javanization.

Still, many Javanese do not object to the term at all. Most often, they have a form of cultural imperialism in mind rather than the practice and ideology of government or the lavish display of status. For them, the spreading of Javanese culture throughout Indonesian society is taken for granted, a historical necessity that is already adumbrated in the myth-making school teaching of history, in which Majapahit, the last Hindu-Buddhist Javanese empire, once united the whole archipelago,

5 *Peta, Pembela Tanah Air* (Defenders of the Fatherland), Indonesian army corps established by, and allied to, the Japanese; precursor of the Indonesian armed forces. *Heibo*, indigenous auxiliary troops, technically part of the Japanese army.

6 They are not the first to protest these exorbitant potentialities of court culture (Anderson,1990:213-37). These traits are also criticized by Pramoedya A. Toer in *This Earth of Mankind* (APPENDIX H).

and in which the current Republic is pictured as the legitimate successor state after the disgraceful interval of colonialism.[7]

With unsettling ease, they proclaim that many Javanese things have already become accepted as Indonesian such as the Javanese costume, the *gamelan* orchestra, the *wayang* shadow play, or official ceremonial ways. Others plainly predict that the products of Javanese high culture, such as refined dancing and the art of music, will experience a revival, and be accepted by all Indonesians, as their national heritage. This overbearingness that often smacks of conceit comes 'naturally' to a self-image that is convinced of Javanese cultural superiority and the island's dominant position in the polity. It also reveals a deeper trait, of which the ideas of power and hierarchy are mere epiphenomena, namely, the drive for oneness, for wholeness and unity.

Oneness

In reading through newspapers, official statements, or school books for that matter, the newcomer must be struck by the frequent occurrence of words such as *kebulatan* and *keutuhan*, completeness and oneness; or combinations, such as *selaras, serasi, seimbang*, in harmony, fitting and balanced; and *kesatuan dan persatuan*, unity and integrity; and increasingly also *seragam*, uniform, even to the extent that the colour of Jakartan garden fences has been ordered to become *seragam*. Although fondness for uniformity may come naturally to the military mind, there is more to it than this, because uniformity means conformity, and conformity means adaptation and harmony; all combines in the notion of *keselarasan*.

Conceptions about oneness are not derived from mathematics, but rather culturally elaborated; they range from the absolute oneness of God to the oneness of juxtaposed complementary principles (e.g. *yin* and *yang*) up to ideas about unity in diversity. Some ways of thinking may emphasize synthesis, while others will be more tolerant of inherent duality and variety. In order to explore the Javanese conceptualization,

7 For instance, Sartono Kartodirdjo, Marwati Djoened Poesponegoro, Nugroho Notosusanto (eds), *Sejarah Nasional Indonesia* I, II. Jakarta: Departemen P. dan K., 1975.

we may take our point of departure in two related sets of symbolic thought, namely, about kingship and mysticism.

It has been a long time since the king was seen as in some sense divine, who thus, as a religious figure, commanded the veneration and service not only of the priests, but also of the inhabitants of his realm. This image gave way to that of the inspired king, the bridge between the supernatural power and the society of ordinary men who beneficially bathed in it. As the exemplary centre of the realm, he was the axis around which all revolved, his motionlessness proving his control. Guided by divine inspiration *(wahyu, wangsit)*, he demonstrated his being perfectly in step with supernatural purpose and volition, being at the same time the container and the content of wisdom, the unifier of the realm, and its fusion between the sacred and the mundane, the invisible and the manifested.

In this imagery, the king is both at the centre and the summit of social life. As a quasi-religious figure, people should revere and submit to him; he symbolizes the integrity of the realm and all that it contains; there can be no comparison, there is no equal at his side: he is absolute lord, the embodiment of the state, transcending the diversity that is fused in undifferentiated oneness.

Javanese mysticical thinking, at least the variety that is known as *ngèlmu kasampurnan*, the 'science' of perfection, is a way to unity, or, if alternately interpreted, an escape from diversity. It views the mystical path from the bottom upwards and begins with the individual life situation that is characterized by outer *(lair)* aspects, such as having a body, five senses, lust, cravings and rationality, and refined qualities, such as the sixth sense or intuition *(rasa)*; these latter qualities relate to the secret inner core *(batin)* that harbours a spark of one's origin in *Hyang Suksma*, 'God', or the All-Soul.

The mystical quest aims to subdue the complexity of the material conditions of passions and desires, of corporal drives and planning, by overcoming it, by reducing it to irrelevance. The ordinary situation of life is confusing and an obstacle to developing a stable, strong *batin*, and a refined, sensitive *rasa*. Needless to say, this requires discipline, ascetic and concentration exercises, isolation and meditation.

To follow this path is by no means easy, not only because of the strength of one's drives and the demands of everyday life, but also because it seems to be well provided with pitfalls, obstacles and temptations. It is like travelling through the jungle where the right path is often unclear, where wood-nymphs and fauns may lead one astray, and where spirits and magical forces may pose as friends and deceive the traveller in his purpose, namely, to seek guidance from and ultimately unification with 'God'.

To develop the inner core and intuition requires training and guidance from those who are more experienced, and it is generally thought that it is dangerous for the young or neophytes to engage in the practice of *kebatinan* mysticism on their own. They may easily fall prey to temptations, the lure of magic, and the abuse of the supernatural powers they come into contact with, because they are subconsciously being guided by egoistic motives *(pamrih)*. They may also gravely damage the functioning of their minds.

To engage in pure mysticism is to seek perfection, is to attune oneself to the divine, to the force of life that animates all, and is fuelled by the desire to reach one's origin, to fuse with one's origin and destination, to reunite with the All-Soul, to be fully in step with Life, not only to be guided by its inspiration but to experience mystical union, the joining of mystical servant and Master *(manunggaling kawula-Gusti)*.

In this way of thinking, the mystical adept seeks a oneness that negates differences, that has overcome diversity. Through the exercise of his inner attributes, *batin* and *rasa*,[8] they expand, as it were, dominating the visible aspects of life and relegating them to irrelevance. The unity sought after is fusion with the Master, representing the peak, the

8 Depending upon whom one seeks information from, mystics may differ in opinion about what is *batin* and what is *rasa*, sometimes even equating them, especially if they emphasize the secret nature of both. *Batin* then becomes the private, reserved inner core by which a person is connected to his origin in the All-Soul. In its meaning of essence, *rasa* holds the same signification, and often such adepts will take pleasure in playing on the words *rahasya*, or *rahsa*, secret, hidden, and *rasa*: they are so similar that they must be the same.

In this study, *batin* and *rasa* are differentiated; in mystical parlance I interpret *batin* as just explained and see *rasa* as the active, sensing agent. In colloquial speech, *batin* refers to inner man, even character and sincerity, while *rasa* becomes intuition, the means to empathize. *Rasa*'s ordinary meanings of taste, taste of, sense, feeling, and semen, do not occur in this report.

centre, and the all, one's origin and destiny, a reunion in which the self disappears. Diverse identity and the complexities of life have been conquered, perfection has been reached.

From these two examples it becomes clear that oneness is, on the one hand, an ideal state worth striving after, and, on the other, a hierarchical notion, superior and antagonistic to diversity. In this idea of unity diversity disappears. One has to prevail over the others, man over woman, Pendawa over Kurawa,[9] king over subjects, *Gusti* over *kawula*.

To the Javanese mind, achieving oneness is a noble endeavour that has very little to do with harmony among oppositing principles, or tolerance of diversity. The group, society, is one with the king; the individual is one with the group; and these ideas also colour conceptions of leadership (chapter 4) and social order. So, what to some appears as military and dictatorial thought is a concept that also finds strong support in the culture. To be able to grasp diversity is very difficult in this mind set, that always seeks to synthesize, to subdue the variety that is recognized as threatening and chaotic.

There is, therefore, nothing wrong in enforcing conformity, because conformity is a sign of good order, of 'harmony'. At the national day of the press, the army commander observes that the press should be one with the army, should voice the same opinion *(sependapat)*. Village heads issue arbitrary orders, even conduct political censuses, and expect the population to follow suit, to conform. Also, Samin villagers, who are thought to be notoriously obstinate in sticking to their own customs and thinking, in which marriage is their most sacred and meaningful institution, are forced *en masse* to remarry according to the rites of one of the five recognized religions — in this case Buddhism — under the threat of being exiled to somewhere in the Outer Islands, a fate that befell their original spiritual leader, Surontiko Samin.[10]

In the above way, the newspapers provide many instances of Javanese-Indonesian thought that often, at first sniff, reek of military-inspired thinking, but that also happen to dovetail neatly with the time-

9 Pendawa and Kurawa, the epic factions that stand for righteousness and disorder, respectively. See p. 107.

10 For background information, see Harry J. Benda and Lance Castles, The Samin Movement. *Bijdragen van het KITLV* 125/2 (1969):207-40. Also Saminism and Buddhism. Niels Mulder, *Java-Thailand. A Comparative Perspective.* Yogyakarta: Gadjah Mada University Press, 1983:62-7.

honoured principles of Javanese conceptualizations. This latter corre-
spondence will become much clearer in the following paragraphs where
we bring mystery and causation into focus.

Mystery and causation

Whether expressed in the kingly idiom of concentrating cosmic
potency, or in the mystical pursuit of union with the All, oneness
remains an elusive goal because it is the realization of a state of perfection. There is no doubt that it exists, and it is certainly not beyond
human possibilities either, but it is difficult to realize, hard to grasp,
and mysterious. The quest for oneness, for perfection, is a quest for
essence, for the real and deepest meaning, also called *rasa*.

Just as revelation and inspiration descend on those who attune
their movements to the rhythms of cosmic purpose, so signs and formulas that contain the essential condition may also be discovered or
revealed in other fields. The most common manifestation of this is the
Pancasila that is often spoken of as the origin and destination of the
Indonesian people. If people could but understand and practise the
Pancasila,[11] a perfect society would have been attained, but to understand fully, let alone to practise, is difficult, and so we can often read
sentences observing that the behaviour of civil servants — executives of
New Order Indonesia — is not yet in accord with the Pancasila and
should therefore be corrected.

The government also likes to call the New Order the Order of
Development and the Order of Pancasila. These various terms serve the
same purposes of legitimation: the idea of the *Orde Baru* is good, must
be good because it originated from *Supersemar*[12] that, as a God-given
miracle *(mukjizat)*, protected the Indonesians from communism, and
opened a new historical phase for the Indonesian people on the way to
the realization of the Pancasila society. The sacred (*sakti* (I)) formula of

11 Pancasila, the five basic principles of the Republic of Indonesia: the belief in Almighty Divinity (*ke-
Tuhanan Yang Mahaesa*, see Mulder, 1989:6-9); humanity that is just and civilized; the unity of Indonesia;
democracy guided by the wisdom of representative deliberation; social justice for all Indonesians.
12 The mark of the official transition from the Old to the New Order. See p. 59-60.

the Pancasila is a pilot giving direction, is an amulet giving protection, and a guarantor of the oneness and integrity of Indonesia. It is the dearest possession of the nation.

The Pancasila — as much as a holy mantra — is, and evokes, protective *sakti* power, but its effectiveness can be thwarted by shortsightedness. Blinded by egoistic motives and factional or special group interests, people fail to recognize the redeeming power of the formula, and thus fall out of step with revelation, and like those straying in the wilderness, they seem to have lost any sense of direction. They therefore need to be trained to understand; once they know, society will be on track.

To appreciate the Pancasila is not easy. The New Order government had first to order a unitary interpretation of the formula that was then disseminated throughout the country in special seminars and in school. Later, in 1984, the Pancasila became by law the ideological basis of each and every social organization, whether religious, political, or otherwise. But even so, is the Pancasila already fully clarified? From the mass media one may learn that the Pancasila is *final*, definitive, what it, being perfect, must be, but also that people are still searching for its deep meaning because, after all, perfection, like oneness, is and remains mysterious.

Moreover, mere teaching and cognitive understanding can never lead to the heart of an enigma that can only be reached by intuition, be felt. Teaching, as a process of handing down rules, may stimulate a desire for conformity, a disciplining of the manner of life, but a real comprehension of these rules can only result from a deeper-seated recognition of their moral benefit. Such insight is a personal matter, touching one's *rasa*; it is an attuning of one's *batin* to the secret, then merging with it. Reaching real appreciation of the Pancasila is, therefore, a long quest motivated by fascination with mystery, and the conviction that the symbol — mantra, formula, name, slogan — can reveal the right way and destination.

If things are plain and simple, they are mere routine, and therefore not so interesting. So there is a tendency to make them more attractive by veiling them, by hiding common things in symbols and slogans. This art shows itself to full advantage in the traditional construction of Javanese chronograms, the *candrasengkala*, in which numbers are indicated by words or allusions to their meanings, king, God, star, or navel standing for 1, and so forth, and in which the year is given in reverse, the sentence *resi tiga trusthaning nata*, three learned men please the king, means 7-3-9-1, thus 1937.[13]

A modern way of hiding meaning and giving things a secretive flavour is cloaking them in Sanskrit-derived neologisms or opaque abbreviations and acronyms. So it was decided to call the mouth-filling yet plain Directive for the Full Understanding and Practice of the Pancasila,[14] popularly known as *P4*, the mouth-watering but esoteric *Ekaprasetia Pancakarsa*. This new clothing, of course, needs a clarification that is given in the *P4* teaching materials,

> Ekaprasetia Pancakarsa derives from Sanskrit. Literally "eka" means one or one and only, "prasetia" means promise or resolve, "panca" means five, and "karsa" means strong desire. Ekaprasetia Pancakarsa thus means the oneness of resolve to implement the five wishes ... these five strong wishes are the desire to cause the five moral principles of the Pancasila to materialize. It is called the oneness of resolve because this will is very strong and unshakable (*Bahan Penataran*, 1990:27).

In this way, apparently simple things can be drenched in mystery, and mysterious things can be made more esoteric still. When that has been accomplished, people can start speculating about meaning, truth and significance, train their *rasa* in order to achieve insight, and delight in the play of words. So much is certain, however, the object of speculation has the potential to reveal truth, a future condition and latent historical necessity that will materialize when its time has come. A simple illustration of this thinking lies in the popularity of lottery prediction, especially of the last two figures of the official draw of the *Sumbangan Dana Sosial Berhadiah* or *SDSB*, normally translated as the Philanthropic Donation with Prizes. Ahead of time, people seek revealing signs that anticipate the outcome, but that still need interpretation to get at it. Basically the result is already there, inevitably so; it must come out, because it has been so conditioned. It is not a chance occurrence, but a necessity. The thing to know, therefore, is the conditions and the signs

13 Th. Pigeaud, *Javaans-Nederlands Handwoordenboek*. Groningen (etc): J.B. Wolters, n.y.: xi-xii.

14 *Pedoman Penghayatan dan Pengamalan Pancasila*.

they produce that lead to the inevitable result (APPENDIX B).

Naturally, not every ordinary thing is revealing; the signs sought for must by themselves have an aura of conundrum, being, for instance, highly coincidental and connected to the spiritual, the hidden realm of life. Dreams may reveal, inspiration be obtained through meditation, or through the behaviour of a spiritually powerful person, or even objects associated with him. So, even Catholic priests, who are certainly not in favour of giving lottery predictions, may be watched for any revealing signs that they might emanate. Inexplicable facts are also interesting, as, for example, why one candle out of seven in a chandelier at a headman's ceremony apparently did not want to light. Does that mean that 6 or 1, or any of their combinations, are strong possibilities?

By scrutinizing the signs, the final outcome of any event, or the appropriate date to set out on a venture, may be figured out. Important happenings take place on important days, they co-incide, and it was no chance that Independence was declared on the 17th of August 1945. Since then, this holy figure, 17-8-1945, has given rise to a vast magical literature, and civil servants are still supposed to dress in uniform for the the-17th-of-every-month celebrations. While the date of Independence was not pre-calculated — although many will hold that it was correctly predicted hundreds of years ago in the Joyoboyo prophecies — the dates for future undertakings can and should be calculated, certainly for marriages, or a major burglary, and sometimes they seem so auspicious that they, by themselves, become inevitable.

The event in mind happened on 11 March 1966 when the then lameduck President Sukarno ordered Major General Soeharto, the chief of the Strategic Reserve Command *Kostrad*, to take over the reins of government. The written document of this assignment became known as *Supersemar*, the felicitous and powerful onomatopoeia of *Surat Perintah Sebelas Maret*, thus alluding to Semar, the most mystically enigmatic character in the *wayang* mythology. According to many of the adepts, Semar is the real god of Java, originator and redeemer of the Javanese, and thus date and name formed an auspicious mantra inaugurating the *Orde Baru*.

The underlying thinking is that events are preconditioned, that happenings fulfil historical necessity. They are manifestations of God's omnipotence or the power of nature, of *kodrat*. The working of this power is not haphazard, but regulated, preordained as it were, making for an ordered cosmos of ineluctable manifestations. These 'effects' are the result of co-ordination, which means to say that manifestations are produced by the meeting of co-ordinates. Visualized as lines that are always being drawn, or travelling, they cross each other, or coincide, as when persons walking across town from different points of departure meet, such a meeting being a pre-co-ordinated co-incidence.

So, what one searches for in a lottery prediction is signs of coordinates that are still developing and that, upon their meeting, bring the outcome to light. Yet also the very act of becoming involved in the co-ordinating may contribute toward bringing the desired result about, as with *Supersemar* or the mystic's attuning himself to the All-Soul. This is also expressed in the most common of Javanese rituals, the *slametan* in which people seek auspicious continuity *(slamet)*, or the blessing of 'God'[15] and ancestors. The *slametan*, though, can only produce the desired result if it demonstrates by itself that harmonious, well-ordered and peaceful relations among the participants already prevail, which is the essential precondition for receiving the blessing sought.

Things, therefore, are manifestations of co-incidence, of *kebener-an*. This co-inciding is not mere accident or chance but a result of what was latently and necessarily given. Upon meeting, the givens produce a result, a visible effect that has not so much been caused as unfolded from preordination. Latently, it was there all the time; it had only to arise, to become veridical *(bener)*, truthful through co-inciding with reality.

In this conceptualization, things become because they are verifiable; thus they are manifestly true *(bener* (J); *betul* (I)). They are the product of co-incidence *(kebeneran; kebetulan)*, of the inevitability that precludes the idea of chance as an accidental happening, as a haphazard occurrence. All manifest things, even history, the whole of reality in short, is the shaping of necessity.

For the adepts, these various principles are exemplified by the *wayang purwa* shadow plays that enact the Javanese version of the Mahabharata mythology. To them, life on earth itself is seen as a mere

15 In single quotation marks, 'God' refers to the more immanent *kejawèn* concept; without them, God refers to the more transcendent Middle-Eastern idea.

shadow *(wayangan)*, a reflection of cosmic happenings and divine will. Thus Javanese history and society is seen as a microcosm of a more encompassing one, its evolution already fixed by inescapable cosmic law, the *ukum pinesthi.*

Sometimes, also, the performance of the *wayang* plays is thought to be powerful in itself, generating *sekti* potency that is projected into society or individuals. This is apparent, for instance, in the *ruwatan*, the ceremony of dispelling the threat of misfortune resulting from a malign cosmological alignment afflicting certain persons. By projecting a certain play *(lakon)* into the world, the evil spell is unbound and the person(s) concerned freed.

Negative results may also be produced by *wayang.* When I did my first research in Yogyakarta at the end of the 1960s, some people were still fond of relating how the performance of the violent mythology of the Great War, the *Bharata Yuddha*, had an effect on life in Indonesia. On the evening of 30 November 1957, the *lakon* was performed in which the hero Karno is killed; that same night, students from Bima threw five grenades at his namesake, President Sukarno, at Cikini in Jakarta.

While it may be true that the belief in the projective power of *wayang* is waning, the ideas of co-incidence, right moment, compelling *sakti*-inspired formulas, necessity, and the goal of perfection (*kesempurnaan* (I)) are certainly still very full of vital juices. This is demonstrated by the many slogans that, as holy mantras, are repeated over and over again as if they were spells that could bring about the development of Indonesian society. One of them is certainly Pancasila that, as *pusaka* (holy heirloom), is thought to harbour efficaciousness in itself, so protecting the nation and guaranteeing its unity and progress.

Although the Pancasila society may still be a remote — yet inevitable — possibility, more mundane statements also appear to share some of the qualities of magic formulae. Periodic election rituals are always preceded by lengthy campaigns in which everybody is summoned and appealed to "to make the elections a success". The endless repetition of Development *(Pembangunan)* seems to contribute to bringing about development, and if things can be justified in its name, such as land expropriation for a dam, factory, or golf course, it must be a morally good necessity, an unavoidable part of history. Also, the following stages of development are foreseen, summoned up as it were by the constant use of the word, so that even the dictionary quotes the jargon that "In the 6th Five-Year Plan Indonesia will take off *(tinggal landas)* to become an industrialized nation" (Echols, 1989).

The idea of take off, *tinggal landas,* points up not only the popularity of long abandoned theories of development in Indonesia, but with the words being iterated and reiterated in speeches and the media, the idea of inevitability is created. What it precisely means, few people seem to know, but in the same vein as Joyoboyo's prophecies, it must, in the fullness of time, come true.

What is given is revelations of the co-ordinates that will have to develop to the point of meeting in the *kebeneran* of the Pancasila society. So much is known, and these revelations are considered final, as a given perfection that remains to be filled with substance. So, a bent for legalistic thinking is certainly not at the roots of the unwearying references to documents, such as the Constitution of 1945, *Supersemar,* or the *P4:* all provide co-ordinates, the rails that have to be travelled. It is already written and no word should be changed: it only awaits fulfilment.

Javanization?

The protestations of some intellectuals about the state of Javanese culture in Jakarta are really beside the point. Culture is process; process is change; new culture, finally, is always in the making, with the old often being relegated to the museum and folklore. What has been carried to the current capital is fragments of Javanese culture that have been interacting both with other Indonesian elements and also many ideas that have flowed in from the outside. Furthermore, this amalgam of ideas has had to be applied in wholly new situations, such as economic development, nation-building, and international influences, that all demand original thinking and novel approaches.

The increasing weight of the national centre and the ideas it generates have already outstripped the cultural importance of the Javanese centres of its production, and set the model for Javanese and Indonesian society. What is being created is a Javanese-Indonesian culture that, in certain of its aspects, is heavily Javanized, showing clear traces of its Javanese origin, but that equally obviously displays a process of selective derivation. The *kraton* and its regal culture of refinement, etiquette, art and inspired literature, has been firmly left behind in the courts of Mataram. Yet high-cultural production has also long been languishing there, and literary production almost ceased with Ronggawarsita (died 1873), the self-proclaimed closing figure of the court poets (Anderson 1990:24-3). What he foresaw was a time of cultural malaise, of darkness, and a *zaman édan*, a crazy period in which order would be upset, the greedy and fools would thrive, the lazy be rewarded, and people would no longer know manners or shame. Of course, all that sounds very contrary to the dominant ideal of order, or is it perhaps merely a sign of the emergence of ordinary people onto the stage of history, replacing the ruling class of old?

Even if the transplanting of culture to a new centre resulted in a few deeply rooted plants being left behind, while some others failed to flourish in the new Javanese-Indonesian situation, nonetheless, others still have quickly taken root in the novel environment and are thriving on the nourishment it provides. In that process, some aspects of the culture may be transformed. For example, court entertainments are no longer staged, but there is a marked taste for lavish celebrations at luxury hotels. Such types of activities are known as the *neo-priyayi-isme* of the OKB, the *orang kaya baru*, or parvenus. It is at least in part due to their wealth that good quality *wayang* performances prosper in the capital and that Javanese dress is maintained on ceremonial occasions.

Some of the more important mystical movements, such as Pangestu and Subud, have long established centres in the Jakarta region from which they propagate their Javanese ideas to a national or even an international audience.[16] And while it may be argued that the production of *belles-lettres*, mostly in the Indonesian language but with a strong Javanese flavour, mainly takes place in the Javanese heart land,

---

16 Subud, *Susila Budhi Dharma*, interpreted as 'Living Attuned to God', is a Javanese spiritual sect that gained many foreign followers, several among them publishing about their experiences. For instances, Emmanuel Elliot, *Revelation Subud* (Los Angeles: Dawn Chorus, 1991); Robert Lyle, *A Way through the World* (Hillegom: Altamira, 1985); Dominic Rieu, *A Life within a Life; an Introduction to Subud* (Kent: Humanus, 1983); Husein Rofé, *The Path of Subud* (Berkeley: Hummingbird Books, 1988).

government propaganda and moral education activities are so distinctly Javanese as to warrant the idea that a new moralizing quasi-regal tradition has been established. This supposition is at least given some weight by the publication of the *Grains of Javanese Wisdom,* a collection of wise sayings in which the president not only poses as a very Javanese father to his children *(anak-anaku),* to whom the book is dedicated, but also — in the image of a Javanese king speaking *sabda pandita ratu* — as a guru in relation to the public to whom the book is distributed and sold.[17]

While some people may underrate the importance of the said wisdom once they read dictums such as "Children are born of parents", others will point to the Javanese world of thought in which such a statement becomes meaningful. Are not parents closer to the Origin — and thus worthy of worship and respect — and who would children be without them? Similarly, the five categories of legitimate lies *(bohong sembada)* have drawn some flak, but the president's pronouncement that the nonpunishable lies are "those you tell in a social gathering, those you tell your bride on your wedding day, those you tell to protect your wealth, those necessary to protect your life, and those you need to protect your family" serves, of course, a deeper purpose, such as the peacefulness of life, both of the personal *batin* and within family or community.

Whether certain Universitas Indonesia professors like it or not, there can be no denying that the Javanese input in Jakarta-centred Indonesian culture is very tangible indeed. This Javanization becomes clear when scrutinizing basic categories of thinking about oneness, mystery, and necessity that seem to characterize the dominant practice of government. The execution of power has probably always been far divorced from the lofty ideals of Javanese high culture, and did not have much to learn from Japanese militarism. It is a way of acting that is inspired by fundamental thinking about hierarchy and concentration that inform the ideology of leadership, such as formulated in the official moral education programme (next chapter). This programme also emphasizes basic familial values that are readily recognizable, and that

17 Soeharto, *Butir-butir Budaya Jawa.* Edited by Hardiyanti Rukmana. Jakarta: Yayasan Purna Bhakti Pertiwi, 1990.

are remote from the European values the intellectual fathers of the Republic wrote into the Constitution and the Pancasila. Devoid of this western inspiration, and stripped of the trappings of courtly refinement, the present development of Javanese-Indonesian culture reflects the commoner, but rooted, origins of its bearers, who are influenced by a mixture of Javanese civilization, Development, and consumer culture (chapter 8).

CHAPTER 4

The ideology of Javanese-Indonesian leadership

Moral and hierarchical principles

In the 1980s, the regularly recurring phrase "Certain individuals or groups stirring social unrest" was almost certainly intended to impute the blame to 'communists' for any form of protest. These days, the enemy within causing social unrest, referred to by the very same words, is those individuals or groups that are suffused with an overdose of 'individualism' or 'liberalism' and a false understanding of the meaning of basic human rights.

This shift in emphasis can be understood in the light of the official (and *final*) interpretation of the Pancasila, the state ideology that is presented as the compass setting by which the nation and its individual inhabitants should sail on their voyage to a perfect society. Communism is clearly incompatible with a doctrine that proceeds from "Belief in God", but so are 'individualism' and 'liberalism' that, according to the Indonesian interpretation, give undue importance to the freedom and interests of the person.

A recurrent theme of the Pancasila Moral Education *PMP*,[1] that all pupils have to study up to the very end of their high school days, is the subordination of the individual to community/society *(masyarakat)* and state *(negara)*. It is the latter two that embody the common good *(kepentingan bersama)* that should prevail over private, or individual, interests. This subordination is accompanied by a persistent parallel emphasis that all rights come with obligations to others, to society and the state. The twin themes of subordination and obligations to social units larger than the individual are then combined and employed to construct the argument that the western belief in the concept of 'basic human rights' is not a universally valid statement about human dignity. This proposition is then used to justify a specifically Indonesian inter-

---

1 *Pendidikan Moral Pancasila.*

pretation of the latter (*PMP* I:136). And so a hierarchical element is introduced that is at odds with notions of basic human equality (APPENDIX I).

The course repeatedly discusses the idea of the equality of community members, but however often this principle is reiterated, especially in the chapters about mutual deliberation *(musyawarah)* and cooperation *(gotong-royong)*, the main emphasis there is also on the subordination of the individual to the common unanimous decision *(mufakat)* that expresses the group's unified will *(kebulatan kehendak)*, and the common desire to live in peace with each other *(rukun)*. This *rukun* is expressed in the willingness to compromise, which is most often taken to mean accommodation to the point of conformity. The key word leading to an understanding of Pancasila democracy's version of human rights lies therefore not in any notion of equality but in the idea of *kekeluargaan*, in functioning as a family.

According to the lessons devoted to this subject, *kekeluargaan*, paired with the principle of sharing burdens *(gotong-royong)*, is the basic principle of the Indonesian nation and state. It means that in social life harmony should come about as in the family, in the consciousness that the common interest transcends that of individuals (*PMP* II:86-7). This thought is elaborated by reasoning that if the common good is attained, so also are all individual goals, while it is not at all certain that the satisfaction of private interests means that the common good has been served, too (*PMP* I:128). The important thing, then, is to know who decides what the common interest is.

While we shall return to this question further on, it may here be useful to note that this thinking about common and private, or individual, interests basically equates them: what is good for all is good for one; such reasoning apparently does not differentiate between *res privata* and *res publica*.[2] The nation is seen as a family, or at least as guided by the principles of family life; its common good is a shared private interest that should be protected against non-family members, and from those who do not behave in accordance with the family code.

The Pancasila course is about ideology and is thus not necessarily good sociology. It does not touch on the structure of the family, although it has much to say — as we shall see later — about the func-

---

2 See discussion on pp. 141 and 161-2.

tion and role of the state as the embodiment and protector of the national family. First, however, I want to trace some basic principles of Javanese family life that seem to underlie the political elite's thinking about leadership and state.

It is a bedrock premise in the official course material that the family is a moral unit and the basis of the social identity of all men. The individual cannot be thought of independently from the others who give birth to and bring him up. This fact of being primarily a social creature, of belonging to others and to each other, carries obligations all around. To be a fully grown adult means to become a parent, and parents must care for and teach children. This in turn obliges these children to honour their parents, to follow their advice, to be obedient, and, ultimately, to marry. The consciousness of these obligations is well developed (Mulder, 1989:21-36).

The course material is clear about the respect and obedience due to parents and elders (*PMP* II:24-5), but then, deliberately or not, fudges the issue. While constantly emphasizing the communality of interests and the obligations of individuals, it also postulates the equality of family members, of the importance of practising *musyawarah* style deliberations and consultations (*PMP* III:68-70), while not even touching on the principles of leadership. Such a refusal, or inability, to face up to plain facts that cannot, or at least should not, be ignored, makes clear why the whole problem of societal organization is never discussed. Social hierarchy, moral and practical inequality, leader-follower relationships, and so forth, do not fit the vague image of Pancasila society that is offered in school.

In Javanese thinking, though, the family is more than a little moral world characterized by mutual obligations. First of all, as everybody involved is aware, these obligations are unequal, which provides the moral underpinnings for the existence of hierarchy, and the obligation of some to guide and lead the others. Elders, teachers, and especially parents are the subject of extreme reverence, of worship *(pepundhèn)*, a place that they deserve because of their care, protection, and teaching.

In other words, the family is a steeply graded hierarchical moral world that should be guided by the principle of solidarity, and certainly not by equality. Parents have to guide and teach — they must — and it is the children's obligation to accept and follow *(turut)*. Hopefully, the leadership that parents provide will be in accordance with the Taman Siswa principles[3] that recur in the Pancasila course for adults, the *P4*. There, in the 'Latin'[4] of New Order Indonesia, it is stated that Pancasila-inspired leadership should be *ing ngarso sung tulodo*, so exemplary that people will follow out of conviction, *ing madya mangun karso*, stimulating their own will and creativity, while *tut wuri handayani*, fostering initiative and responsibility. A leader must thus have the qualities of a guardian, or protector *(pengasuh)*, who stimulates, leads and guides the ones he has to bring up *(asuhannya)* *(Bahan Penataran* 1990:33).[5] A Pancasila leader therefore equates with the ideal father.

The above conceptualizations provide the key for the practice and the theory of Javanese-inspired leadership in Indonesia today. The practical image is military, or feudal, in which followers gather under the banner of their leader, to whom they are expected to be fiercely loyal. He is a *Bapak*, a father and reliable patron who should be honoured and followed, whose every whim and wish is a command, and who cares for his subjects *(anak buah)*.

This image of social organization is rooted in the family and is projected onto society as a whole. In order to advance in life, one needs patrons, protectors in the world outside the home. Such patrons should be resourceful, capable of attracting and protecting followers, and so all share in a common interest: if the benefactor thrives, so will his clients.

By its very nature, patronage is hierarchical, tying people together

3 The Taman Siswa school system, founded by *Ki* Hadjar Dewantara in Yogyakarta in 1922, was based on, at that time, very modern humanist ideas combined with elements of Javanese educational practice. See Ruth Th. McVey, Taman Siswa and the Indonesian national awakening. *Indonesia* 4:128-49 (1967).

4 To make things more weighty and deeply significant, official Indonesian is steadily enriched with opaque neologisms derived from Sanskrit or Old Javanese. In the present case, modern Javanese is used, apparently in the belief that it conveys a depth of meaning better than Indonesian can. Not all Indonesians are happy with such signs of the Javanization of the polity.

5 The manipulation of language in the *Bahan* is interesting. By making the leader a *pengasuh*, the people are pushed into the position of children whose initiative should be curbed. The Taman Siswa idea translates more precisely as leading 'by example in the front, inspiring in the midst of people, encouraging from behind'.

in personal bonds of unequal moral and material worth, in which the higher cares and the lower obeys and follows. Arousing feelings of awe and love *(wedi-asih)*, the superior should empathize *(tepa slira)* with the inferior; such sympathy is not expected of the underling. After all, *tepa slira*, literally, to measure against oneself, means to judge, from what one's own reactions would be in a similar case if the positions were reversed, how one's deeds will affect others. And how is the lowly follower to do this for himself in matters concerning the decisions, wisdom and responsibilities of a patron or father? To attempt that would not only be presumptuous but also sheer churlishness *(kurang ajar*, falling short in — moral — comprehension). The client's role, then, is to underscore the highly honourable status of his patron by a display of respectful deference, and it is an ominous sign indeed for all concerned if a leader cannot command respect any longer.

Elaborating on this, and taking it now on the level of the state, the thrust of the Pancasila course becomes understandable. In it, the Government of the Republic is portrayed as the umbrella that shelters the whole territory and all the population (*PMP* II:79). This protection explicitly entails obligations, and thus people are urged to work hard and support the State *(Negara)* (*PMP* II:95). The paragraph continues with the observation that "The Government of the Republic of Indonesia is the authority that regulates the social life of the State of the Republic of Indonesia. Because of this, we Indonesian nationals *(warga negara)*[6] are obliged to submit to *(tunduk)* and to obey *(patuh)* all the regulations that emanate from the legitimate government. We are convinced that the purpose of the Government with all its regulations is to improve the life of its nationals. The success of this governmental task also depends on the attitude of these nationals ..." (95-6). In the next paragraph, we learn that "Apart from being submissive and obedient to the given regulations, we are also obliged to respect *(hormat)* the officials who carry out the administration ..." (96). Further on, this is followed by "We believe that if all Indonesian nationals fulfil their obligations to the State, the State shall also satisfy hers, namely, to guarantee the rights of each national", which is, of course, supplemented by "The

---

6 Normally, *warga negara* is glossed as 'citizen'. Since I think that the idea of citizenship is confusing if applied to Indonesia, I prefer to translate with 'national'; 'subject' would be another possibility.

good Indonesian national will always give precedence to his obligations over his rights" (97).

While consistent with the observations about the family, all this remains fairly abstract so far, and one would like to know who is in charge. Well, "The executive of the Government of the Republic of Indonesia is the President of the Republic of Indonesia ... The Presidency... is a high office that is occupied by a national who is selected, praiseworthy, reliable, and respected" (94).

By exposing the hidden assumptions about *kekeluargaan*, the functioning of the state as a big family with a father at its head becomes clear. Father State protects and guides, the population submits and follows. To instil the necessary attitudes, the state, just as a good father, should teach the populace so that people will become fully mature, respectable members of the national family, real Pancasila men.[7] This task is given shape in the teaching materials and the great effort to spread the national ideology, in school by way of the *Pendidikan Moral Pancasila*, the Pancasila Moral Education course, and outside of it through the *P4*, the *Pedoman Penghayatan dan Pengamalan Pancasila*, or the Guidelines for the Internalization and Implementation of the Pancasila. Once everybody has learned enough, then individuals' moral awareness will lead them to live virtuously (*à la* Pancasila) and no obstacles will thwart the natural evolution of an ideal just and prosperous society.

The question this begs, though, is whether the model and ideology of the family can be applied to the state. The family is a moral entity that is thought to be anchored in 'natural fact', and in the quasi-religious obligation to carry on the family line. As representatives of Life who protect and bestow blessing on their children, reverence is due to parents. In other words, it is this 'natural' and 'religious' condition — or unquestioned mythology — that legitimizes the family as a moral hierarchy.

The family is a small world of people who feel they belong and

---

7 In Javanese education, young children are considered to be *durung jawa*, not yet Javanese. Through socialization — teaching and learning — they will hopefully become *wis jawa*, Javanized. Being deficient in learning (falling short in it is the literal meaning of *kurang ajar*) must, by its own nature, lead to insolent behaviour.

have obligations to each other; they know each other personally. To expand their world, they may seek patronage, personal connections to people who can distribute favours. But can an abstract entity, such as the State or the Government of the Republic of Indonesia, act as a patron, let alone a pater familias? Even granting that such vague and vast claims can inspire loyalty and nationalism, in the course of every-day life they will be more usually experienced as compulsions and im-positions.Their power is felt. But is it recognized to be morally legitimate?

The fact that there is power, and that some profit from it while others suffer, is indisputable. Whether in the hands of kings, governors general, presidents, marshals and other high officers, technocrats, or economic bosses, the exercise of minority dominance will generally be experienced as a necessary, or at least unavoidable, condition that one has to accept. However, when measured against the scale of family val-ues, it may well be difficult to recognize such overarching power and its exercise in moral terms. Perhaps it was the case that some Javanese kings did indeed succeed in legitimizing the dynastic organization of their realms in the eyes of the ordinary people. Nonetheless, such past public acceptance of, or acquiescence to, this ideology of hegemony should not blind us to the very real possibility that the inner circle of life, with family members, relatives, friends, and possibly including patrons, was recognized as moral, whereas by contrast, life in the outer circle was experienced as dominated by amoral power. Consequently, going against parents drew automatic supernatural sanction *(walat)*,[8] while acting or speaking against the king — the incorporation of the state — was rebellious *(balélo)* and *lèse-majesté* indeed, so thoroughly deserving of heavy, worldly punishment.

The present-day Javanese-Indonesian elite's exercise and under-standing of power and leadership comes closer to the regal dynastic doctrine than to *kekeluargaan*, even if we allow for the strong hierar-chical dimensions of the functioning of the family. It is an authoritarian practice that is highly sensitive to exterior, and intolerant of any form of

---

8 In an interesting way, this thinking is illustrated in Achdiat K. Mihardja's *Atheis* (*The Atheist*, 1949). This book does not so much discuss whether the main character is irreligious, denying the existence of God, but highlights the fact that he leaves home and goes against his parents wishes, and thus has to lead a miserable life.

interior, criticism or doubt about its righteousness. People should be guided and educated so that they will behave responsibly, know their obligations and their place. They are seen to constitute a floating mass that is excluded from political participation, and they can thus not be held responsible for the successful operation of the whole. They do not really participate as family members conscious of duty, but are expected to respond obediently to commands.

The populace is regarded as an aggregate of individuals, possibly vaguely organized in corporate 'functional' groups, that together form a society that is embodied, represented, and transcended by its ruler, with, in the present circumstances, the leadership functioning as a patron in the guise of the State, which effectively means the government itself replicates the role of monarch. To go against one's exalted lord can never be right, because the whole incorporates the righteousness with which the individual should unite. The best would thus be if all individual members were to be uniform in purpose and wish, driven by the mystical desire to *manunggaling kawula-Gusti*, to become one with the Lord.

Hierarchy and the individual

The authoritarian 'paternalistic' form of political leadership fits the way society is seen and experienced by most Javanese. The small organizational kernels consist basically of (multigenerational) nuclear families that exist alongside and apart from each other. Such individual units take care of themselves, and do not tend to act through corporate organization. Although relatives, and especially siblings, unite for ritual occasions, their households are economically separate, and there are no transcending clustering principles — such as the clan or the lineage — that institutionally organize related people.[9]

9 In his fine dissertation, Frans Hüsken (1996) offers a vast amount of convincing material to prove family cohesion among the village elite in defence of their property, power, and privilege; class thus becoming the clustering principle at the top of the pile. They consolidate their position through strategic marriages and sometimes take pride in, and formalize, their pedigree to safeguard their prestige (chapter 11; see also next footnote).

The bilateral organization of kinship is limited in both depth and time — only those people who have been personally known, such as parents and grandparents, are remembered and honoured at their graves.[10] This does not prevent individuals from building up far-flung networks among favourite relatives, friends, and patrons, but these networks are individually specific: they are based on their personally knowing and relating to particular aunts, cousins, a grandfather and others. The fact of their being related is obviously the cause of their acquaintance with each other in the first place, but the basic organizing principle is still the forging of dyadic, or paired, links between two concretely known individuals. This type of organization, that is characterized by the absence of encompassing structuring principles among relatives and the dyadic nature of interpersonal ties, has become known as "loose structure" (Mulder, 1996:75).

The only encompassing organization is the administrative one imposed by the state, by means of which the state is able to control a loosely structured population. While in 'feudal' times people were personally tied to and controlled by 'liegemen' and functionaries *(priyayi)* of the king, in colonial times such impositions led to the territorial organization and the 'invention of the village' as a 'natural', 'solidary', 'family-like' unit, represented by a *volkshoofd*, a 'natural' paternalistic leader (Breman, 1988). This territorial principle still persists, and has meanwhile been refined, organizing people in smaller units still, such as neighbourhood *(RW, Rukun Warga)*, and neighbour groups *(RT, Rukun Tetangga)* (Sullivan, 1992).

From the vantage point of the state, order should be imposed on an otherwise intractable and unruly, unorganized populace *(rakyat* (I)) that appears as an aggregate of individual *marhaen*, as a mass of little people who, each and all, fend for themselves. The New Order regime even institutionalized this view with its floating mass policy, in which

10 This is not true for those few who trace their descent from an apical ancestor and feel a sense of belonging to a lineage *(trab)*, as is usual for the nobility and *priyayi* who take pride in their pedigree. These lineages show more cohesiveness and sense of obligation than the arbitrarily widespread 'networks' of relatives among ordinary people. Nowadays, such *trab* are also organized among commoners who seek to strengthen solidarity among relatives in order to assist each other, consolidate property, and/or enhance prestige. See Sairin, 1982, and APPENDIX D:191).

people are not supposed to be politically active and may only organize in bodies approved of by the state.

The ideas of unruliness and order find a strong parallel in Javanese education, that may be understood as an effort to discipline the individual and make him submit to his group by conformist behaviour. When still a small child, he is considered to be subject to his emotions; in growing up he is taught to become a Javanese, learning the rules of his culture and mastering his drives and impulses. By living thus, he demonstrates his humanity, his Javaneseness.

In other words, it is claimed there is a need for this imposition of order from above due to the inherent basic unruliness of individuals; such persons cannot be trusted and are not seen as the fundamental units of society. If imagined individually, they are thought to be somehow outside the social order, like wandering ascetics, thieves, or roaming souls and spirits. People become part of society by, of course, socialization, which, in Java, means becoming part of a group that defines identity and to which they submit.

For many, these very impositions stimulate a stubborn quest to live out their individuality and to feel free from hierarchical constraints. Of old, this has been possible in the practice of *kebatinan*; through the cultivation of the *batin*, inner man, the outward, phenomenal world of hierarchy, pressure and conformity loses its relevance. In *kebatinan*, the accent is squarely on the inner life of the person, on his intuition, or sixth sense *(rasa)*, that becomes the centre of experience and truth, proclaiming one's subjectivity to be the most important thing in life. In a way, *kebatinan*, with its related practice of asceticism, takes place apart from society, in undomesticated territory; it is also a quest for individual potency, such as character, strength, and efficaciousness in life, or invulnerability and health. It is therefore more than a temporary escape from hierarchy, because it declares individuality.

For quite different reasons than fascination with one's inner life, individualism and social indifference seem to thrive these days. This is stimulated by the rapid opening-up of society, strongly increased mobility and anonymity, and the growth in personal wealth and opportunity that sets people free to do their own thing. Also, quite ordinary, mainly younger, people in Yogyakarta apparently do not feel oppressed by the weight of hierarchy. Since the erosion of the order of the sultanate and the opening-up to the outside world, people have been liberated from the mould of encompassing hierarchy and behave freely, unhindered by the formerly prevailing *sungkan, rikuh* and *pakéwuh*, which all refer to feelings of inhibition vis-à-vis superiors. In some sense, the old points of orientation in a highly regulated order have given way to a measure of structural vagueness, in which the little people *(wong cilik, rakyat)* as true *marhaen* seem to feel well at home, belying the often heard opinion that the sense of, and honour for, hierarchy are innate, are part of Javanese life blood.

If there is anything 'innate', it is probably the gut feeling of leaders and power holders that there are strong tendencies towards 'individualism' and anarchy among ordinary Javanese if they are not controlled by their social environment and the reins of hierarchy. If that control has strong moral elements, such as in the family, it may be accepted 'spontaneously'; when moral legitimation grows weaker, the carrot of privilege and material progress, or Development *(Pembangunan)*, may keep people in line, until the stick of power and compulsion must be used. There do not seem to them to be any imaginable alternatives, and so Javanese-Indonesian leadership will remain obsessed by maintaining order by whatever means.

Conflict

Order is not only threatened by individualism and diversity but also by conflict. We have noted that people who go against their leaders, who are critical or go their own way, are considered 'rebellious' *(duraka, balélo)*. In the case of misbehaviour towards parents, such actions will be punished by supernature, and in severe cases, where it is felt that the good name of the family has been injured, parents may even disavow the child concerned, cutting the links because the obnoxious behaviour reflects badly on the elders' social status and self-respect, while affecting their psychical balance and well-being.

Self-respect and reputation are closely linked, and open conflict, or rebellious behaviour that may be observed by others, is particularly painful, not only because it jeopardizes a family's status, but also as it shows that people are in discord, not united and in harmony *(rukun)* as they should be. However much the neighbours may relish such a spectacle and indulge in gossip, so much is certain; open conflict is distasteful. It exposes one to criticism for the weakness of not being capable of living an agreeable existence.

The disorder of open conflict, protest, or criticism reflects directly on the power of a leader, demonstrates its decline, and is thus intolerable. As a sign that he is not able to keep those who follow under control and in order, it threatens his good fame, and raises the spectre of derision; the worst thing to suffer. To be treated with disrespect means doubt arising about one's potency, about one's character and capabilities. Lack of respect is thus gravely insulting.

When students demonstrate, or workers strike, it is not readily understood as an appeal for serious discussion; on the contrary, it shows that *musyawarah* has failed, that the government or the boss has been disgraced — yet this also reflects on the protesters themselves, open conflict being inelegant all around. Seen from the top, opposition is threatening, ominous, and its open expression must thus be promptly suppressed; it is no invitation to dialogue. Parliament cannot function other than as a rubber stamp for the executive, while students are threatened by tanks; reputable people who sign a petition for reform are still hassled by officials for as long as twelve years after the event; labourers are forced to humbly request their own dismissals; villagers are intimidated into 'voluntarily' selling their land at very special prices indeed; peaceful demonstrators may be shot; would-be political candidates may suddenly lose their jobs and find themselves avoided by people who were formerly close to them. And books may be burned, newspapers closed down, magazines censored. There should be no signs of open disagreement or criticism.

To underscore just how repugant the powers-that-be find any casting of aspersions on their mandate to rule, thus rousing in themselves fears of declining potency, it may still be worth recounting a story that took place in 1976. The event may be seen as just one more mystical excursion, but the minor civil servant, Sawito, who figures in this tale also received the backing of prominent Sumatrans, such as former Vice President Mohammad Hatta, retired General T.B. Simatupang, and the national Moslem leader Hamka, when he claimed that President Soeharto no longer held the *wahyu*, which is the sacred mandate to rule.[11] Because of that, he should step down and hand over the affairs of state to the one to whom the charisma had been transferred, Sawito.

This affair was taken very seriously indeed by the government because it touches on truly basic categories of legitimation. A ruler demonstrates his charisma by attracting followers who submit spontaneously to his leadership. This charisma is the *wahyu*, the divine legitimacy that is the mandate to rule. This political authority derives from higher sources and is the almost tangible power and prestige that attracts the partisans and adherents.

So, when doubt was expressed, backed by the authority of several respected national leaders, also including Cardinal Darmoyuwono of Semarang and former Police Chief Sukanto Tjokrodiatmojo, this was no laughing matter, and Sawito thus had to be silenced and removed from public view. After due process of law, he was found guilty of subversion, criticizing the government, and sent to prison for seven years (Bourchier, 1984).

What in other places would be judged as overreaction to a kind of practical joke makes sense in Javanese thinking about leadership and conflict. The Sawito affair touched on the rawest of nerves: prestige, and in that there is nothing to laugh about. This same theme even surfaced in another context in 1992 when the American general Colin Powell expressed his disagreement with a military action proposed by President Bush. The Indonesian newspaper headline announced the event with the word *balélo*, rebellious behaviour (that must be suppressed). In this context, the idea that things can be discussed, and that presidents are not necessarily the fountainheads of wisdom, or repositories of compelling charisma, is difficult to grasp.

Fathers or presidents, department heads or village chiefs embody the groups or institutions they stand for, and so it is difficult to disentangle person from prestige, and from the group he represents. Their reputation may be seen as a defensive shield, guarding the unity of those under it. Disunity or conflict threatens this protection and thus conformity and integrity must be enforced from above, while 'troublemakers' are excluded by denying them justice, access to resources, or

11 In a different context, the loss of *wahyu* is elaborated by Harijadi S. Hartowardojo in his *Perjanjian dengan Maut* (*Date with Death*, 1976).

entry into the country. Those who remain under the shield while demonstrating their loyalty and agreement are rewarded with privilege, and the opportunity to abuse their positions for personal profit, or pleasure, as in the case of a notorious disturber of the village peace who retorted when questioned about his behaviour, "My father is the headman here".

It is easy to draw a seven year prison sentence for insulting the government, the country, or the state, let alone the president. Basically, these four are equivalent, embodying the righteousness of the nation that equates with its prestige and reputation. Hence the intolerance of disagreement. People who have been critical of the *Negara* may lose their right of re-entry and have to live in exile abroad, the State not being their national home any longer; they are repudiated as obnoxious children and excluded from the civilized process of discussion and deliberation, for which the only imaginable outcome is spontaneous unanimity, *kebulatan kehendak*.[12]

All this is not so different from interpersonal life situations where people are very much concerned not to cause others to suffer indignity, because status and prestige are a man's best possessions, and any affront to these is taken personally, becoming a prime cause of conflict. It is thus bettter to conform to expectations, to side-step threatening situations, and to avoid confrontation. Conflict should be suppressed, or denied, because there are no good mechanisms to negotiate it, and if it bursts into the open, it can only be fought out, such as in the endless battles between the Kurawa and the Pendawa, in which the righteous party always prevails, killing his opponents, and thus 'solving' the conflict. There is no real resolution of the tension and compromise cannot occur, because any giving in equates with losing; conflicts are not so much solved as terminated. In this sense, the Javanese moral universe is flint-hard.

The inevitable vicissitudes of life make it wise to cultivate smooth

---

12 On 4 March 1992, it became legal to ban the re-entry of citizens who "have tarnished Indonesia's image abroad". This Army Faction-sponsored bill gained the support of Golkar and PPP. In the debates, the PDI argued that travel bans violate human rights while running counter to the Constitution (of 1945) and the legal system. According to the supporters of the ban, "the public's interests should be put above those of individuals".

relationships with each other and to ritually invoke the state of *slamet*, of auspicious continuity. Yet people often feel worried, exist in a state of solicitude *(prihatin)* that nurtures the determination to keep oneself under control, to exercise self-mastery by the practice of minor ascecis that is at the same time thought to bring about favourable circumstances, and to accept life as it comes, because it is wise to strive for accommodation.

This complaisance is part of the acceptance of, and the quest for, leadership. The world is an uncertain place, and it is good to have people in charge of controlling it, of keeping it in predictable order. If the price for that is surrender to authority, or to the demands of group life, it is not too high, because continuity and a state of peacefulness are the higher good. Submission to hierarchical order is therefore a moral act, and a way of avoiding disagreement. Such a stratified order imposes strict rules, demanding obedience and a rigid etiquette *(tatakrama)* that ties people to their station in life and incumbent duties, and that serves as an excellent means to keep open conflict at bay.

CHAPTER 5

Images of men and women

Most Javanese are not aware of the Islamic origin of the oft quoted saying "Heaven is located at the soles of mother's feet". Some who are feministically inclined will stress the fact of its recent propagation in the government's campaign to encourage the country's women to perform their 'traditional' roles of housekeeper and mother. While in Islamic understanding the expression is meant to underscore the boon of goodness that flows from mother to her child, many Javanese may more readily interpret the sentence in light of hierarchical notions of their culture that emphasizes the obligation to honour one's mother as the first and most essential step towards a blessed existence.

Respect, of course, is expressed by tractability, and obedience to one's mother is a sign of living a moral life. So, when the leader of the Nahdatul Ulama Islamic mass movement was sailing through some rough political waters, a sympathetic newspaper interviewed his mother, who supported her son by declaring in a front page report that he had always submitted to her, implying that he must be a good person.

Obedience as a sign of moral behaviour does not solely concern the children; it also involves the moral exemplariness of the mother. By giving birth and nurture, she is the living symbol of self-sacrifice; by being accessible and attentive to her offspring, she extends trust and emotional warmth; as the first teacher, she lays the foundation for the evolution of the child on its way to becoming fully Javanese, fully human. Altogether, this makes her the most important person in early life, creating an emotional bond that is most often not undone by the passage of time.

The father, being the elder and the progenitor, is entitled to the highest honour, and is hierarchically far away. In contrast to the approachable and emotional mother, the symbol of warmth and homeliness, who earns her honour because of self-sacrificial care, the father seems to embody prestige per se. In that position, he needs to be dignified, in charge without much to do, somewhat remote from his children, and often from his wife, too. He especially represents life outside the home, the world of work and male affairs, and the family's prestige. Whatever respect children and wife may earn for themselves, their main honour in life lies in their belonging to him.

The symbolic value of men and women appears to be dramatically differentiated, indicating their supremacy in different realms in life. The male area is the outside world of politics and power, of work, position, prestige and hierarchy; the female centres on the home, the children, education and care. This is not to say that men or women are practically confined to the areas they symbolize, and that their realms are exclusive preserves: there are women generals, village heads, politicians, professors, and many are known for their business acumen. There are also men who fulfil tasks classified as female, but women seem to have the greater freedom in 'border-crossing'.

This relative licence has often been noted but only recently written about (Errington; Hatley; Keeler, 1990). Women, in this schema, are supposedly more earthy, actively caring for things, earning and handling the family's resources, emotional and not so restrained in their behaviour, whereas men are expected to be dignified, somewhat removed from daily cares and activities, pursuing, shaping, and expressing the prestige of the family. Their dignity reflects self-restraint and strong inner resources, or what Keeler likes to call potency (1987).

Of course, women may also cultivate their inner strength, refined manners and mastery of speech, and by so doing express themselves in the hierarchically ordered area of life, where they may achieve rank and position, power and influence, or just strengthen the prestige of husband and family. Generally, however, they are thought to be second in such things to men, less refined, less spiritual, less potent, more spontaneous, more emotional, and thus less deserving of prestige. It almost goes without saying that in a hierarchizing environment, prestige is far more important than control of the purse-strings.

All this does not mean that women are less appreciated than men. They share in the same humanity, complementing each other. Unlike in China or India, there is no preference for male children — many parents prefer a daughter as their first child because they can rely on her for care, even after marriage — and the ranking of the children is on the basis of their relative ages. If resources permit, both sexes receive the same educational opportunities, and there is nothing comparable to the active disdain women are subject to in the above two regions adjacent to Southeast Asia, where they are held to be 'useless' and inferior.

The direct influence of Islam on these ideas seems small indeed; irrespective of great religious traditions, this thinking about gender and prestige appears to be Southeast Asian, at least in that part of it that is joined by the South China and Java Seas (Reid, 1988; Mulder, 1996). In Indonesia, this ideology is now actively propagated as the *Panca Dharma Wanita*, a doctrine requiring the compulsory organization of the wives of officials, the latter themselves being organized in the *Korpri*, the Indonesian Civil Service Corps.

According to the publications of the *Dharma Wanita* association — the name can be translated as the mission of women — the roles or duties of women are (1) to function as the assistant *(pendamping)* of the husband, (2) who takes responsibility for the household tasks, and (3) rears and raises the children. As (4) a member of society, she serves husband and children, and, if necessary, (5) she may seek supplementary income.[1]

From these five *(panca)* rules it appears that, at least in the official view, the task of women is to function as the auxiliary of the husband, shouldering the domestic tasks. This implies the idea that activities outside the home are less appropriate for her, certainly if these lead to the neglect of her primary duties. So, even when the home is well provided with servants or grown-up children, while her husband happens to be sick, a woman is not supposed to show her face in public, say, to attend a seminar for a few hours at the university. Such a visit away from home will be thought ill of and penalized by backbiting, most probably by the other women present. It is clear that men who leave their spouses in comparable circumstances are not slandered in this way; after all, their area is outside.

To become a mother — and thus to be a wife — is thought to be fulfilling nature's course; it certainly is the fulfilment seen as preordained by the culture. And women are supposed to live in (nuclear) families, as are also men, that are managed, though, by the female part-

---

1 Noviana Titin H., *Sebuah catatan tentang "gender ideology" yang merugikan wanita* (Note on a "gender ideology" that is harmful to women). *Kritis, Jurnal Universitas Kristen Satya Wacana* 2/1 (1987):44-8.

ner. Rearing children and caring for the home is an important task and, in order to execute it, women are guided by the official development organization Family Welfare *(Kesejahtaraan Keluarga)*. Besides this, she may still need to seek some income to support the family, but since these earnings are explicitly understood as supplementary, it directly justifies the practice of paying women — whether they are married or not — less than men for the same work.

Endlessly repeated by the mass media and school education, the *Dharma Wanita* doctrine seeks to perpetuate traditional perceptions of the appropriate places of the sexes in society, since it is cut to fit the prevailing ideas about hierarchy and moral order that assign mutually unequal tasks and obligations, the execution of which equates with moral fulfilment. It also fits Moslem concepts about gender relations, and the current process of Islamicization of Javanese society may very well reinforce this dominant ideology, especially among the urban middle classes where, in spite of tolerated public appearances and the professionalization of women, strong tendencies toward "housewifization" can also be noted. The first task of women appears to be woman, and the Five Duties of Women outline this.

All this may be more than a little depressing for Indonesian feminists, who also complain that the regimentation of the nation even leads to state control of family life. Based on the concept that the country is an organic integrated whole, individuals and groups can only be comprehended as parts of that totality who cannot exist free from it. The caretaker of the state, the strong government, thus prevails over its subjects, who it can even sacrifice for the well-being of the whole.

The household, or (nuclear) family, is acknowledged to constitute the smallest unit of the nation; if that building block is in good order, so will the republic be. This is even more the case for the country's civil servants who can only devote themselves full-heartedly to their task if they are not hampered by family problems. Their conjugal existence should thus be controlled, its moral and sexual life regulated, not only by way of family planning programmes, but also through the organization of the wives of army personnel and functionaries in the *Dharma Pertiwi* and *Dharma Wanita* respectively.

The husbands owe their first loyalty to the state, the wives to their husbands, and to keep the matrimonial relationships peaceful, marriage, divorce, and polygyny — polygamous wives are unthinkable — should be regulated, while wives should be protected from the more adventurous exploits of their men. Consequently, soldiers and civil servants should ask for the permission of their superiors before they divorce or marry a second wife, while all other relevant mutations in the family must be reported. Cohabitation without the benefit of nuptials is forbidden. Through these controls and each department head's command over the salaries, the morality of civil servants, and their married lives, can be checked up on. It may also force people to discuss very private matters with bureaucratic superiors, a situation that most would like to avoid (Suryakusuma, 1991).

The undifferentiated family as an organic unit of society in which men and women play complementary, yet hierarchically unequal roles, is an official ideal akin to widely held views. This thinking emphasizes the important moral position of the mother and recognizes the wholesome home as the wellspring of identity and virtue. Because of this ethical burden, it is very difficult to gain access behind the scenes to assess critically the everyday experience of family life, and the common circumstances that may give rise to problems. The walls seem to be high and the tenor of everyday marital life obscured by an ideological fog. This seems to be reassuring for most, however far divorced it may be from actual individual experiences. Due to the above, there is widespread reluctance to face and analyse, or even to discuss, personal problems, to uncover the realities of the less than ideal circumstances, which the majority feel should remain hidden from the public view.

None of this is particularly helpful to the cause of feminism, to the mutual emancipation of the sexes, and to a new thinking about gender relationships. There are so many disturbing questions that need raising about prevailing relationships that the task seems overawing. For instance, is it really possible to question the idea that hierarchy, or inequality, is moral per se? That women must become mothers and thus shoulder the burden of moral preceptor? Caught in a golden cage and put on a pedestal, it will be very difficult for any woman, as a mother, to step down to earth and to acquire the independent personhood that some progressives think to be her right.

Most people would find it hard to conceive of even asking such questions, not only because they cut across the grain of their culture, but also because such a deed would be out of joint with prevailing consciousness. Feminism and democracy are products of a different historical experience and other structures of thought. They are grounded in the acknowledgement of human equality and the subsequent emancipation movements in the evolution of western society, leading up to the formulation of a doctrine of human rights. This evolved against a historical backdrop of the emancipation of colonials from the colonizer, of the citizen from the dynast, of the slaves from their owners, of the working class from the bourgeoisie, of women from patriarchy, of children from parents. In this long drawn out development, in which emancipation is a central theme, sociology, reflection upon societal complexity, and political ideology to remedy social arrangements, evolved in fits and starts over centuries with one step leading through inexorable logic to the next.

This new awareness had involved the analysts distancing themselves from concrete situations and experience, building theories to understand what was going on, and asking questions about social structure while tracing its historical evolution. Who are rich and who are poor, and why? Who is oppressor and who is oppressed, and why? By abstracting from concrete situations, answers could be given, inequalities analyzed and causes assigned, stereotypes and ideologies unmasked, dominant thought patterns recognized, and the enfranchisement of most people from these prevailing ideas achieved. This type of consciousness is hardly existent in Indonesia today, and typical feminist questions, let alone specific theory, are unlikely to be formulated with much clarity, and even if so, cannot expect to be understood by all those who still sail on a self-righteous moral compass bearing (see p. 117-9).

In this pre-scientific environment, society is still experienced as concrete social relationships to known people, and womanhood still formulated in the terms of religion and *Dharma Wanita*. The sexes are still thought of as naturally given, as biology rather than as gender. Consequently, problems of emancipation, women's rights, gender equality, and so forth, will be treated as moral questions and be largely obscured by the ideological fog that hides them from close scrutiny.

But, however much men dominate life outside the home and however much prestige is allocated to them, it is hardly correct to talk about innate chauvinism in the Indonesian situation. That is because, in this cultural constellation, the categorization of life in two symbolic realms that are complementary, yet of unequal prestige, appears entirely natural to most of those involved. In such a hierarchical setting that always assigns unequal obligations, the fulfilment of which is moral and equally binding on all, the thought of emancipation is an aberration. People are mutually unequal and dependent.

A male chauvinist is one who defends his prerogatives in a historical situation that does not recognize his rights to such privilege any longer, let alone its moral underpinnings. Western men, therefore, who deny women access to what they arrogate to themselves, are swimming against the currents of their own history and culture, and it is fair to take issue with that. Where the equality of rights is a supreme moral principle, emancipation becomes an imperative to be supported. Both as a practical situation and an ideology, all this still appears way beyond the horizon in Indonesia, where militarization and its influence over concomitant bureaucratization reinforce authoritarianism, hierarchy, male prestige, and a 'virility cult'.

It seems that, for the time being, gender separation and its sustaining cultural stereotypes will persist in spite of women entering the professions and the general labour market. This is not only because of the official propaganda that reinforces conservative thinking, while aiming at strengthening the family as the basic unit of society, but also because of a style of socialization that stresses differences in role and moral value, and a psychology that is strongly relational. In that construction, it is very hard to imagine oneself as free from the roles and relationships to others that define one's basic identity. Seen from the point of personality development, people do not experience the self independently, meaning that their degree of individuation tends to be comparatively low, and they are thus not capable of looking at interpersonal situations in an impersonal, objective manner, as we shall see in the next chapter. So, if Indonesian feminists want to discover the roots of gender separation, they still need to travel down a long road that will lead them far beyond the immediate issues of prostitution, unequal pay, and other social 'injustices'. Once having achieved that distancing, these latter burning preoccupations will be revealed as the mere epiphenomena of a very complex situation.

Gender categorization is a refractory part of the culture, buttressed by a conception of morality and a psychology that combined together make it particularly resistant to change. This classification is not just ideology, but is practically expressed in patterns of association. Women befriend women, men befriend men, and there appear to be many obstacles to free flowing communication between the sexes. Often both are very low in self-confidence in dealing with each other, a psychological uncertainty that does not promote serious conversation and interchanges. Even marriage itself tends to reinforce institutionalized roles and gender separation, rather than fostering intensified communication.

There is more to this than ideological gender separation and practical segregation. Free flowing communication, the frank negotiation of feelings and opinion, may be felt as confrontational, as threatening conflict. The delightful observation of Hildred Geertz illustrates this point when she describes the case of a young, married man who avoided talking with his wife as much as possible, which he saw as the best strategy to maintain the peace (1961).

It is never good manners to be straightforward or explicit, and good, refined *(alus)* people are masters of indirectness, often evasive and devious, dissembling intentions, always avoiding the hazard of causing others to suffer loss of face. This part of the culture enjoys higher validation than frank communication, which may disrupt good order. Of course, the boss can allow himself to be candid, to give orders, but he also should be careful not to criticize his underlings in front of others, because it would result in their suffering acute embarrassment, and so being less committed in carrying out his commands.

With all these things standing in the way of communication — hierarchy, moral inequality, gender ideology, sex, roles, caution, etiquette — it would be wildly optimistic to anticipate a fluent and frank discourse developing, about whatever type of problems, in the immediate future. This is especially so, then, for one concerning the most 'sacred' of institutions, the family and gender relationships.

CHAPTER 6

About psychology, women, and conflict

Amazingly little is known about the experience of growing up in a Javanese environment. What is best known about the family is its ideology and, of course, some of the observable and statistical consequences, such as distant fathers representing the world outside, and near mothers, symbolizing the inside, who also run the household and become the central figure in the home. This situation is often described by the term matrifocality, meaning that the domestic affairs revolve around the mother more than the father, with the former, and commonly also her relatives, providing the primary source of stability and identity for the children, bilaleral descent notwithstanding.[1]

Yet, what all this means precisely for the development of the child and its experience of family relationships can only be speculated about. Local research in these matters of culture and psychology faithfully follows the methods and thoughts of western textbooks, and researchers are still blinkered by family and gender ideology. So all one can do at this stage is to theorize on the basis of the little that is known, largely from the observations of anthropologists, and the contributions of Filipino psychologists and psychiatrists who have advanced far further in a cultural environment that is more comparable to the Javanese one than the imported Euro-American notions that at present serve to inspire Indonesian social science.

In the Philippines, the western psychological notion of personality has been questioned. According to Enriquez, familiar people are so close to each other that they share in each other's personality.[2] Their

---

1 The best observations about Javanese family life are still Hildred Geertz's (1961); about the undoing of the marital bonds, see Hisako Nakamura, *Divorce in Java: a Study of the Dissolution of Marriage among Javanese Muslims*. Yogyakarta: Gadjah Mada University Press, 1983.

2 Enriquez, V.G., *Kapwa*: a core concept in Filipino social psychology. V.G. Enriquez (ed), *Philippine World View*. Singapore: Institute of South-East Asian Studies, 1986:9-12.

identity feelings overlap, or interpenetrate, and they cannot define themselves as personalities independent of others. This is grounded in socialization, in always being together with others, and the demand to be sensitive to mutual feelings, to be careful with, and mindful of, one's fellows while maintaining workable relationships.

The cultivation of operational mutuality was also noted by Lynch, who made social acceptance and getting along with each other harmoniously the key-stones of his interpretation. SIR, smooth interpersonal relationships, are so central to Filipino behaviour that people submit to them, not only to avoid trouble but, more especially, to gain acceptance, thus giving in to others while enjoying the pleasure of association.[3]

This corresponds with psychiatrist Lapuz's observation that the interpersonal world becomes the primary source of emotional gratification, and that the successful negotiation of one's affairs with family and friends brings reassurance, recognition, and the material resources that are needed to feel secure and accepted.[4]

This easily leads to the recurrent observation, also in the literature about Java, that a person's self-esteem derives from how he is perceived by others, thus making for conformity with expectations, along with timidity and unassertiveness. Security derives from the correct enactment of status requirements and role. In Bulatao's opinion, this often results in an "inferiority complex" that sprouts from the suffocatingly close ties that allow for insufficient development of the self.[5]

According to the same author, family-type relationships, socialization practices, and inescapable togetherness, all these foster the intensive experience of oneself as a member of a closed group rather than as a separate being. He describes this phenomenon with the comparative notion of "unindividuated ego" (1964:430). From this position, he then proceeds to describe the Filipino as somebody whose individual core is identifiable, but whose ego-boundaries blend with those of others (431).

3 Lynch, F., Social acceptance reconsidered (1973). A.A. Yengoyan and P.Q. Makil (eds), *Philippine Society and the Individual*. Ann Arbor: University of Michigan, 1984.

4 Lapuz, L.V., *A study of psychopathology*. Quezon City: New Day Publishers, 1978.

5 Bulatao, S.J., J.C., Hiya. *Philippine Studies* 12 (1964):424-38.

He perceives himself as a member of a group and has therefore a dependent identity. So the basic unit of society is not the individual but the closed group that absorbs the person, the nuclear family being the prime example.

In passing, we may note that this last psychological observation corresponds with the Javanese-Indonesian ideological position that we exposed in the previous chapter: the individual is subsumed by his group, his family. But apart from ideology, the Filipino assumptions also seem probably applicable statements about Javanese identity and personality. Furthermore, the Javanese experience of life is strongly relational and centres on near persons, with whom one is not necessarily intimate, but with whom one must share narrow space. People are close in a physical sense and acutely aware of needing each other (Mulder, 1989:55; APPENDIX F). In this setting, there is constant interference in each other's lives, a continuous reference to others with whom one tries to get along as well as possible by strategies that may range from avoidance to tolerance, from dissembling to sensitivity, from conformity to role-playing. It appears likely that these very similar circumstances in Java may also lead to a relatively low degree of individuation and a high need for acceptance.

People mutually control each other, poking their noses into others' affairs, becoming mutual superego representatives. It is the eyes and ears, the opinions of others that need to be managed. These latter are a very prominent part of one's existence, because they can cause loss of face, shame — and thus undermine one's self-respect — while they can also enhance self-satisfaction by indicating acceptance and, possibly, praise. In this experience, conscience — and part of identity, too — becomes consciousness of others.

It seems that the concept and possible practice of *kebatinan* mitigates the validity of too much comparison with the Philippines. While it is certainly true that Filipinos have fewer cultural means to retreat from the pressures of social space, and also that *kebatinan* promotes self-centredness, its practice does not necessarily affect "individuation", the experience of the self as an independent personality. *Kebatinan* celebrates individuality, that is individualization in the sense of temporarily placing the adept apart from society; it is a retreat, a holiday that, according to certain psychiatrists, is definitely beneficial to mental health (Dipojono, 1969; 1972).[6] It is a recharging of the battery and, if resulting in the strengthening of the inner resources, certainly personality-building. All this makes a person less vulnerable at the hands of others, it may foster leadership capabilities, but whether it results in a socially independent identity experience, when one once more needs to function among others, remains an open question. While granting that a preoccupation with *kebatinan* — which is mainly found among males — may contribute to personal independence, the social preoccupation with prestige — also generally a concern of men — makes them continually dependent on social acceptance, resulting in a self-experience that is constantly evaluated by others.

This polarity of fields of self-expression may result in its own pathogeny. We have already noted that the mystical practice of *kebatinan* does not always lead to happiness or perfection, and may disrupt psychological balance, especially among those who are less adept, the young and neophytes. But the practical and culturally validated possibility of retreat into the self can also lead to particular problems. This is reportedly often the case among those gentlemen who are extremely conscious of their dignity, of the prestige with which they identify on the social stage, which not only comprises their public and professional appearances, but also their association with family members. As distant fathers and dignified husbands, they are unable to communicate with progeny and spouse, their emotional life silting up, as it were, since kept to themselves. This type of retreat seems to be stimulated by status anxiety, by a permanent worrying about the impression they make on others, and leads to its own pathology. In a way, it is a caricature of what *kebatinan*, as the cultivation of inner resources, of a real inner core and equanimity, stands for, but it remains a real possibility.

The idea that status anxiety could be a common affliction in an environment that is highly conscious of hierarchy, self-presentation and social performance, seems obvious. It is one aspect of Lapuz's general idea that the permanent pressure of the presence of others — actual or

6 This position was recently reaffirmed by a quantitative research project of the Faculty of Medicine of Gadjah Mada University. Inu Wicaksana *et al.*, *Aspek falsafah hidup (Jawa) terhadap depresi pada warga beberapa kelompok kejawèn di Yogyakarta* (Relationship between living in accordance with the Javanese philosophy of life and suffering from depressions). *Jiwa, Majalah Psikiatri* 22/3 (1989):53-71.

imagined — is a prime cause of psychological malfunctioning, suppressing individual self-expression and other personality needs. By contrast, she points out that the stress on individual performance, such as standing on one's own feet, managing personal affairs by oneself, proving one's autonomy and independence, is a common cause of psychopathology in western countries.

Here is not the place to elaborate on the possible causes of mental disturbances in as far as they can be traced to living arrangements and socialization, but rather to explore how these latter normal experiences generate common, yet often implicit, expectations about psychological functioning. In view of the ideological and practical importance of the mother figure, we should begin with her.

In Southeast Asia, I am always struck by the tendency to idolize the mother, who seems to impress herself really deeply on the emotional life of her children. In every discussion about the subject, some people will take the opportunity of praising their mothers, and in my interview material she regularly surfaces as the only person in the world who really cares and can fully be trusted. The mother is close to her children, accessible, radiating warmth and consolation, living for her offspring and becoming the centre of their lives.

This matrifocality is enhanced by the cult of the mother and its pervasive ideological underpinnings. As the symbol of morality, goodness, self-sacrifice, endurance, responsibility, women as mothers carry a heavy ideational burden that also provides the reasons why mother should be honoured above all else. The emotional experience of closeness to her and the indoctrination in her moral impeccability combine to make the mother the dominant figure of the consciousness and conscience of her children, she becoming the primary superego representative. Disobedience, or going against her wishes, hurting her in any way, is about the worst thing imaginable, causing severe feelings of guilt, referred to as *rasa berdosa* (I), feelings of being burdened by sin.

To have a good relationship with the mother, to be devoted to her, also becomes of extraordinary importance, therefore, for one's own feelings of self-respect. Neglect of her feelings, say, going against her wishes even if she will never know, is often felt as treachery to this most important of relations, thus damaging the self. So, when her mother mildly objected to her taking up a job in Jakarta — perhaps the mother was merely worried about life in the city, or might feel lonely because of her absence — a female factory worker (28) felt uneasy for as long as she had not visited her mother again in the small town she hailed from. Upon being reunited, she could, with some pride, show that her new existence was a relative success, not only because she sent money home, but also because of her rapid promotion to overseer that demonstrated her competence. When she went back to the capital, she felt much better because her mother had expressed trust in her decision to pursue a career in town. She felt accepted as a good person, her conscience unburdened.

In contrast, Harjanto's feelings were uneasy because of his failure to fulfil his moral obligations to his mother. At night, I met him regularly at the place where I often dropped by for a drink before retiring. He was an extrovert, given to boasting about his resourcefulness and obviously enjoying his financial success and independence. At thirty-seven, he had made it as a tailor, receiving steady orders from army officers who commissioned their dress uniforms from him. Yet, almost every time we met, and after drinking a glass of beer, he also talked about his aging mother and her hopes of seeing him married before she died. In view of their ages, he was in a fix. In his mother's view, he was still a child, unsettled, and not satisfying his duty to his parents. His predicament was that he had to choose between his personal preference for a free lifestyle and his mother's peace of mind.

An older informant related agonizing over his moral dilemma when he was about to be incarcerated as a political prisoner. Should his ideological principles prevail, or should he consider the suffering that his punishment would cause to his mother? He decided to recant, because the idea of her anxiety was the more repugnant, also causing himself psychical distress. Mother's welfare should take precedence over more mundane politics, her tranquillity being the higher good.

The closeness to the mother and her importance in one's emotional life may even be expressed after death in cases where a choice can be made between visiting the spiritually more powerful grave of the father or the more homely one of the mother. Most often, the latter one will be the destination of the yearly pilgrimage, honouring her in reminiscence of the emotional warmth that she had always bestowed, while feeling close to her in spirit once again.

The interest of these stories derives from their being told by people who were well advanced into adulthood, the mother apparently remaining important in their emotional life and claiming an important part of their conscience. While the mother figure is an important super-ego representative for any small child, western psychology would argue that children should free themselves of parental dominance around the age of puberty — often simply understood as protest against tutelage — and seriously begin to develop an independent conscience. In Java, puberty is only understood in its biological sense of young people becoming functionally capable of procreation, while the superego role of the parents continues in function, often extending throughout one's adult life. This situation of being tied to others, that is often treated as problematical, even as mildly pathological, in western psychology, is definitely the norm in much of Southeast Asia, and can better be understood in terms of a relative degree of individuation, as proposed, for instance by Bulatao.

Seemingly, conscience rests on consciousness of others and is anchored in concrete relationships with personally known people, a situation that apparently builds from the qualities of the most important of relationships. Yet it cannot be expected that more remote people will give rise to the same intensity of feelings, and transgressions do not evoke the guilt that gainsaying one's parents stimulates. It is rather the feeling of being at fault, *rasa bersalah* (I), that surfaces in such contexts, which is also wrong-doing, but is apparently negotiable, though giving rise to the discomfort of 'shame'.

While it is true that the great, abstract principles of Good and Evil do not seem to have made much impression on the Southeast-Asian mind — their acceptance is perhaps related to a greater degree of individuation of the person — the widespread fear of shame does not preclude the existence alongside it of very tangible feelings of guilt, as well. These lead to the psychical self-flagellation that some modern people recognize as *walat*, the punishment sent in retribution for infractions against what should be morally inviolable.

The emphasis on status in a hierarchizing environment corresponds with the assumed relatively low degree of individuation. For status recognition, a person is dependent on others, who attribute the prestige that becomes one's self-esteem. What's more, a person's private self-definition always includes others. Seeing self and others relationally brings status and role aspects to the fore, and these thus become more prominent at the personal level than one's psychological constitution. In other words, there is a strong tendency to identify with expectations.

This is highlighted in literature about 'traditional' Javanese women written by male authors. In his story *Sumarah*, Umar Kayam presents us with a woman who finds her satisfaction in adapting herself fully to the wishes of her environment, serving her husband hand and foot. Also Linus Suryadi's *Pariyem* can only see and understand herself as the faithful servant of a ranking family, her being equating with her role. It is from this identification that she derives her personhood. There is no conflict apparent between the individual's psychical make-up and environmental expectations; if there ever was, it has been transcended, the two seemingly having united.

These idealistic descriptions may oversimplify matters greatly, yet they expose clearly the palpable reality of identification with role, especially among women. While everybody is expected to marry, the pressure on girls to do so is very considerable. Not to marry is shameful, an embarrassment for the parents and a blot on their reputation, also reflecting badly on their daughter. And if the non-marrying woman has younger sisters, she may even delay their entry into the conjugal state, because some still hold that the elder one should marry first. Moreover, marriage is an obligation owed to parents, and having descendants is one's duty in life. This ideological construction has an inbuilt self-fulfilling character and few are the people who remain unwed.

Children are reared to marry, and the girls in addition are trained and expected to become housewives. Being forever fussed over by a lowly individuated mother, who finds her fulfilment in having sons and daughters who depend on her, and whom she likes to dominate — an act often necessary to assert her own identity — girls will be reproduced who again will seek their satisfaction in mothering. This has become second nature to them during their upbringing, erasing the boundaries between self and expectations, while prodding them to find security in role performance.

Very often parents are overprotective of their daughters, whom they feel they have to worry about more than sons. They, and especially mothers, constantly interfere in their lives and intervene in decisions, a situation that is of course buttressed by the ideological moral role that presiding females are thought to exemplify. This may contribute to low self-confidence on the part of subordinate women and the seeking of acceptance through the execution of tasks. And from an early age on, these are continually part of the fabric of life. Daughters are expected to help in the household, to take responsibility, and to show restraint when associating with the opposite sex. This training in identification with task, duty, and role also spills over into the reputation of women in contemporary life in Southeast-Asian cities, where managers almost invariably agree that, other things being equal, women are the better, the more conscientious workers, or even as students for that matter, they are seen as more capable and responsible than their male peers.

From the foregoing, one thing should be clear. Boys obviously receive a somewhat different education. Compared with the girls, they enjoy a much greater freedom of movement and are far less burdened with tasks and responsibilities. Theirs is the wide world outside the home. This relatively privileged position is a form of pampering that is reinforced by the tendency to pay more attention to the whims and wishes of the boys. Naturally, this often results in spoiled sons who remain very dependent on signs of affection, acceptance and care, for which they rely heavily on their mother and, by extension, the other females in the home environment.

In this construction, mothers impress themselves on their son's psyches as the source from which goodness flows, and I have often been amazed in listening to the eulogy on "My Mother" by men of all ages. It is perhaps for men even more so than for women that the maternal figure grows to cultic proportions, so the quality of the relationship to her remains a prime marker of identity, self-respect, and ethical behaviour. Later on, when married, the mother may still remain so dominant in the consciousness of men that they take her side, following her wishes as against those of their spouse.

Compared with the girls, who learn to identify with their role that also moulds their self-confidence, the expectations surrounding boys are far more diffuse. Since 'boys will be boys', a measure of irresponsibility and naughtiness on their side is tolerated. After all, the symbolic load that they carry is very different. Males are not seen as the reliable centre of the home or the symbol of morality. They represent the world outside that they will have to subdue, and that place is not necessarily moral. It is a relatively competitive place where status and prestige are the important prizes.

The normally rather distant and authoritarian father offers little to immediately identify with other than the prestige of the family that he incorporates. In most cases, he is content to leave the matters of the home in the hands of his wife; his affairs are on the other side of the fence, separate from female worries and cares. This division of concerns results in practice in distinct areas of activity and identification. Although there is no law that says so, the sexes are each allocated their realms in life and there seems to be comparatively little overlap. The need for communication is therefore low and the security of role-playing high, which may contribute to a relative insecurity of the sexes vis-à-vis each other.

This, of course, is to be expected among people who tend to be low in individuation. Deeper communication is stimulated by greater overlap of realms and roles, opening more concerns to common experience and deliberation. In that process, people need to face each other, to assume mutually high profiles, to crystallize so to say, as personalities. This, for the time being, seems unlikely, and not for reasons of the prevailing gender ideology alone. It is mainly due to the anchoring in a psychology in which identification with role or status determine self-confidence. In leaving these positions, people would have to seek their security in their own personality, standing independently on their own feet, all of which runs counter to training and experience.

Dependence is the normal thing, not (moral) autonomy, and the original social environment is crucial for one's self-concept. Because of the initial vagueness of their role, of being pampered, and of later consciousness of status — requiring to be served — males grow up much more dependent on women than the latter on men. Often husbands turn into a kind of eldest son to their spouses, a situation that wives refer to as having a *bayi tuwa*, an old baby, in the house.

In the dependent, unindividuated conscience, the mother tends to remain very important. Often the wife takes over as a superego representative, or becomes one more, juxtaposed with the mother. It is this psychological function plus the symbolic load of motherhood that often stand in the way of a wife developing an erotic relationship with her spouse. She may be praised and idealized romantically, being the impeccable mother, but as such and as the embodiment of conscience she is in an awkward position to become the focus of her man's sexual drives.

The separation of realms and the different symbolisms they represent are pernicious. We have noted how they function as obstacles to communication between the sexes that marriage is often unable to dissolve, with women opting for their prescribed roles of mother and devoted wife, and the men for dignified fatherhood and provider. Since the man's area is the amoral world outside, he can release his erotic drives there, seeking women who do not symbolize morality. After all, who wants to sleep with his conscience?

For men, sex away from home is not really a moral issue and little stigma attaches to it as long as it is done discreetly. Wives may not like it, but the double standard is firmly in place, in spite of the prudery of the New Order state. The entrenchment of two different norms, one for women and one for men, has, of course, much to do with gender ideology, but also with a socialization that results in a psychological construction that stimulates identification with role rather than individuation and communication.

Generally speaking, the Javanese of the sultanates are cautious about expressing themselves, even to their spouses. Opening oneself up is dangerous, exposing vulnerabilities, and threatening to oneself while placing one's prestige in the hands of others, or, as an old saying has it, "A person's self-esteem is at his lips". What one says is also a potential menace to the partner in conversation, who may feel irritated, offended, slighted, pressured, criticized, in brief, confronted. It is therefore much better to keep the conversation irrelevant, to allow each other all ways out while maintaining the form one's role prescribes.

The socio-psychology of conflict

Quite early in life, people learn to suppress their negative feelings and to master their emotions so as not to disturb each other unduly. The initiative is with the nurturing mother, or her representative, who takes very close care of the child, sheltering it from disturbance and indulging it at the slightest signs of displeasure. As a result of this, autonomy is late in arising, dependence is regarded as positive, and attuning one's sensibilities to the presence of others becomes 'innate'.

In other words, people not only learn to side-step confrontation but also give it little chance to arise. Siblings learn to share, to play games for the sake of playing and not of competing, and if quarrels break out, all involved are most likely punished. Contentions among siblings are disgraceful, and possible negative feelings should be restrained.

Conflicts with parents are viewed as almost sacrilegious and characteristically their very existence is denied — but if one should burst into the open, it is experienced as socially most shameful and destructive of one's self. Discord among brothers and sisters should also be muted, although the feelings of resentment it gives rise to may often be vented in the private company of a good friend. Since mutual avoidance in the family is almost impossible, in cases of strife, parents may take an active role in reconciling their children with each other, and in restoring the semblance of peace and harmony. However, where suppression of conflict is a norm, a veneer of normalcy may hide true feelings and tensions that simmer on long.

People learn to experience themselves as members of a solidary group that defines part of their identity, and from which they derive a good deal of their self-assurance. Within that group, they enjoy a rather low degree of ego-autonomy, and accept hierarchy and deference for age as unquestioned moral criteria. In consequence, they equably tolerate a measure of interference in 'their' affairs, including criticism from relevant others.

The relatively dependent identity and other-directedness make for a high degree of vulnerability at the hands of others, of the easy arousing of feelings of shame and wounded dignity. Since people know this of themselves and of each other, they are given to caution, to avoidance and tolerance, and to being wary of each other. Sensing the feelings of others thus becomes an art, the art of staying out of trouble and, naturally, of getting one's way.

Emotion and feeling, intuition, empathy and sympathy, self-consciousness and appreciation of each other's dignity, these are the valid guides in interaction, along with the suppression of conflict, the denial of frustration, and the mastery of negative emotions. Often one's own strong, dark feelings are felt to be as threatening as the presumed critical opinions of others.

Yet despite all that, tensions and frustrations may build up and need to be released. While men may have recourse to talking with friends about negative experiences, the culture also advises a more self-centred way to relax tension in the cultivation of the inner self and a calm mind.[7] By declaring the *batin* to contain a truth superior to whatever may be the reality of the social world, many Javanese are able to handle their distressing experiences, learning to accept *(nrima)* rather than letting themselves be overwhelmed by them. Their safety valve, so to say, is within themselves.

Most women need more social space to release frustrations. To them, relationships with each other are a vital element in organizing life and restoring disturbed equilibrium. Gregariousness, conversation, and gossip are means that allow them to let off steam. They are believed to be by nature less restrained than men, and so enjoy a somewhat greater freedom to voice frustrations, thus 'getting them out of their systems'.

In a private world that is conceived of and experienced as highly interpersonal and interdependent, it is rewarding to pay close attention to the avoidance of open, solidarity-threatening conflict. Often, people stay out of trouble by not involving themselves at all, by indifference, or by avoiding controversial contacts while ignoring *(nengnengan)* actual and potential opponents.

Although avoidance behaviour suits people who do not live under a common roof, silence may also be practised within the home as a way of either softening or carrying on a conflict. To talk about it, to try to deal with it by discussing the problem, is usually felt to be too confrontational an approach to the resolution of such tensions. In all sorts of relationships, one may find that people are rather inhibited, guarding themselves, and normally unable to pin-point what precisely plagues

---

7 The development of a strong inner core and a refined intuition is primarily an endeavour of men. Not that women are excluded from, or incapable of, generating potency and efficacy, but they are held to be less gifted in these things, their very nature throwing up more obstacles than those encountered by men. Or, possibly, women are just less interested in the pursuit of *kebatinan*. In passing, though, we have noted that the widespread lower-middle-class *aliran* Sapta Darma is headed by a woman, *Sri* Pawenang.

them emotionally. Generally, negative feelings need to be left to soften up over time — avoidance and the use of intermediaries being excellent means.

Wives may refuse to talk to husbands for days on end, or retire for some time to mother's. Often there are a plenty of reasons for such behaviour: infidelity, trouble with in-laws, conflicts of loyalty (between parents and spouse), the husband's spending too much time away from home, and gambling, all being the roots of much conjugal discord. Yet, in the marital abode the need for reconciliation, or at least peaceful coexistence, is high, and thus many wives choose to confine themselves to their roles of housekeeper and mother (rather than spouse and lover) and men opt to be mere bread-winners rather than emotionally involving themselves with their women and the affairs of the children.

Discussing problems appears to be difficult. If it occurs, it is top down, parents telling children what to do, and so on, though children are not supposed to answer back — as with subordinates outside the home. Criticism or rebuke of children should preferably be done in private and never in front of others — and so it should be in other extra-familial relationships. But even private hierarchical communication may be startling *(kejut-kejut-atiné)* and cause much psychical discomfort *(sungkan)*, such as demonstrated by the servant of my Javanese housekeeper. Addressing him directly, and so jumbling the good order of the compound, made him feel confronted, and so my innocent request — "See to it that there is always a rag hanging here for wiping my motorcycle" — perplexed him so much that he left the house the same day.

Direct interaction carries the seed of conflict, and yet people need to work together and cannot avoid associating with each other. Keeping each other at a certain distance helps, and so do good manners, indirectness, shyness and giggling, sensitivity to the mood of others, respect for authority, tolerance and low privacy requirements, conformity to expectations, and fear of gossip and backbiting. Altogether, to keep relationships in good order and operational takes a lot of conscientious effort. People know that harmony, *rukun*, does not come for free.

In brief, the way in which Javanese live with conflict in everyday life is very much coloured by the effort to avoid it, and to skirt situations that may provoke or challenge others. The anger of others is often felt as physically or magically threatening, in the same way as harsh words, or talking about an inappropriate subject, may cause upset. But while gossip falls in the category of bad words, it is sometimes also positively appreciated as a means of getting to know of the neighbours' irritation about one's behaviour, so that the offence can be avoided in the future. The best thing, of course, is to give no cause for gossip, and people feel morally good when others have no critical things to say about them. After all, it is these others who guide one's conscience, the superego being located in relationships, in the consciousness of others. Consequently, it is there, in these relationships, that one is vulnerable, and thus it becomes imperative to avoid conflict and promote solidarity.

A common strategy for dealing with, or avoiding, conflict is (unconscious) denial of its existence, which sometimes leads to nervous problems that are subsequently drowned in over-activity or (excessive) gregariousness among women, or side-stepped in the self-centred practice of *kebatinan* among men. Another way, cultivated by both sexes, but particularly by women, is to live up to one's obligations, even in adversity, by complying with the wishes of others *(sumarah)*. Other strategies that are less overtly psychological are staying away from where one has no business, being tolerant of, or indifferent to, what happens around one, withdrawing from contact when anticipating trouble or controversy, denying their existence by behaving as if everything is normal, acknowledging the moral right of superiors and following their wishes, or passivity and inaction even in the company of others. These self-repressive strategies may sometimes lead to typical, culturally induced psychopathology.

Summarizing patterns of thought

Order versus disorder

The Javanese preoccupation with the ideals of unity and order, that often appear to mean the same thing, may be interpreted as the desire to escape from pluriformity and confusion. Unity and order mean peacefulness, quiet continuity, mastery, success and well-being, a moral way of life, that all seem to be threatened by the chaotic forces of non-domesticated nature, the untamed drives and desires of the individual, and the lure of the spirit world.

While it is wise to do everything possible to maintain order and guarantee continuity, for all that, turbulent currents may be flowing beneath the calm surface. On occasion, encounters with disorder are unavoidable. There are historical periods when, however much people might like to distance themselves from it, they are inexorably caught up in strife. This, for the Javanese, is symbolized by the great myth of the battle of the Mahabharata between the Pendawa and the Kurawa.

It is the Kurawa who symbolize the forces of passion and greed, of unbridled desire and egoistic motives. They are arrogant and boastful, although also valiant knights, and in spite of their natural allies, the dreadful demons and giants *(reksasa)*, they must lose to the Pendawa, the faction that stands for order, control, steadfastness, justice and elegance.

This symbolism recurs in the thinking of those who strive after a pure life by the practice of *kebatinan*. Through training their inner resources *(batin; rasa)*, they aim at overcoming their passions, sensual desires and egoistic motives, taming their nature, as it were, while generating discipline, insight, endurance, steadfastness in purpose, and inner quiet. Imperturbable, they demonstrate the power of their *batin* and the subtlety of their *rasa* (sixth sense), holding sway over and anticipating events. Apparently attuned to the great scheme of necessity, *kodrat*, they naturally attract disciples and followers, and if they opt to do so, they can become potent leaders.

This is also the picture that the president projects of himself (Soeharto, 1989). His *Orde Baru* is a historical necessity on Indonesia's road to perfection, and that order revolves around his person, his concentrated potency that inspires it.[1] He is therefore not indebted to anybody at all, each of the other prominent adherents of the New Order being attracted by the power of his *batin*, mere henchmen and followers. The only person who needs positive recognition in his autobiography is thus his legitimator and predecessor, Sukarno, Soeharto himself thus becoming a kind of shadow crown prince, a secretive and necessary co-ordinate moving through Indonesian events until *Supersemar*, as the great *kebeneran*, draws him out on to the centre stage of history.[2]

Kebatinan aims at concentrating potency, which may then radiate, control and inspire. The serious practitioner should pursue it for its own sake, for the perfection of life. According to many, he should not set himself up to teach others, because that could stimulate self-satisfaction and vanity, egotistical motives that should be avoided. Others are not in agreement and become gurus, often relishing the limelight, and some of them may even become teachers of the science of invulnerability, give lottery predictions, reveal auspicious dates, or simply counsel and advice. Among them, there are quite a few who practise healing. Because of their advanced training and self-discipline, they become sources from which a curative force flows. Thanks to the inspiration that they derive from asceticism and meditation, and because of the refinement of their *rasa*, they can feel what ails their patient, and can thus diagnose and give advice. This combination, of possessing healing energy, inspiration, plus their trained intuition, makes them the source of beneficial power. Since they are not supposed to be propelled by ego-motives, they are expected not to charge for their services. In the

1 For an overview of the historical depth and roots of 'Javanization', and the continuing relevance of *kejawèn* as an aid to understanding the republican present, see Denys Lombard (1990), especially part III, *L'héritage des royaumes concentriques*.

2 From my reading of the excerpt of a speech by Sukarno that Anderson presents (1990:83-5), I think it safe to conclude that the first president, at least during the years of Guided Democracy when he had become the Great Leader of the Revolution, also saw himself as the embodiment of historical necessity.

pure tradition of *kebatinan*, their self-discipline and activities make the world a better, a more beautiful place *(mamayu hayuning buwana)*.

The above reasoning explains why a steady informant and old friend was not pleased when I happily showed him the place where he figured in my book. There, in the first edition, I referred to him as practitioner of Javanese medicine which I glossed with *dhukun*. That word, meanwhile, has been suffering some downward mobility that makes it less acceptable these days, but the reasons for my friend's displeasure went deeper than that. For him, they lay in my faulty understanding.

In his self-image, he was a *sepuh*, a respected elder whose guidance was sought in many fields of life and who had acquired a reputation for healing. Because he was an advanced practitioner of *kebatinan*, he radiated a curative mesmerism, directly influencing the state of health of his patients.

Dhukun, he explained, are mere intermediaries, mediators between the supernatural and the patient. They seek their inspiration in the disorderly realm of those lower forces that are represented by the Kurawa, are possessed by spirits and souls, and practise magic. Often their behaviour and activities should be deemed sinful, going against good order, and motivated by desire for personal gain. While there is no denying that their advice may be often sought and their influence efficacious, they draw inspiration from a different source. Moreover, as mediums, *préwangan*, they do not harbour power; without their spiritual possessors, their riders, they are impotent. Inevitably, the esteem in which they are held is ambiguous, and their familiarity with invisible forces and magic makes people fear rather than trust them.[3]

3 My friend distinguished between three types of healers; the exemplary, wise and respected older people, or *wong tuwa (eyang; sepuh; ki; kiai)* who want to help others, whom he contrasted with *dhukun* and *préwangan* who function as mediums, befriending souls and evil spirits, and practise magic, most often for personal gain; he allowed for the existence of those who practise for the exclusive benefit of their clients, too. The third category he recognized, were physical healers, such as the *dhukun bayi* (midwife) and *dukhun pijit* (masseur).

His classification corresponds with Rosalia Sciortino's. She found that local notions about healing separated secular, outward knowledge (*ilmu lahir* (I)) from the spiritual *ilmu batin* (I) practised by both *dhukun préwangan* and *wong tuwa*. See her *The Caretakers of Cure: A Study of Health Centre Nurses in Rural Central Java*. University of Amsterdam: dissertation, 1992:ch.8.

His lesson was lucid, and since I was in the process of revising the book, I could present the situation more clearly straightaway in the new edition, which I had the pleasure of showing him not long before I left (Mulder, 1989/1992:61).

Obligation

A sense of obligation should be at the heart of life, and is not merely a matter concerning inferiors in their relations with superiors. Parents also have their obligations vis-à-vis their children, whom they have to rear and protect, to teach and worry about. That is their task: they must prepare their offspring for life, see to it that they grow up human and respectable, conscious of others and the precariousness of existence. In preparing their children for life, they will arm their charges with good example and right teaching, while parents express their anxiety *(prihatin)* about this endeavour in austerities, minor forms of asceticism, *slametan* rituals and self-sacrifice.

In all this, the child appears to be on the receiving end, as the one who benefits from nurture and care, attention and teaching. This lays the basis of one of the most important attributes of personhood; the sense of gratitude, of obligation, of dependence and origin, or identity. Alone, nobody can survive; as social beings, people depend on each other, first of all on morally superior parents; this, in turn gives rise to obligations of respect, submission, and especially the recognition of sacrifice, and thus of gratitude. In a general sense, to be in the care of somebody places the recipient under a moral obligation *(utang budi)*, a debt of gratitude. Not to acknowledge such a debt is more than despicable; it is to be morally defective.

This sense of obligation to others is a salient and crucial element in Javanese existence; it is its moral touchstone, and the cement of social relationships. As a theme, it surfaces all the time in the Pancasila moral education programme, in which obligation is rooted in dependence and so, by implication, it censures those who are so presumptuous and arrogant as to think that they did it all alone, that they achieved their success independently, that they are 'self-made men'. Such 'individualism' verges on culpable self-glorification. It equates with not knowing gratitude, of negating one's essential humanity, of losing one's Javanese personhood. When people comment *"Ia sudah kehilangan kejawaannya"* (I), "He lost his Javanese qualities" — and it is a way certain public figures are talked about in Jakarta — they mean that such persons must be considered to be beyond the pale of civilized life, since exalted position has blinded them to obligation and morality.

While hierarchy is thought to be moral in itself and imposes an order on otherwise unrelated people, the essential experiential element is the recognition of beneficence received and the obligation to be grateful for it. Goodness bestowed creates loyalty and gratitude, and so, as soon as one steps outside the familiar hierarchy, one should know who is obliged to whom, what the content of the relationship is, what 'burden' this carries in order to be able to predict the ways others will act.

Such 'burdens' (*beban* (I)) can only arise between people who are concretely known to each other; it pairs individuals who relate dyadically, and who personally experience the relationship in which one feels obligated to the other. In other words, a moral element is inherent to such relationships that, if not honoured, will certainly cause shame and loss of face. In this conception, moral equality occurs only between persons who have nothing to do with each other, or who refuse to be the recipients of unsought favours.

Religious preoccupations

The position of parents is quasi-religious. As elders, they are closer to the Origin, to the sources of identity and wisdom, to Life, the line of which they must continue by procreating and rearing children. The fulfilment of this task makes them worthy of the highest respect and justifies the 'cult of the parents', in which they become an object of worship *(pepundhèn)* in themselves. The religious dimension of this 'cult' becomes clearer still from the dependence of children on their elders blessing *(pangèstu)*. Even when already well established and financially independent, at least once a year, at the *Lebaran* festival at the end of the fasting month of *Pasa* (Ramadan), siblings should gather at the ancestral home to ask for parental forgiveness and favour. This dependency continues when the parents have passed away, because children are expected to visit their graves *(nyadran)*, preferably during the month of *Ruwah* that precedes *Pasa*, or at least before *Lebaran*, to make offerings and to seek the beneficence they need in order to enjoy a peaceful and prosperous existence.

An interesting aspect of the parent-child relationship is that it locates certain 'religious' elements squarely in this world, such as the obligation to revere parents, the necessity to seek their blessing, while sins are in the first place committed against them, obstinacy and insolence not only invoking supernatural punishment *(walat)*, but also causing concrete feelings of guilt *(rumasa dosa)*. Altogether, it is safe to say that the relationship between parents and children provides the solid ground for the idea of moral hierarchy, ultimately stretching up to 'God', but firmly rooted in certain key relationships.

The primacy of social life is clearly expressed in the idea that "Whoever honours his parents, his elder siblings, his teacher, and his ruler, already honours 'God'" This dictum means that respect for social order is one's foremost obligation, and that good community relations transcend personal interests. This striving is also expressed in the core ritual of the *slametan* that seeks the blessing of ancestors and souls for *slamet*, quiet and peaceful, continuity. It demonstrates the nearness and accessibility of supernature and the desire to live in harmony with its beneficial forces. Some of these are located at graves, especially those of mystically inspired religious teachers *(kiai; wali)* and kings, that become *pepundhèn* or *kramatan*, spots where the faithful seek inspiration, potency, or lottery numbers, a quest that is often accomplished by ascetic practice at these places — such as staying awake throughout the night. In order to ward off inauspiciousness, ritual may be needed to avoid or reverse bad constellations, and offerings *(sesajèn)* are brought to appease or cajole invisible *(alus)*, yet near, spiritual beings.

It is clearly impossible to analyse these ideas in terms of the sacred and the profane, as is sometimes done in western sociology. Javanese thinking emphasizes the oneness of life, in which the condition of the cosmos is reflected by life on earth, and in which supernatural events penetrate everyday experiences. Supernature seems to be inhabited by all kinds of spiritual beings, whose intentions and potential may be beneficial or disruptive, but, so much is certain, their powers affect those in the visible realm of life. People are therefore preoccupied with the acquisition of blessing from those who can protect and with increasing personnel efficacy. In brief, religious practice is a relationship with power that is future-directed, not so much toward an afterlife, but as an activity seeking auspiciousness in the here-and-now. This quality is also exemplified by the practice of *kebatinan* for the sake of generating potency and efficacy.

Be that as it may, *kebatinan* also reveals an essential trait of the *kejawèn* philosophy of life and the shaping of its culture. Religious practice and mystical *kebatinan* are parts of *kejawèn*, and although the religious element is not necessarily dominant, neither can it be eliminated from a style of conceptualization that emphasizes wholeness and the unity of Life. In the Pancasila, the nature of this unity is referred to as *ke-Tuhanan*, the Divine, that may either be thought of as a transcendent God or an encompassing All-Soul *(Hyang Suksma)*. This latter less personal notion allows for equating the Divine with Life *(Urip)*, or with Necessity *(Kodrat)* and preordination, with *kebatinan* becoming the endeavour — quasi-secular, quasi-religious — to be attuned to what is greater than man, and to feel this in one's inner being.

We have noted that this exercise aims at a strong character *(batin)* and a refined, accomplished *rasa*, personal attributes that underscore individuality, subjectivism, and that proclaim the validity of individual experience and personal feeling as the ultimale touchstones for truth. This subjective trait that stands in opposition to the requirements of social discipline — the pressure to conform to society and the wishes of the powers-that-be is very considerable — generates a general distaste for religious dogmatism, and a fascination with mystery and esoteric affairs. Things that are clear and simple are not that interesting, and a mystical discovery tour is entertaining. One's religious life, therefore, is felt to be a private affair. This does not negate the usefulness of regular religious practice, of following the rules of the faith, or of seeking God in Mecca, but people who want to go another way should be free to do so, religious practice being an open-ended quest for safety, efficacy, blessing, and personal fulfilment.

Syncretism?

Discipline is obviously a matter that belongs to the public realm of status and etiquette, social control and duty. In that world, one always has to stand on tiptoe, to be alert and apprehensive; it is not a place to relax in. To the outer world also belong the five senses, passions and desires, pride and conceit that need to be restrained and controlled if somebody wants to develop his inner potentialities. When the outer realm has been brought under control, the inner can thrive. Living according to expectations and obligations frees the inner life from worry and the need for planning, while good manners serve as a protective fence behind which people can go their own way, undisturbed by happenings in society. In fact, quite the reverse. It should be one's developed *batin* and secret inward resources that influence the manifested world.

Social life has rigidity, is disciplined by the reins of hierarchy and power that fear the unrestrained individual, his initiative and creativity. In a similar way, the practitioner of *kebatinan* has to check his emotions, creating the outer order that frees his inner resources to develop, to explore the mystery of life, to listen to the voice in the silence, to seek unity with the divine, to have visions, to create, and, possibly, to dominate visible existence.

This recurrent contrast and relationship between discipline and regulation versus unrestrainedness and exploration, between clarity and mystery, stimulates the desire to reserve the inner life for oneself, to have freedom there at least. And since that inner life also comprises one's relationship with supernature, religious development should be a personal business. Morality is contained in concrete social relationships; in the relationships with the spiritual, people should be autonomous.

This recognition of a basic individual area of self-determination results in a multitude of mystical theories and practices that, however much their similarities, are always claimed to be the personal revelations of each guru, *kiai*, or individual virtuoso. In this atmosphere, one can imagine that there is a general distaste for religious dogma, proclaimed orthodoxy, or systematic theology; it is the individual visionary encounters that are held to reveal experiential, direct truth.

This general stance allows for the incorporation of all kinds of elements from other discourses that have come to the attention of the adepts. Some generously mix in Moslem ideas with the Hindu-Buddhist heritage from the period that preceded the advent of Islam, others juxtapose Catholicism, ancestor worship and theosophy, while others still relish combining cabalism, freemasonry and Javanese concepts of biology, without ever bothering for a moment about questions of compatibility. This licence is often labelled syncretism.

I am not convinced that this term explains what is going on; it merely establishes the fact of mixing, but does not delve into the cultural constellation in which the blending takes place, and so it is not descriptive of causes or the field of action. Personal speculation may be seen as a generic trait of Javanese religious thinking. After all, religion is concerned with the unseen and mysterious, and its location is more within the person than in social life. Syncretism, then, is merely a logical outcome of these basic conditions that should be first of all understood.

In the *kejawèn* frame of mind, rationality is always combined with intuition, it is *rasa*-thinking[4] grounded in the recognition that there is always something that is non-explicit and not graspable by reason within almost every phenomenon and experience. This also inspires the sense of distrust towards western science and linear rationality. Some Javanese are very ready to point out that, for them, the way the sciences claim to progress at once shows up their basic flaw. Science, in its search for true statements, reasons deductively from premises that, at the same time, it attempts to disprove and reject, nothing apparently having any permanent status, and so, what can be the value of the 'truth' arrived at?

Javanese reasoning, in contrast, is more inductive, analyzing experience and necessity while grasping the essence (also *rasa*, the truth in and behind phenomena) intuitively, that is to say, directly, without tor-

---

4 Restricting her analysis to social relationships, Unni Wikan observes a comparable type of "feel-think knowledge". If rationality is not combined with feeling, with sympathy and empathy, a person will be bereft of moral guidance. In relating to each other, shared human experience should be the measure, or what Javanese would call *tepa slira*. See *Managing Turbulent Hearts: a Balinese Formula for Living*. Chicago (etc): University of Chicago Press, 1990: last chapter. It is interesting to note that this idealized perception of relationships is also the key to Enriquez's *kapwa*-psychology; p. 91.

tuous theoretical constructions and tedious research. Perhaps this is one reason, too, why science fails to flourish in Indonesia and why there is little indigenous cultural input as far as the social branches are concerned. As part of prestigious modernity, and in response to the demand for education, the western sciences are taught as systems of terms, concepts and rules that are taken straight from the foreign-written textbooks. When translated into research, formal procedures that appear to have worked themselves free from any theoretical coherence are applied to particular phenomena, yielding single statements about the ethos of work of underpaid labourers in factories, or the non-innovativeness of native entrepreneurship, without considering access to credit.

While there are many other reasons for the uninspired intellectual life at many a university that will be treated in following chapters, two factors may well contribute to the failure of indigenous higher education in making a meaningful contribution to shaping modern life so far. The first is a general approach to knowledge that surfaces clearly in the religious mentality that takes pleasure in mystical speculation, and the second the relative rigidity of social life that suppresses creativity. Yet most people are unfazed by such critical observations as the above, because the scientific enterprise has been cut loose from its western moorings and has become localized in a syncretizing, or rather a synthetizing, environment, where there is little awareness that the path science follows is logical and analytical, rather than constructive and compounding.

Thanks to the generous infusions of all kinds of uncritical assumptions and undigested theories and approaches from western universities, discussions in Indonesia remain extremely blurred and irrelevant. The country is on its way to the Pancasila society, it will take off to become an industrial nation that will be steeped in a culture of *IPTEK*,[5] science and technology, producing a new type of man who is innovative, democratic and meritocratic. To reach this, a new cultural strategy is needed that is functional, integrative, aiming at building a new ethos of work with international standards and that will overcome the collectivism that is characteristic of the village, which then leads to the amoral familism

5 *Ilmu Pengetahuan TEKnologi.*

that is the source of clanism, ethnicism, and groupism (Sularto, 1990:54-6).

The above is not presented as balderdash. This type of jumble of concepts occurs not infrequently in serious discussions among people, most of them holding degrees from reputable universities, who are deeply concerned about the course the nation is steering. Their deliberations come across as unrealistic, their assumptions as wild, and their vision as fantastic. What they are doing is syncretizing; they are not analyzing the situation on the ground, they are not scrutinizing structure or looking for basic causes. The course of Indonesian society is given, its development inevitable, and people need to be prepared for it, and so textbooks are written about Pancasila economy, sociology and philosophy. The production of books, treatises, and mystifications about Pancasila — written by all sorts of academics — is so impressive that it probably runs second to (comparable) religious and mystical writings. In such an intellectual climate nobody should be amazed if one university or another opens a department of Pancasilalogy in the years to come.

I think that this delight in stirring all kinds of unconnected things together, of compounding them, is, on the one hand, related to *rasa*-thinking and, on the other, also to the obsession with oneness. This drive toward unity always subsumes distinctions, striving upwards, away from facts and analylical hair-splitting. In that process, incompatibilities gradually disappear, and it is therefore different from just syncretizing. What it seeks to accomplish is synthesis, the quiet order of undifferentiated union.

Scientific versus moralistic thinking

According to one of Indonesia's own keenest social critics, the priest-author-architect Y.B. Mangunwijaya, the culture has not reached the stage of the Enlightenment yet (Sularto, 1990:144). Thinking is still mythological, the individual still dominated by the group, and society by dynastic rule. Few and frustrated are the people who have grasped what western science is about, and who are adept at handling theory as a system of suppositions serving to get a firm grip on observable reali-

ties, and yet, who see clearly that these suppositions are not to be
equated with the phenomena to be explained. Systematic, disciplined
abstraction is difficult to comprehend, and so truth remains derivable
from experience and pleasant speculation.

It is still very hard for most to distance themselves from what they
personally experience, while such abstract ideas as the public interest
or the rule of law are extremely difficult for them to conceive of.
Society is still seen as it is experienced, as ties to concretely known
individuals, whose common good is phrased in terms of mutual claims
and obligations, and whose just, or ethical, behaviour depends on their
status so defined.

Equating a person with his status, power, or obligations, makes
him very tangible and sets him far apart from the abstracted 'general-
ized other'. If for no other reason than this one, the working of political
democracy becomes a non-probability already. It simply cannot be
imagined. Needless to say, in such a situation political ideologies —
being theoretical by their nature — cannot thrive, and the sociological
imagination does not develop. Society is then perceived as an aggregate
of individuals who cluster in families, and who need to be hierarchically
controlled. Seen from this viewpoint, it is not poverty that is the problem, but the presence of many poor people.

Solutions to social problems are thought to be rooted in individual
ethical behaviour. If people know their place and fulfil its inherent
obligations, are faithful in living their religious duties, and strive to live
according to the Pancasila, problems will evaporate and social life will
become exemplary, with Indonesia shining as a beacon for the world.

Consequently, problems originate from individual moral decay,
and thus individuals need guidance, teaching, leadership to keep them
on the right track. They need to be constantly exhorted to discipline
themselves, to cooperate, to make the election a success, devote themselves to society, to plan their families, to live according to the
Pancasila/Pancakarsa/Panca Dharma Wanita, and so on.

These admonishments show more than just a delight in slogans
and self-fulfilling mantras. They also demonstrate an approach to societal questions that is moral and intuitive. It is not a systematic theoretical approximation of reality, however often maxims are dressed up in
modern gear. The overuse of terms, such as human rights, take-off,

innovation, democracy, development, rule of law, only demonstrates that they have been freed from any context in which they make sense. The content of these dictums is no more than a moral appeal to help shape the destiny that is, anyway, inevitable.

While the social sciences can only develop by drawing inferences from observed facts in their quest for theoretical development, and thus must devote a great deal of attention to actual circumstances and facts — 'reading', analyzing, diagnosing them — and often producing mercilessly objective assessments of situations, the moralistic approach is not so much interested in carefully dissecting the actual situation and its history. It is future-oriented, more interested in where we are heading than in where we are, while seeking direction more in inspiration than in the confrontation with obdurate facts.

Ethics

Oneness in the sense of unity means good order, smooth relationships, the absence of disturbance; it means harmony and conformity, a static state that is calm and pleasing. It is a sign of mastery. The contrary situation, disunity, means conflict and strife, opposition and unruliness. It is mastery lost, unpleasant, exciting and wild. It is graceless.

Things should be presented in fine order, be accomplished gracefully and elegantly executed. Such smoothness, such refinement, such elegance, or grace is *alus*. It is culture at its best. And so it is *alus* to demonstrate mastery and to speak High Javanese well, to be aware of etiquette, to have fine manners and a modest bearing. These are the marks of a civilized person, reflecting his inner discipline and calm. His accomplished self-presentation adorns the world, makes it a more beautiful, a better place. Such a person is good.

Alus contrasts with *kasar*; this latter is the absence of good manners, the stir of monkeys, the turmoil of emotions, the lack of education, the pretension of clowns, the threat of 'communists', the straightforwardness of criticism, the rebelliousness of disagreement, the openness of conflict, and the lack of diplomacy. Untamed is *kasar*, is closeness to nature, while falling short in civilization.

119

The imposition of order is good in itself, because order is what should be. To do so, power is needed, be it the power of self-discipline to achieve inner calm, or the power to make others follow and obey. The exercise of it can be *alus*, as in the image of the exemplary leader whose charisma commands spontaneous submission, or gross, such as firing into crowds of unarmed demonstrators.

This latter habit is quite widespread in the Southeast Asian region, massacres — whether at Mendiola or on the island of Negros, on Rajdamnoen or at Thammasat, in Dili, the Lampongs, or Tanjungpriok — apparently being a ready means to compel obedience, and the serene order of the cemetery.[6] The violence is warranted, because rebellious behaviour is disgraceful, is questioning the authority of the 'legally' constituted sovereign government, is an offence and gross behaviour.

The end justifies the means, although it is better if the means are *alus* too. Mysterious murders[7] are therefore far more acceptable, and the eradication of a Sumbawan village attracted so little publicity that the insult of disagreement did not lead to the injury of loss of face. Yet, basically, these violent means are felt to be suitable for dealing with *kasar* people, who can only be reined in by force because that is the only thing they seem to understand.[8]

Command can be *alus* too, a compelling hint, a polite appeal (*imbauan* (I)) that nobody will ignore or refuse. And if, in civil society, people still politely protest by signing a petition, by declaring themselves presidential candidates, or by voicing displeasing opinions while abroad, then *alus* means will be mobilized. Perhaps their relatives will

6 The cases referred to here are the Mendiola massacre at the presidential palace in Manila, February 1987, the one at Escalante on Negros, September 1985, at the Democracy Monument in Bangkok, May 1992, at Thammasat University there, October 1976, in Dili, East Timor, November 1992, the Lampongs, South Sumatra, early 1989, and in the port district of Jakarta, September 1984.

7 Reference is to the so-called *petrus* executions *(penembakan misterius)*, the 'mysterious' killings of petty criminals without any trial by covert murder squads, and sanctioned behind the scenes by the highest authorities, as became obvious in the Soeharto biography (1989).

8 This attitude, that is shared in common with the outdated *priyayi* two-class perception of society, is still very widespread among educated and powerful people. They hold that measures aimed at the improvement of life — Family Planning, Development — should initially be forced upon the small people *(wong cilik)*; later, when they understand the benefits, they will certainly be grateful.

be dismissed from their jobs, or be refused access to the university; perhaps they find that they cannot open a bank account or are found ineligible to obtain credit; maybe they suddenly find that former associates are avoiding them, and thatthey cannot get a passport if they want to travel. In extreme cases they will be promoted to the status of *doctorandus*, Drs., when they are placed under house arrest *(di-rumah-sajakan)*,[9] or they may enjoy the full hospitality of the state in the prisons called *Lembaga Permasyarakatan*, or socialization institutions, that should from their very name prepare inmates for re-entry into society at a point which, in all too many cases, appears to be located in the graveyard.[10]

The more refined the better, both in the aesthetical and ethical senses. Order is not only a good, it is good as such. Good and beautiful belong together; to speak High Javanese is to speak good language, to obey one's parents is good behaviour, a sign of mature morality, and the less stir one causes makes one a more graceful and moral man. Conflict is disgusting and distasteful; it must be eradicated to restore the stillness of unity that is in itself the sign of ethically accomplished life.

9 *Doktorandus*, abbreviated as *Drs.*, is an academic title, and corresponds to the d r s in *di-rumah-sajakan*, to be placed under house arrest.

10 This relates to the frequent executions of prominent communist notables in the 1980s and 1990, after periods of imprisonment of up to 25 years.

CHAPTER 8

The evolution of culture under the New Order

When I came to the country in 1969, the New Order was new indeed and still far from having shaken down into its present shape. After the turmoil of the later Sukarno years and Indonesia's increasing isolation, it seemed as if the nation was turning back to the world again. Of course, the New Order was repressive of those it accused of involvement in the murky affairs of the 30th of September 1965, or of membership in communist organizations, but compulsion had not yet become its overriding characteristic. I entered on a tourist visa, and when I reached Jakarta it took just a few days of bureaucratic routine to arrange for a research visa with the *LIPI* academy of sciences.[1] I was made welcome and I well remember the director involved saying that Indonesia had opened up wide to the world once more.

A critical press was alive and well. *Indonesia Raya* broke many racy stories, *Harian Kami* proved itself a fortress of righteousness, and *Mahasiswa Indonesia* was quick to point out abuse and deviations in government circles. The old political parties circulated their opinions and their presence was visible on billboards at their branches and offices, and, although controversial, the first president commanded the respect of many, his rhetoric still reverberating in their minds. In brief, there was diversity in the unity of Indonesia and a continuity in its national history.

That history can be retraced to the 1920s. Due to the late development of modern education in the colony, Indonesian nationalism was tardy in arising. Its precursory movements — all in the 20th century — may have been anti-colonial in content, but nobody yet dreamt of an Indonesian nation.[2] The birth of this idea was the central highpoint of

---

1 *Lembaga Ilmu Pengetahuan Indonesia.*

2 See B. Anderson, *Imagined Communities: Reflections on the Origin and Spread of Nationalism.* London: Verso Ed., 1983.

the youth congress of 1928 when the oath "One nation, one country, one language" was formulated. The choice of language was felicitous; Malay, as an old lingua franca, had spread throughout the archipelago. This decision gave an initial advantage to the Sumatrans, who, as native speakers, also wrote the nation's first modern novels.

To avoid choosing Javanese, the language of the majority after all, not only side-stepped controversy, but was also almost inevitable for the young, comparatively well-educated people who had enjoyed considerable exposure to liberal western ideas and the traditions of European humanism. While this influence naturally gave rise to feelings of nationalism, it also stimulated the formation of the idea of the basic equality of the citizens of the future country. This latter notion is natural to popular Malay though not to Javanese, which continually stresses relative rankings among persons. Besides this, it was very much a symbol of the Javanese nobility and upper class who had compromised themselves in the eyes of the independence movement by their collaboration with the Dutch in their highly hierarchically structured administration.

Early Indonesian nationalism thus contained the moral principle of equality, of the basic right to similar treatment before the law, while standing against privilege, special statuses, and the exploitation of the weak that these imply. Such ideas were brought fully to the fore in Sukarno's famous defence oration, *Indonesia Accuses*, that expressed the basic immorality of colonialism, its discrimination, injustice, and contempt for the humanity of the ordinary people under its sway (Paget, 1975). Because of this, independence became a moral issue, a basic right.

The road toward that independence proved to be a rocky one, the tenacious opposition of the Dutch deepening and widening the moral dimensions of Indonesian nationalism, with the later physical revolution strengthening feelings of solidarity and zest in the common struggle. It was these emotions that were constantly fed by Sukarno during his turbulent presidency. He became the symbol of a living Indonesia, of a new nation that had a message for the world and its own, now emancipated, citizens, and although everyone recognized that not all was well, still people were proud to be Indonesians.

Less than a year after the recognition of the United States of

Indonesia *(RIS)*, this guileful legacy of Dutch colonialism was abrogated and the unitary state came into place, in conformity with the ideals of the anti-imperialist struggle. This did not mean there was immediate concord. In West Java, for instance, the Darul Islam movement staged a long drawn-out running battle with the central government, and the forces of regionalism and religious antagonism weakened the effective authority of the state. The ravaged economy and unsettled conditions, poverty and political protest, the revolutionary zeal and active aggression first directed to the liberation of New Guinea, then against the creation of Malaysia, all kept on the boil by the flamboyant first president, led to inflation, instability, international isolation, and political polarization, but fanned the flames of nationalism.

Seen from within, many people were not so certain about the blessings of independence. It certainly had not ushered in a golden period of prosperity and justice. The high price of war and revolution is searingly recorded in the works of Indonesia's most powerful prose-writer, Pramoedya Ananta Toer. In his analysis of the post-war years,[3] he penetratingly reveals the starkness of the times, the egoism of motives, the cruelty, the powerlessness of individuals, the total destruction of family life, integrity, and every humanitarian quality. His characters appear to be merely victims of a life beyond their control.

His later *Stories from Jakarta* (1957) elaborate on the same themes. They deal with the life and experiences of the poor and suffering rejects of society. The revolution has run its course; what remains is disappointment, meaninglessness, and disorientation. People are eternal losers, everybody being alone, outsiders to each other and mere observers. For the poor, the price of belonging is too high, everybody having to fend for himself. "In our neighbourhood, poverty killed all ideals."

Yet it was not just destitution that killed them. Opportunity and privilege seemed to have similar effects. In *Twilight in Jakarta* (1957), Mochtar Lubis's composite picture of life in the capital during the early Sukarno period, students discuss events endlessly, trying to find a road to a productive future in times that appear to be out of joint, where

---

3 See his collections *Subuh* (*Dawn*, 1950), *Pertjikan Revolusi* (*Splatters of the Revolution*, 1950), and the novel *Keluarga Gerilja* (*Guerrilla Family*, 1950).

some profit immensely and others are ground into the dirt. In an atmosphere of cynicism, words turn hollow, lose all meaning, or serve to cover apathy or ruthless exploitation of position.

In his prize-winning *Afterpains of the Revolution* (1968), Ramadhan K.H. analyses this seizure of opportunity by focusing on the life of a student whose integrity and self-respect contrast with the destruction of the ideals of Independence. The post-revolutionary period brought corruption, selfishness, false ambition, competition for power, and oppression of the masses, leading to the bitter disappointment and frustration of the idealists, and to the cynicism of most.[4]

The only things that seemed to be in place toward the end of the Sukarno period were the slogans of the president, but they had long lost their mantraic efficacy. *Trikora, Konfrontasi, Nasakom, Manipol-Usdek, Tahun Vivere Periculoso*,[5] all may earlier have invigorated the Indonesian nation, but they could no longer conceal the mess into which the country had blundered. When the final explosion came in the frenzy of 1965-66, people were horror-struck, suffering a shock from which it would take years to recover. It was the big bang that gave birth to the *Orde Baru*.

When I came back to Indonesia in 1973, the New Order was shaping up. Before flying there, I had asked LIPI to sponsor my visit, but since I planned to spend only three months in the country, they advised me to come on a tourist visa because things were not that simple any more. The newspapers now offered a much tamer fare than before, and at the same time that Sukarno slogans were fading from memory, others were being introduced, especially the ideas of *Pembangunan* (Development), *Pemilu* (General elections), and *Repelita* (Five-year-planning), while the ideas of *musyawarah* and *gotong-royong* persisted. Elections had been held for the first time since 1955 and a diversity of parties had participated, but this time the politicians had been largely

4 For more information about novels mentioned in the text, see A. Teeuw, *Modern Indonesian Literature* I, II. The Hague: Martinus Nijhoff, 1967, 1979.

5 *Trikora, Tri Komando Rakyat*, the mobilization of the country to wrest Western New Guinea from the Dutch; *Konfrontasi*, or the Crush Malaysia campaign; *Nasakom*, Sukarno's balancing act between nationalism, religion, and communism; *Manipol-Usdek*, the 1959 manifesto of political reorganization; *Tahun Vivere Periculoso*, the Mussolini-derived phrase for the three years of dangerous living.

defanged while parties were expected to refrain from stirring up emotions between official campaign periods.

It was indeed development all around. Streets were being widened, buildings constructed, while the military saw to it that feeder roads were 'voluntarily' constructed by undernourished villagers; gotong-royong was the slogan employed to mobilize people for all sorts of projects. Agricultural intensification (BIMAS)[6] was forced on the peasants. Village communities were organized as units (BUUD),[7] while money began to circulate. All kinds of research projects were commissioned, and this brought some prosperity and life to certain university departments. The penetration of society by the state even went as far as the womb, with women of child-bearing age 'volunteering' to have IUDs inserted.

A new society was becoming apparent in which security, economic and technocratic reasoning prevailed over all other considerations. In its early, army-dominated evolution, a characteristic no-nonsense approach forced the government's plans and projects down the throats of a dubious population. This way of accomplishing the aims of the state derived from the military mentality of the new leadership. Suspicious of the subversive civilians and the devious politicians, they believed that life in the country should be depoliticized, opinion censored, religion controlled, universities subdued, with the great legitimizers for this becoming Development and Security, elevated to canonical status in the double mission (dwifungsi) doctrine of the armed forces.

The army does things. As the self-appointed saviour of the republic, it is possessed by a sense of righteousness that sees all forms of hesitation and reluctance as the recalcitrance of civilians who have to be brought to heel. They should obey, execute orders. The populace is seen as basically wayward, therefore its role must be to take the bit in its mouth so as to allow the government in its wisdom to control the masses through the reins of power. And if the mount should prove

---

6 *Bimas, bimbingan masal,* massive guidance, a package-deal agricultural credit plan extended by the government. See Booth, 1988.

7 *BUUD, Badan Usaha Unit Desa,* a kind of cooperative organization of the village; one of the forceful efforts to raise yields and to create a national buffer stock in order to stabilize the price of rice. See Mulder, 1980:95; Booth, 1988.

intractable, then the rider would keep it blinkered and on a short rein. Given the government's unyielding stance, wholehearted participation was not easy for those of independent nature, whose opinions apparently did not count. Inevitably, in its further evolution, the authority of the New Order would be regularly challenged by students, religious opposition, dispossessed farmers, and even a would-be Just King (ratu adil). All these, and other, signs of frustration were normally met with a still sharper tug on the reins, with stricter censorship, and intimidation.

The dominance of the military after 1966 was thus naturally not to everybody's liking, although many welcomed a measure of 'normalcy'[8] and regularity after the turbulent years of early independence. What people soon missed, however, was the inspiration that had emanated from the centre in Sukarno's days. The New Order government seemed to lack charisma, in spite of the auspiciousness of *Supersemar* that had given birth to it. Yet, after the trauma of the large scale killing in Java and Bali, the country had to get on its feet again, and so the first five year plan of 1968 and the elections of 1971 provided rays of hope that Indonesia was finally on track to that elusive goal of a just and prosperous society.

Disillusion with how the New Order had evolved, and the concomitant 'greening'[9] of the country, surfaced regularly during my encounters in 1973, when people had grown apprehensive about the ethical quality of the state. Court justice was palpably in short supply; greed appeared to fuel the rapid careers of some notables; the role of foreign funding, and thus dependence, became blatantly obvious; and idealism was buried under *Pembangunan*. Gone were pride in the country's struggle and defiance of imperialism, in its role in the forefront of the movement of the non-aligned nations, and in the potency of Sukarno. The national myths became Development and the heroism of

8 Normal times, *zaman normal*, is still a reference to the colonial period in which the Dutch cherished the ideal of *rust en orde*, tranquillity and order. Interesting in this connexion is Pramoedya's *Glass House* (APPENDIX H).

9 'Greening', *penghijauan*, officially reforestation, in popular parlance a reference to the spreading of military personnel to occupy all kinds of civilian positions, from village head to provincial governor. Speaking about Java, some wryly observe that Development is really a success; under the Dutch there was only one Governor General, while now there are at least three governors who are generals.

the Revolution; too little to fire the imagination. What counted was pelf and power.

In 1973, the Muslims in parliament demonstrated that they had not been reduced to a negligible quantity. They successfully blocked the passage of the government-proposed secular civil marriage law that they found to be in contradiction with Islamic usage. The discussions inside and outside the halls of popular representation became so heated that the watered down version of 1974 changed virtually nothing (Emmerson, 1976:229-45). On the 15th of January that year, Jakarta was the scene of widespread anti-Japanese rioting; it signalled the end of whatever was left of the freedom of the press. In 1976, the arising of a self-styled Just King was denounced in the newspapers as a plot to topple the president; the civil servant concerned, Sawito, had the backing of an older generation of moral leaders widely respected for their role in Indonesian history. It was these heavy ethical undertones that prompted the government to take this affair extremely seriously, so that in the subsequent court cases the accusers managed to isolate Sawito, in order to make it appear that he had tricked the honourable notables into supporting him, and that he had basically acted on his own initiative (Bourchier, 1984).

Three years later another spectacular show trial was staged in Bandung. In 1978, students demonstrated against the unopposed re-election of Soeharto to the presidency. In reaction, the authorities sent in the military to quell campus unrest, and in its wake they arrested approximately one hundred student leaders nation-wide, thirty of whom were brought to trial. They were represented by the courageous human rights' activists of the Legal Aid Institute *LBH (Lembaga Bantuan Hukum)*, so both the court proceedings and the defence oration of Heri Akhmadi (1981) are of special interest.

Heri's published retort — banned, as a matter of course, almost immediately after it was printed — shows a remarkable similarity to Sukarno's famous *Indonesia Accuses* of 1930. In the same way that Sukarno then claimed to incorporate the nation's consciousness, Heri professed that role for the student movement. His defence contains an interesting denunciation of the New Order policies of social and economic development, criticizing widespread corruption, the growing gap between rich and poor, and the reliance on foreign capital. At the same time, he praised the Pancasila as the correct ethical basis of the state. By openly inveighing against the elite and the 'excesses of development', he obfuscated the issue of his moral opposition. So, while the students saw the process as a debate about the interpretation and application of the country's ideological foundation, the judges were more impressed by its spirit of opposition and confrontation. As a result, they did not honour his 'objective' analysis of the political economy, but convicted him for "insult of the head of state", which equates with endangering national stability.

Meanwhile, the government had further tightened its grip on political life by reducing its complexity, through forcing the different parties to fuse. The remnants of the Partai Nasional Indonesia (PNI) joined the small non-Moslem denominational parties, so forming the Partai Demokrasi Indonesia (PDI), and the various Islamic streams were brought together in the Partai Persatuan Pembangunan (PPP), initially resulting in a rather strong representation in parliament. Existing in the shadow of the vast official Golkar, the governmental corporate organization of 'functional groups', the new parties had little political clout, but voting for the non-government parties expressed at least an affirmation of identity, a moral stance, and a refusal to be absorbed in New Order uniformity.[10] It thus came as an unpleasant surprise for the government when the PPP won a majority in symbolically important Jakarta in 1977. Since that time, the government has steadily attempted to further emasculate the parties by exercising strong influence on the selection of leadership, and by making every organization subscribe to the principles of the Pancasila as their, and everybody else's, *azas tunggal*, one and only foundation.[11]

10 The most principled way of expressing disillusionment with the New Order is to cast a blank vote in the once-every-five-years elections for minority representation, most delegates being nominated by the government. It is difficult to estimate the number of blank-voters, or *golput* (*golongan putih*, white group); propagating the practice, predictably, is discouraged.

11 Especially in the 1980s, the government was very successful in weakening the political credibility of the civilian parties, particularly of Islam, and the advance of Golkar seemed steady and irresistable. But given the outcome of the 1992 election exercise, it is apparent that people are growing tired of the present dispensation, which is reflected in the performance of Golkar. While the government bulldozer won — of course — the absolute majority in 27 provinces, it did not get more than 60% of the vote anywhere in Java,

Yet, controlling organizational life is not the same as dominating society and dictating people's sense of justice. Expropriation in the name of development may seem warranted from the side of the powers-that-be, but the victims may have a different interpretation, especially if they experience the procedure as plain land-grabbing, or when compensation is grossly unfair or not forthcoming. So, quite regularly, villagers' frustrations come to the fore and may sometimes surface in the press. To attract such publicity, however, peasants need to do more than suffer. Perhaps they must travel to Jakarta and demonstrate in front of parliament, which they did in 1979, when they even got the sympathetic ear of the then vice-president, Adam Malik (Mulder,1989:123). Or they must physically oppose government policy and fight their case with the backing of the fairly influential NGOs, such as in the Kedungombo case of 1987-91.

To counter rural unrest, the government decided to co-opt the village elite, not only through the opportunities they enjoy because of agricultural intensification and other development programs, but also by incorporating the headmanship into the structure of the state. Through becoming a member of the lowest echelon in the official hierarchy, a *lurah* now enjoys powerful backing and can no longer be considered to be a representative of the people. Together with the other privileged administrators of his little territory, he symbolizes both the state, of which he, or she, has become an instrument, and the class of property owners, who fare well under the present dispensation.

There is more to control than the countryside in a period of rapid change and urbanization in which many make a comfortable living and

....

polling a mere 52% in Jakarta. This result may express Java's relative advantage in development, its population being more urban, modern, educated, informed, and industrialized, giving rise to new middle classes whose interests are thwarted by governmental centralization and favouritism. Another factor may be the disenchantment of the military, who now feel insufficiently involved in the political process to exert pressure to assure Golkar victory. The national count was:

	1987	1992
Golkar	73%	67%
PPP	16%	17.7%
PDI	11%	15.3%

some even grow very rich, but in which vast numbers of other people feel left behind. Development is a highly uneven process from which some profit, but it is not always those who ostentatiously display their new-won wealth who become the target of frustration. In November 1980, anti-Chinese rioting broke out in Solo and Semarang, swiftly spreading to other, smaller towns of Central Java. Others may display their restlessness by joining strange sects that somehow prove to be irrepressible, such as the Islam Jama'ah that was officially banned in 1971 but is still going strong. Class unrest and intolerable exploitation may also lead to people rallying under the religious banner, such as in Tanjungpriok in 1984, when the army was sent in to fire into the crowd. And even fifty respectable people may express their disapproval of a rigidifying New Order by bringing a petition to the attention of the authorities, who predictably reacted with irritation.

The most massive programme of the government to exercise control is ideological. From the time when the voice of *Bung* Karno was no longer heard in the land,[12] Indonesia somehow lost substance and ideological direction. What remained was to be Development-oriented and anti-communistic, which was pretty nebulous, offering little to identify with. To fill this void, the government launched its moral education drive, popularly known as *P4* if it is directed at officials, functionaries, employees, and even businessmen and other adults, or as *PMP*, the Pancasila Moral Education course, if the indoctrination is to take place in school. During the first years after its introduction toward the end of 1978, the programme enjoyed the support of many who were apprehensive about Indonesia's ideological direction in an environment where the old ethical points of orientation seemed vague to the point of vanishing.

It was also the period of the *pop* novel, with their plots invariably involving the children of the newly rich, or *OKB*, who came up as a moneyed class in the wake of vast international credits, Development, and the oil crisis. As their fortunes grew in step with the mushrooming of high-rises, hotels, massage parlours and gambling dens, Jakarta quickly lost its image of a village that had outgrown its strength, soon

---

12 *Bung* is the affectionate title given some popular leaders of the struggle for independence, for instance, *Bung* Hatta, Brother Hatta.

becoming a booming third world capital with its starkly contrasting life-styles, between those in the modern and the 'informal' sectors of the economy.

The *pop* novels are set among the nouveaux riches and their progeny, now the new generation of managers and wheeler-dealers. Then the latter were still at school, exploring life and enjoying the money their parents amassed through lottery or lucrative business, through corruption or privileged concessions. With the pursuit of money so central to the preoccupations of their elders, the young relished the freedom of diminished control and the pleasures that were now obtainable, such as a ride with a girl friend in daddy's car. While fathers spent money on status symbols and mothers were fully taken up with showing themselves off at lavish parties and philanthropic meetings, or just shopping their days away in the new malls of Jakarta and Singapore, sons philandered with their old men's mistresses while daughters flirted with their teachers.[13]

Whether the *pop* novels give an accurate picture of moral life at the end of the 1970s is not really to the point. The interesting fact is that such writings were published, quite deliberately outrageous and ostentatious as they were, thereby thumbing their noses at the ethical arrangements a more traditionally educated generation still went by. In these books, the authors were playing ducks and drakes with the reverence for age and the inviolable position of parents, thus signalling the beginnings of a youth culture that purposively distances itself from former wisdom and ways. In their growing apart, and because of their money, the old and the young created different fashions, each following their own fads and fancies, until we can now watch a full unfolding of the 'lifestyle' phenomenon.

This marking of 'individuality' is fuelled by advertising and publishing that aims at convincing groups of people to try to distinguish themselves from others, by promoting the use of a panoply of consumer goods, trips to modish travel destinations, exclusive fashions and penthouse-living. The thing one therefore needs most is money to visit the air-conditioned shopping malls where all the imported goodies can be

13 One of the most delightful *pop* novels of the period sketching these aberrations is Yudhistira Ardi Noegraha's *Arjuna Mencari Cinta* (*Arjuna in Quest of Love*, 1977).

bought.[14] Lifestyle peddling does not aim exclusively at the better-off, and indeed finds a huge market for cheaper, fast-moving items among all those who want to demonstrate their 'urbanity' through sporting blue jeans, cropped hair, imitation Lacoste shirts, carefully copied Rolex or Cartier watches, and the possession of status products, such as recorders and pirated music and video tapes. The fashions all follow the international trends, including fast food and the Americanization of TV-programming, a sort of globalization of consumer culture that is most pathetically highlighted by the attempts to introduce local colour in luxury hotels and airports.[15]

Local colour is primarily laid on for visiting foreigners. Those who cater to the home market had better style themselves after the McDonald's formula, because to look American, sterile, or international shows that one is really advanced and abreast of the times. So it is the pop music of the world, the violent action movies, and the American comedy shows that colonize the minds of the young; the competition these offer to Indonesian productions is certainly considerable. If, ten years ago, the content of TV programmes was still dominated by boring Indonesian fare — endless regional dances, ethnic costume shows, *kroncong* ensembles — now the foreign-produced or -modelled features figure prominently on the screen. With the sudden appearance of commercial broadcasting, western songs seem to be greatly preferred to market the goods. On state-run TV, ethnicity-focussed distractions continue, as they have already for a long time, in order to keep the multifaceted cultural heritage alive, albeit as mere folklore.

14 Things become desirable if they are imported. In contrast to what is usual in western Europe, local Mars Brand Super shag tobacco finds itself good enough to advertise as 'import quality'.

15 In the first volume of his monumental 'essay' (1990), Denys Lombard discusses the limits of westernization and cautions against eurocentric exaggeration. I agree: behind modern images one soon meets the indigenous mentality — always on the move — and the quest for authenticity and roots, the creation of an Indonesian identity. Should the current New Order-rush towards Progress and Development — that Lombard does not discuss — be considered as 'westernization'? I do not think so; the large scale introduction of the essentially capitalist mode of production leads to the 'globalization of culture' characterized by consumerism, but this global culture is stripped of the value and intellectual content of western civilization and thus unable to westernize the mind of the Indonesian recipient who remains bound to the moral understanding of his local traditions.

Mass cultural promotion styles have also reached into the palace where, during the Independence Day celebrations of 17-8-1991, prepackaged food was distributed with the compliments of Coca Cola, and other messages from sponsors providing crackers and snacks. If such is the symbolism of the most important national day at the focal point of the country, then Mangunwijaya's diagnosis that the country has entered its post-Indonesian period, may be accurate (Sularto, 1990:105-9). Widely open to foreign capital and culture, history is fast losing its relevance. The bogus information filling two or three pages of the daily newspaper keeps the reader in the know about the exploits of the international sports-heroes Boris Becker and Maradona, while also giving incisive analysis of the matches of the Dutch soccer league. In order to do better still, *Kompas* even commissioned a column by legendary football player Franz Beckenbauer for authoritative commentary... really, on what? More concerned with local events are the society pages that feature, for instance, who is breaking the Ramadan fast with whom at which luxury hotel, or who has staged the greatest extravaganza in marrying off a child.

The fashion of prodigal feasting is commented upon in a variety of ways. Sometimes newspapers devote as much as half a page to analysing the cost of the munificence by interviewing the host, or by asking for the quotation for such receptions from the organizing hotel. Some people are irritated and show disdain about this expression of what they call neo-feudalism or neo-*priyayi-ism*. In school, students are taught that the Pancasila style of life is plain and unpretentious, and in official quarters the potlatch to underscore status aspirations is discouraged, not so much because it would be unbefitting the modern Indonesian man, but because it demonstrates the extreme distortion of income distribution in a country, where a few appear to be very privileged indeed while most toil in deprivation. This type of inequality may promote jealousy and so endanger social stability, and should thus be less conspiciously celebrated.

With status and prestige so central to the mind of most, it will be extremely difficult to discourage ceremonial elaboration, and the official admonishment — similar to most Pancasila rhetoric — is halfhearted at best. Moreover, modern business-based economic development is founded on money circulating and not being hoarded. When Spanish singer Julio Iglesias appeared at the Hotel Said, seats could be had for as little as US$375, and the house was packed. Sogo department store, Block M Plaza shopping mall, with many others to follow, are firmly ensconced, although the labourers building those places may earn less than $2 a day, while low-level civil servants do not take home more than $30-50 a month. It is clear that they should listen to other performers and shop in different places, although they are free to hang out in the luxury of an air-conditioned department store on a Sunday afternoon.

One way or another, consumer culture affects the life of all, enticing people to surround themselves with all kinds of goods that become indispensable as markers of urban ways. It also makes money inordinately important. As the new 'great tradition' of city-centred culture, it directs the attention to international life, the outside, the future, the foreign example, while setting up lifestyles and fashions as the new criteria by which people are judged. And it provides entertainment, endless and senseless diversions, ranging from loud pop music in the exhibition hall in the basement of the national monument *(Monas)* to inescapable sound on buses and in supermarkets, from tedious TV programmes without end to the musical religious revival rallies, from sports festivals to real Surabayan soccer hooliganism, from fast food to slot machines, computer games, tabloid newspapers, movies, star cults, snooker parlours, disco dancing, smutty *dangdut* shows, comic strips, gossip and lifestyle magazines, with golf courses for the rich.

Advertising teaches people what to want and how to live, as much as tradition may have had that function for earlier generations. It sets the example and its symbols dominate the urban landscape, such as the private car, the fly-over, the high-rise hotel, the office tower, the bank building, the department store; all these overshadow the minarets of mosques and spires of churches. In orienting attention towards progress and the future, this fixation directs awareness away from the past, relegating it to insignificance, while giving birth to a new kind of 'people without history', without much political interest, rather indifferent to their wider social surroundings, each and everybody basically caring for himself and the small group of others who provide his deeper identity in the sea of urban anonymity.

The recent availablity of consumer culture is especially important in setting patterns of life for the upwardly mobile people in town. As *homines novi*, they are new on the urban scene and so in search of models that they can imitate to shape their existence. Since such an urban culture is new to Indonesia too, they can only seek ideas to express their identity by drawing inspiration from the lifestyle of the Javanese upper class and from abroad, and by this means giving form to something that must perhaps pass for Indonesian culture, but that fails to express the nation. It is a mongrel with which it is hard to identify, having no moral content of its own and lacking any substance to fire the imagination.

In this cultural vacuity, the national character needs to be recreated, and in the absence of a person like Sukarno, who fired the fantasy with his oratory, people are now urged to shape and identify with the *Manusia Pancasila*, the exemplary Pancasila man who embodies the true Indonesia. Such is the purpose of the moral education programme. This activity, though, is flawed by the grave contradictions in the teaching material itself, aiming both at teaching citizenship and the creation of obedient subjects, and by the even more serious perversions of morality that the student observes and experiences in social life. So, while at the beginning of the indoctrination, quite a few people wanted to give it a chance, the very words *P4* or *PMP* now produce sardonic smiles.

The counter-productiveness of the programme has been noted by scholars known nation-wide, such as Umar Kayam and Selosoemardjan, who have expressed their apprehensions about the content and a teaching method that alienates the people, kills off their interest, and makes the course a very boring experience, so wasting a lot of valuable school time while failing to stimulate both feelings of pride in nation and also participatory citizenship. The course material is out of joint with reality, and since it is a compulsory examination subject, it can only breed cynicism.

Also, the content of the history course appears to me uninspiring. It centres on the evolution of nationalism, but focuses especially on the role of the present leadership as the heroes of the revolution, as victors over vicious communism, as glorious and righteous army officers, as originators of Development and implementors of Pancasila. Such teaching has a definite whiff of government propaganda and military megalomania but gives little sustenance to any attempt at identification with the national experience, which, anyway, is an elusive concept at the best of times. Seen from the point of view of the students, the course is boring. Following its own official line that people should be trained for development and goaded into obedience, the regime has at least succeeded in giving rise to a generation of pupils whose education took place under the auspices of the New Order, resulting in a crop of *Orde Baru* babies who are not very much interested in anything apart from a regular job, and earning the extra money they need to demonstrate their up-to-dateness. Apolitical and without any feeling for history, they can take off into the skies of progress, unhindered by any burden of humanism, *kebatinan*, or social criticism.

The *Orde Baru* is adept at sterilizing life, taking the sting out of discussion, killing any curiosity or intellectual development. Yoshihara Kunio has recently been honoured by the burning of his book *The Rise of Ersatz Capitalism in South-East Asia.*[16] Robison's writings are on the black list.[17] The best an Indonesian author ever produced about the awakening of the nation is categorically forbidden.[18] Nobody protests, the universities remain silent; at best people are afraid, but, depressingly, many seem to have lost their capacity for critical thought. While in a way the country is wide open to the world, it is the material excesses of consumer culture and capitalist exploitation that have penetrated, rather than the substance of western intellectual and political thinking.

To arrive at an appreciation of the evolution of thought, people need at least to have access to modern knowledge, and so it should be available in a language they can understand. Over the years, knowledge of foreign languages has not developed; the vast majority of university students are unable to read an English text and so they need to rely on whatever is available in Indonesian. Academically speaking, that is not much. Although quite a few books have been translated, the quality is

16 This book was published in 1988 with Oxford University Press, Singapore (etc); on orders of the High Court of the Capital Region, 261 copies of the Indonesian translation by Arief Budiman were burnt (middle of March 1992).

17 Especially irritating to the authorities is R. Robison, *Indonesia: The Rise of Capital.* Sydney: Allen and Unwin, 1986.

18 Reference is to Pramoedya A. Toer's works, especially his tetralogy *This Earth of Mankind* (APPENDIX H).

often questionable. To me, it was a shocking experience to find in my discussions and seminars that the only literature students were familiar with was the same that I had studied in the late fifties and early sixties at the University of Amsterdam. In our debates about development and modernization, their references were to the ideas of innovation as the basis of cultural change, religious evolution according to Bellah, the ethos of work and the Protestant ethic, Lerner's passing of traditional society, McClelland's need for achievement — preferably referred to as *nAch* — Rostow's simile of the flying machine, and Hagen's withdrawal of status respect. So in this context I was startled to discover that somebody had already advanced to literature as recent as 1976 when he mentioned Scott's idea of moral economy, in obvious reference to its Indonesian edition, *Moral Ekonomi Petani* (*The Economic Morality of the Peasant [sic]*).[19]

Compared to other ASEAN countries, academic life in Indonesia seems to take place in a vacuum, with certain academics writing books about Pancasila economics,[20] and almost nobody having any idea at all about the function and use of theory. Many things are 'researched', that is measured, but the why of the endeavour remains unclear because of the absence of context. With the fear having been expressed that East Indonesia was lagging behind in development, so that it might be Java alone that was going to take off and fly into the era of industrialization, the ethos of work of Sumbawan villagers needed to be inspected. No, they were not lazy! When, in the ensuing discussion, a Timorese pointed out that conditions in the area researched were very similar to those in dry, calcareous Gunung Kidul, the Javanese in the audience reacted

19 For instances, H.C. Barnett, *Innovation: the Basis of Cultural Change*, New York (etc): McGraw-Hill, 1953; R.N. Bellah, Religious evolution. *American Sociological Review* 29 (1964):358-74; D. Lerner, *The Passing of Traditional Society, Modernizing the Middle East*; Glencoe, Ill., The Free Press, 1958; W.W. Rostow, *The Stages of Economic Growth*. London: Cambridge University Press, 1960; E.E. Hagen, *On the Theory of Social Change: How Economic Growth Begins*. Homewood, Ill.: Dorsey, 1962; D.C. McClelland, *The Achieving Society*, Princeton: Van Nostrand, 1961.

20 Mubyarto and Boediono (eds), *Ekonomi Pancasila*. Yogyakarta: BPFE, 1981. Also, Mubyarto, *Ekonomi Pancasila. Gagasan dan Kemungkinan (The Pancasila Economy: Concept and Possibilities)*. Jakarta: LP3ES, 1987. This astonishing mixture of morality, 'theology', and development economics has been reviewed in *Bulletin of Indonesian Economic Studies* 25/1 (1989):139-41.

with incredulous laughter. How could someone dare to compare any-thing as primitive as Nusa Tenggara Timor with a starvation region on Java?

At this stage, the universities do not seem to be the loci that will envigorate the nation. The faculties that thrive are those concerned with the subjects that are thought to be relevant to Development, such as economics, technology, engineering, physics. They are *IPTEK*. This acronym stands for science and technology, the necessary ingredients of progress and the handmaidens of the government in reaching its goal. With Development coming first, and with the monetary pervasion of society, the power of the state over the population grows. Its instru-ments are the bureaucracy and the army.

As servants of the monolithic state, these highly hierarchical orga-nizations are supposed to be 100% loyal to their patron, a political prin-ciple known as *monoloyalitas*. They should therefore implement the policies and orders from the top without much ado or questioning, and it is striking that many people who are co-opted by the state somehow lose their individuality, the personality and independent wit for which they were formerly known. Bureaucratization and militarization lead to a decline in creativity and sense of humour; the orientation to planned targets hinders consultation with the people concerned; the pressure to succeed makes for unreliable statistics and an exaggerated picture of performance. In this way, the state functions increasingly as an entity apart from the society that it penetrates and dominates, much in the way the macho male has his way with any maiden.

The army is no longer the preponderant force it once was at the beginning of the New Order. Although the role of the military is very important in maintaining the polity, the Development-oriented state has grown to be dominated by capital, monopolies, and big business rather than by those in green. Its policies are technocratic, economy and national stability-directed, the army so becoming a mere instrument for the maintenance of an order that it no longer commands. In repressing unrest, it serves the continuation in office of the powers-that-be and the integrity of the realm, a role that suits the generation of younger offi-cers who see themselves as military professionals rather than as com-manders of a people's army of freedom fighters responsible for building a new Indonesian society. So, while the official doctrine stresses the *dwifungsi* concept and the army is still well represented in parliament, it has lost much of its former influence over the affairs of Jakarta, along with its image of a popular force serving to integrate the nation.

In the era of the monolithic state, the nation seems to have miscarried. Where a feeling of solidarity once persisted in spite of ethnic and religious differences, and of corruption and political abuse, the nation now seems to be emptied of its moral content and of the imaginative power that brought it to life. The country has been purged of such niceties. They have been replaced by an imposing centre instead, with its powerfully enshrined hierarchies, by *monoloyalitas* and Pancasila indoctrination, by conglomerates, banks and business, by privilege and compulsion. In such a morally depleted environment, corruption is naturally cosily at home, and it may even be questioned whether that word correctly describes the use and abuse of power and position in Indonesia today.

To utilize one's status in a hierarchical, morally unequal structure of society seems a normal thing to do. Not to act so, not to exploit privilege and prebend, is merely stupid. To do so is to profit from a private, positional right. Also the word 'private' is a dubious usage here, because that only has real meaning if paired with 'public', and the problem that should be pondered is whether the idea of 'public affairs' exists at all in a state-dominated polity that is somewat opaque and basically intolerant of democratic procedure and controls. It appears that the benefits of the nationalistic period, and its moral protest against the impositions of colonial rule, have got lost somewhere along the way. Perhaps that is the reason why Pramoedya Ananta Toer's writings are considered to be subversive. It may also be why one of the foremost *budayawan* proclaimed that the country has been put back to 1900, to the time before its national awakening.

The moral vacuousness of present-day Indonesia, that hinders nation-building and thwarts identification with the state, also stands in the way of the evolution of a national culture. This connexion was clearly elaborated by Umar Kayam in his speech to the fourth Cultural Congress of 1991. In his view, the way forward to true modernity is via democracy, which means the opening up of closed hierarchical relationships to general controlling mechanisms and a new readiness on the part of power-holders to be subjected to popular scrutiny. In referring to world history, he noted that the advance to modernity has failed time and again in those states that merely base their attempt on advanced industry, science, sophisticated technology, and a free market economy. If such countries do not also evolve an open, democratic system, they are bound to collapse eventually.

Modernity has one vital need; the enthusiastic and creative participation of a nation's whole population. The people should therefore not be regarded as just statistical units on the planning board. Such a practice only breeds cynicism, while the exclusion of popular participation deadens the potentialities of the populace. It is from them that the nation's culture sprouts and grows, and as it flourishes so does national self-identity. To pave the way for a convincing culture of the nation, Kayam described six crucial conditions for its successful emergence. First of all, there must be the will to face the current situation honestly, to analyse and diagnose it without taking refuge in hypocrisy and deceptive similitudes. This implies, secondly, a democratic, open manner of conducting affairs, with respect for human dignity, and, thirdly, an economy that gives chances to everybody while guaranteeing minimal standards of income, including employment opportunities, and, fourthly, there should be education provided for all. In addition, fifthly, all barriers impeding artistic production, such as censorship and outlawing the works of certain authors, should be lifted, while, sixthly, this tolerance should also be reflected in the attitudes of the different religious groups vis-à-vis each other (*Editor* 5/8, 1991).

Given all this, Kayam could safely deduce that a national culture would be a new thing for Indonesia. It is part of the evolution of a modern, open society, and he doubted whether the 'feudal', hierarchical order of social life was yet ready to allow, and stand aside for, such cultural growth. His pessimism should serve as a stern warning to those in power and to the technocrats who foresee the Second National Awakening as occurring shortly after the initiation of the sixth five-year plan in 1993, when the country is supposed to 'take off'. Or do these people imagine that that Awakening will follow the same revolutionary course as the first?

The moral content of the New Order has reached its lowest ebb, legalizing the money-grabbing and incompetence of its monopoly-holders, while its protagonists stage occasional show-case trials of people who have fallen from grace. The man in the street comments on this, tongue-in-cheek, that there is only one corrupt person in the land, namely, the one before the court at the time. In the early months of 1992, this was Ahmad Thahir.[21]

The same period witnessed the government seizing a heaven-sent opportunity to divert the populace from their by now habitual cynicism. It was provided by the initiative of some Portuguese and Timorese who had decided to sail a decrepit, slow old ferry all the way from Lisbon to Dili in order to lay wreaths on the graves of those massacred there in November 1991 (*Tempo* 2/22:13-24). For weeks on end, the progress of the *Lusitania Expresso* was reported daily in the newspapers, together with the trials of those Timorese who had publicly expressed sympathy for the victims, and their doubts about the legality of the invasion and annexation of East Timor. All this amounted to a threat to the integrity of the state, an insult to Indonesian sovereignty, intolerable international, especially Dutch, criticism, and the heightened visibility of that irritant human rights' organization, the Legal Aid Institute *LBH*.

When it had all blown over, I doubt whether the army and navy had gained much prestige as defenders of the territory. With the Eastern Fleet out in full force to intercept the nefarious ferry boat and direct it on its way back to Darwin, most people could not help but notice that this had been a positively elephantine reaction to what was at best a tame mouse, and they felt let down. So the courageous act of cutting the aid strings still held by the Dutch uncle came as a welcome diversion that helped to revive the spluttering flame of nationalism, at the same time that it cut deeply into the financial support of progressive NGOs, among them the *LBH*.

---

21 *Haji* Thahir died in 1976, and since then the various parties laying claim to his possessions have been at loggerheads. His fortune was built up through the commissions he received as the right hand man of the then director general Ibnu Sutowo. Those wheeler-dealer days resulted in Pertamina's spectacular debt of US$10,500 million (1975), and some well stacked bank accounts. The case between Thahir's widow Kartika and the state oil company Pertamina in the Singapore courts about US$78 million deposited there was reopened in January 1992 and received massive publicity (*Tempo* 48/21, 49/21, 52/21 — main feature, 53/21 — main feature, 1/22). The story of Pertamina as the source of private perks for its top men has been written in the form of a novel by Ramadhan K.H., who has a long standing interest in corruption, for instance, *Royan Revolusi* (*Afterpains of the Revolution*, 1968, op. cit. p.126), *Kemelut Hidup* (*Life's Crisis*, 1977) and, for the present case, *Ladang Perminus* (*The Oil Field*, 1990).

In sum, we may identify the traits of what is nowadays called 'globalization' in the discussions about culture.[22] It contains the idea that all kinds of external processes are exerting their influence on the shaping of Indonesian culture, opening it up to the outside, and, further, that modern communication systems continue to bring in many new ideas. This process has gone so far and had such widespread effects that the ideas of post-nationalism and post-Indonesian identity have been launched.[23] In my analysis I do not disagree. Indonesia as "imagined community" has failed to prosper because it has been emptied of its moral content. It is not the expression of a highly diversified national community any longer but the monopoly of a high- and heavy-handed government that has lapsed from being, or failed to become, an ethically exemplary elite, yet appropriates to itself the task of defining what it is to be Indonesian. Thus people have become alienated, cynical, apathetic, and consumer culture-oriented.

That culture is another aspect of *globalisasi*. Inherent to this is the pursuit of money by all means, display-spending, the OKB and his search for a style and identity, the executive look — western jacket, neck-tie, samsonite case, Seiko watch — pop and youth culture, soccer hooliganism, fights among school gangs. Globalization also means the streaming in of foreign capital in search of quick profit, new technology, a businesslike way of doing things. Taken altogether, it has no moral content and is contrary to true nation-building; it stimulates 'individualism', or at the very least the widespread tendency of everybody only caring for himself, or the *lu lu, gué gué* (you you, I I) syndrome, social and political indifference, and an exalting of foreign examples that are eagerly imitated, thus killing off local creativity, relegating one's own culture to insignificance, disdaining it as old-fashioned and countrified.

Often Jakarta appears to offer an insane existence, an order of life that contrasts with what one would prefer deep down. Parodying life in *Orde Baru Indonesia*, Teater Koma, the self-styled most successful the-

---

22 The money that fires the fever for seminars of all sorts even resulted in a one-day discussion on The Effect of Globalization on the Institution of Marriage. Although I failed to hear anything about the presumed effects, it brought cash to the four participants who presented papers and a good lunch for us all.

23 It is *budayawan* Mangunwijaya who promotes these ideas; he unfolds them in his latest novel, *Burung-burung Rantau* (*Birds of Passage*, 1992).

atre group in Southeast Asia, drew full houses when it staged its *Mental Asylum, R.S.J.*, in which an idealistic physician joins the medical staff. The young man is full of interest for his patients, to whom he listens in the process of trying to come to a sensitive diagnosis. Soon this is recognized as a threat by his seniors, who hold that patients should shut up and swallow the pills prescribed, the doctors knowing what is good for them. The new medical man does not conform to the expectations of his colleagues and the institution, and so has to be brought to heel. By all the tricks of the trade, his life and self-confidence are undermined. The doctor becomes increasingly given to self-doubt and identification with his charges. Gradually, his behaviour turns weird and odd until, finally, he is a patient himself. Is that what is meant by *zaman édan*, the crazy times when the clown becomes king, or is it just a satire of a graceless authoritarian system that tries to force out idealism and diversity?

Alternative ideas

The *Orde Baru* environment is also satirized in the songs of Iwan Fals and thus, in the best tradition of this government, he has been honoured with umpteen military and police interrogations on the pretext that he disturbs national stability or stirs up society. Yet, over the more than ten years of his public performances, he has been hard to silence, because he merely sings about what everybody knows and sees, such as the plight of impoverished teachers, the greed of big business, the indifference of the parvenus, the mysterious killings of petty criminals, the popular opposition to unfair expropriation at Kedungombo, the pollution of culture and the sea, the suffering of servants, the abuse of employees, the arrogance of managers, the insult of prostitution, the loss of self-respect of the jobless, the social imbalance, and other 'sensitive' issues.

But Iwan does not challenge anybody, he merely registers. He does not call for revolution, does not advocate any solutions, and knows which of his songs not to sing at certain occasions and which ones not to record in his albums. Greatly popular as a rock star, he draws crowds of young people, the *Orde Baru* babies 'born to be

145

meek', who have no political ideas, who know nothing about participation, and whose only aspirations are as consumers. His public is not
going to rise, to stir up society, or disturb stability; the enthusiasm he
provokes remains constrained to the occasions of his concerts, and he is
probably right when he sings "Let us not talk about idealism, but rather
about how much money we have in our pocket... Let us not talk about
nationalism, but rather about our oblivious selves".

Others are also unhappy with the twists and turns the New Order
has taken. We have noted already frequent protest, normally of a moral
nature, that emerged during the 1970s and early 1980s. As far as these
were institutionalized, they have been joined by comparable groups,
such as the *Forum Demokrasi* and the *Lembaga Pemulihan Demokrasi*,
the Foundation for the Restoration of Democracy. This name is telling.
While Indonesia poses as a democracy, it is certainly a special case, a
Pancasila democracy, the interpretation of which is dictated by the *Orde
Baru* leadership. In practice, it means a parliament that is almost totally
subservient to the executive branch, made up of a group of politically
emasculated and privileged yes-men who actually have very little to
deliberate and serve rather as the government's rubber stamp.

Whether democracy can be restored is debatable. Restoration sug-
gests that democracy was once in place, that it worked, and that it is
worthwhile re-instating it. I doubt it. Open politics did not work out in
the 1950s, and they are alien to the Javanese environment. It may be
that openness and democratic procedures promise the best potential for
uniting Indonesia's ethnic and cultural diversity, that popularly based
politics can provide the moral transcendence the country needs if it is
ever to become a nation, but it is unlikely that it can easily be established in an environment such as depicted by Iwan Fals.

Be that as it may, one of the interesting voices advocating more
openness and democratic evolution, participation, and active citizenship, is retired general Soemitro's. Having fallen from grace because of
the *Malari* events of 1974, he has recently become quite visible on the
political and even cultural scenes, arguing for change. In a public
speech before the students of Satya Wacana University in Salatiga in
March 1992, he even declared that the *post-Orde Baru* period had
already begun; he also urged the students to join the *Forum Demokrasi*,
a critical movement in which *budayawan* Arief Budiman and Nahdatul

Ulama leader Abdurrachman Wahid are among the nationally respected names. General Soemitro can allow himself to be crusty on occasions: as the influential ideologue of the *Teknologi dan Strategi Militer* magazine, his opinion carries considerable weight in army circles.

Religion

Whatever some people fancy about political reform, it carries little weight if compared to the moral appeal of religion. In the ideologically vacuous environment of the New Order, where money has grown to become the conspicuous idol, congregational religion, whether Islam or Christianity, is faring well. Joining is a means of searching for and expressing a moral identity, one's ethical worth. In mosque and church, a measure of criticism can be voiced against the excesses of development, such as the overwhelming worth of filthy lucre, the overriding priority of pecuniary profit, the race for riches, the disgusting display-spending of the *nouveaux riches*, the Chinese domination of the economy, the opaque monopolies and business conglomerates. Often religious participation, especially in Islam, can also be a means to react against the influence of foreign culture affecting Indonesian life in the form of alien lifestyles, western oriented consumer culture, 'individualism', far-fetched fashions, American pop music, pornography and drugs.

In the absence of other channels though which to express political, social, cultural and moral frustration, religion thrives. Official political life is totally dominated by the government and does not offer the opportunity for meaningful participation or the expression of critical points of view. Trade-unionism is similarly controlled by the state, so the only alternative organizations for expressing one's commitments are religious and communal. They particularly attract members from the middle classes of society, people of modest means and a reasonable measure of education. Such modern people want to participate in what they feel to be their affairs too; this attitude follows from schooling, newspaper-reading, and an orientation to the outside. And whereas many will merely care for their own affairs, others seek a moral identity in religion.

Regional identity

Next to religious self-expression, there is another way of seeking an antidote to the disturbances of being uprooted and transplanted into a modern urban life far from home. Especially in a town like Jakarta, ethnic and district-of-origin associations abound, not only among migrants from the Outer Islands but also among Javanese and Sundanese, who organize in the *paguyuban* that celebrate common origin, so providing a home away from home. Some of these can listen to private broadcasting in their local dialects and languages, and when Great Jakarta looks almost as deserted as its Chinatown, Glodok, in the days following Chinese New Year, you can be sure that it is *Lebaran*, the time after the fasting month when people visit their folks back home and tank up on the local atmosphere, its culture and customs.

This custom, known as *mudik*, when buses and trains threaten to burst at their seams and traffic jams build up all over Java, has the very important function not only of keeping old ties alive, but especially of providing an opportunity for living for a few days a year in an 'authentic', an original, environment that reaffirms identity. Given the near impossibility of identification with a moral community — other than religious and regional associations — in the anonymity of town where business and money dominate life, and where the content of the nation is dictated by the executive branch of government, a retreat to the sphere of a more wholesome 'little tradition' may be an important prop in maintaining mental health.

Islam and the *Orde Baru*

In this connexion, it is interesting to note what happened to Islam under the New Order. As one of the social forces very much opposed to communism, it was mobilized in the destruction of the Indonesian communist party, *PKI*, at the demise of the Sukarno regime, and so it came in as a kind of a natural ally to the military-dominated dispensation that had taken over. Yet the army, and especially its officers with a Javanist background, was suspicious of politically organized Islam and its desire to force Moslem religious discipline on its formal adherents. While the vast majority of Indonesians confess to the religion of the Prophet, most Javanese at that time preferred not be be burdened with the strict observance of religious obligations.[24] Whatever the case, Islam was also too big a social force to ignore.

The initial confluence of opinion in anti-communism soon resulted in the idea that religion is incompatible with the atheistic doctrine of father Marx, and so, that people who acknowledge the supremacy of God cannot at the same time be communists. In this way of reasoning, religion can serve as a weapon against leftist tendencies and should be propagated. It thus became a compulsory subject in elementary and high school. Besides this, everybody was supposed to adhere formally to one of the five officially recognized religions, a membership that is registered on one's residency card.

But then, there also remained distrust. To the nationalistic military, the orientation towards Mecca and the image of a righteous isolation of the ulema-centred Muslims spelled divisiveness. Toward the end of the 1960s, this was still often worded in vitriolic pamphlets and sermons condemning *kejawèn* mysticism and religious practices. If this intolerance had combined with political potential, the recently gained stability as a precondition for national development could easily have been endangered again.

A great number of policy measures aimed at extracting the potential sting of politics, at the same time that the availability of modern education manoeuvred the Islamic community into the mainstream of national life. In the general process of depoliticization, the Moslem masses were also supposed to be demobilized between elections. And while religion became a general subject in ordinary schools, secular teaching was introduced in the many *pesantrèn* religious boarding schools where the pupils, *santri*, henceforward would also be expected to acquire literacy in Indonesian, study English and arithmetic, and possibly useful crafts and skills. The orientation toward a wider world was illustrated when a leading member of the very Javanese Nahdatul Ulama association was the first of that community to obtain a Ph.D. degree at the end of the 1960s.

24 For elaboration and a longer time frame, Martin van Bruinessen, State-Islam relations in contemporary Indonesia. C. van Dijk, A.H. de Groot (eds), *State and Islam*. Leyden University, Research School CNWS, 1995.

Educationally, Muslims did well, in their own and state universities, and in the expanding network of tertiary level state institutes for Islamic religion, the *IAIN*.[25] In producing so many degree-holders — in which they enjoyed a relative advantage because of the decimation of a generation of religiously indifferent *abangan*[26] students — the Moslem community opened up to national life and concerns other than those of religion. As a consequence, the issue of 'secularization' — whatever that means — regularly surfaced in the intra-*ummat*[27] discussions.

All this did not mean, of course, that Islam was suddenly losing its teeth. Electorally it did relatively well during the first three voting exercises, and it decisively defeated the government proposals for the new marriage laws of 1974. This naturally stimulated the executive into trying to domesticate Islam further, for instance, by co-opting ulema to form one of the many subsections of the government party of functional groups, the Golkar. As the most powerful political organization, it could dispense considerable patronage, funding mosques and sponsoring other religious infrastructure, and so was in a position to influence the opinion and actions of, as some will have it, the more opportunistic leaders of the Moslem community. By also exerting strong influence upon those representing the various segments of the *ummat* politically, the government was gradually able to weaken the *PPP* leadership, even before the Nahdatul Ulama association decided to cease functioning as a political organization.

The taming of political Islam had a beneficial effect on the willingness of many to identify openly and actively as Muslims, joining the Friday prayer at the mosque, which they would have been reluctant to do formerly. Islamic study groups flourish, many students listen to the *kuliah subuh*, an early lecture after the morning prayer, and Moslem

---

25 *Institut Agama Islam Negeri.*

26 *Abangan* is a term popularized by Clifford Geertz (1960) to distinguish people who are lax in the performance of Moslem religious obligations. They contrast with the *putihan*, called *santri* by Geertz. All of them, though, are Muslims. Whatever the value the distinction may have had in the period preceding the New Order, the heuristic content of the typology should now be doubted (APPENDIX G), while new issues have come to the fore that divide the Islamic community along different lines. See Zifirdaus Adnan, Islamic religion: yes, Islamic (political) ideology: no! Islam and the state in Indonesia. A. Budiman (ed), 1990:441-77.

27 *Ummat (umma, ummah, umat)*, the members of the, or an, Islamic community.

symbolism further illustrates the pervasiveness of the Islamicization process. Yogyakarta has its first sultan ever to be a *haji*, and the other prince of the realm, *Sri* Paku Alam VIII, is careful to begin his speeches with the Arab greeting *assalam alaikum warahmatullohi wabara-katuh*,[28] and many, more *kejawèn*-oriented people, fear a further penetration of Islam in the *kraton*.

Schooling in religion, and the study of secular subjects in pursuit of advanced degrees, both make for meeting of minds among the more and the less enthusiastic adherents of the *ummat*. Where formerly an almost total lack of comprehension reigned between the products of *pesantrèn* education and more mundane-oriented scholars, the differences are now bridged in the sense that an understanding of each others' points of view contributes to meaningful discussion. In December 1990, this process culminated in the formation of the *ICMI*, the government-sponsored association of Islamic intellectuals.[29] With the secular world now firmly established in the *ummat*, new, but also highly diversified, Moslem identities are being shaped, giving the religion a greater pluriformity.

Differentiation within the Moslem community is nothing new in Indonesia since its own diversity has always been reflected in a variety of political and cultural organizations, often based on specific ethnic traditions or a relative degree of modernity. What has been added now is a set of divergent attitudes to the nation, Development, and life in a changing society, in competition with the orientation to the Middle East. As a result, and under the inspiring leadership of Abdurrachman Wahid, the Nahdatul Ulama, now freed from the corrupting influence of established politics, is opening up and beginning to act as an NGO, aiming at rural modernization, providing small loans to peasants and petty pro-

28 Peace be on you and Allah's mercy and blessing as well.

29 The *Ikatan Cendekiawan Muslim se-Indonesia* was born with the high hopes of being independent of the government and of serving as a channel to express the aspirations of the *ummat*. Under the general chairmanship of the Minister of Research and Technology, B.J. Habibie, this seems rather optimistic, and he himself sees the association rather as a means to reach out to and modernize the Islamic community. It is too early to predict how this nation-wide organization is going to develop and what role it is going to play. Some of the orginal members have already left in disgust when they began to feel the heavy hand of government in *ICMI*'s affairs.

ducers, initialing training programmes in *pesantrèn*, which is altogether a novel, worldly orientation that highlights its transitionary character.

The face of the once modern Muhammadiyah association is also changing, with the ploys and tactics of national politics gaining a growing importance. Under the New Order, the government could penetrate and subvert the Moslem leadership, but it had in turn to make concessions to certain demands that have resulted in a remarkable Islamicization that is now visible in the *jilbab*, the new mosques and prayer houses, the popularity of the *haj*,[30] the teaching of religion in state schools, the crowds at the Friday prayer, the enthusiasm for Ramadan rituals, the craze for fast-breaking at luxury hotels, pop concert-like revival rallies, the industry of designing and propagating the Moslem new look, and the featured prominence of the president at the Istiqlal mosque on important calendar days, when the smiling general poses as *Eyang Kakung Haji* Mohammad Soeharto.[31]

Apparently, the New Order has brought important benefits to Islamic life in Indonesia and the board of Muhammadiyah has been eager to cash in on the patronage of the president, not only by vowing its loyalty, but by petitioning the incumbent to please fill another, sixth term as head of state. The board was clearly acting off its own bat and not all the association's members were happy about it, some of the younger ones even getting furious about this accommodation with the centre of power in Jakarta. How does the penetration of the capital in Islamic affairs reflect on its moral stature? Is the Moslem leadership pulling the strings or is it being masterminded by the state? Who manipulates whom, and does it not in all cases lead to intolerable moral compromise?

These differences of opinion often concern more than the political deals to obtain concessions, and touch on matters of dogma and interpretation, of local traditions and orthodoxy, of secularization and authority, or just on personality differences. From time to time, they become highly visible in the disputes raging between the various stu-

---

30 In April, 102,000 persons had registered to travel to Mecca in 1992. This highest number ever reflects the success of Development.

31 Reference is to O.G. Roeder's *The Smiling General, President Soeharto of Indonesia*. Jakarta: Gunung Agung, 1969. *Eyang Kakung* means grandfather, thus respected elderly person.

dent organizations at the *IAIN*, such as the Muslim Students' Federation, *HMI*, the Indonesian Islamic Students' Federation, *PMII*, and the Association of Muhammadiyah Students, *IMM*. Added to this are the divergent shades of opinion existing within, and the different stances of, the Nahdatul Ulama and Muhammadiyah.

Like all other organizations allowed by the government, these Islamic associations have also been forced to acknowledge that they are primarily based on the Pancasila, while their more purely political branches have openly vowed their loyalty to the state ideology in the period running up to the 1992 elections, with many Moslem leaders going out of their way by praying that Allah may grant the president a new term. Over the years, such kowtowing has brought important concessions that will be difficult to reverse, such as the equation of the juridical competence of the Islamic courts with the state's in matters of family law. What's more, the debates on mixed marriages seem likely to result, eventually, in their prohibition, at least for those who confess to the Faith with non-Muslims.

But it is also the case that the president needs Islam more these days than in the early *Orde Baru* period when the army was his mainstay. The more Development progressed, the more the government policy came to be dominated by economic considerations. As the government's role was transformed into that of a tycoon running a business empire, the civilian props of support gradually grew to be more important, thus relegating the military to an instrumental role, guaranteeing national stability. In this constellation, legitimation by gaining the support of the largest religious community became mandatory.

Whatever the state of discussions and differences of opinion, seen from within, Islam seems to be doing well among the urban middle classes, among civil servants, functionaries, small and bigger businesspeople, and so forth. In step with the trends of the time, it also seems to be developing as a lifestyle with its own fashions, conspicuous fast-breaking, favourite travel destinations, and the revival rallies for the young to the *dangdut* tunes of Rhoma Irama, Rendra's poetry reading, Setiawan Djody's guitar, and topped off by the wise words of charismatic preacher K.H. Zainuddin M.Z. Adorned by these traits of irrepressible consumer culture, the *jilbab* becomes cute, the *haj* fashionable, and revival entertaining.

153

Less amusing, or so it appears to me, is the obligatory teaching of religion in school. If the teaching and examination materials are any guide to go by, they must bore the students halfway to death, and most teachers of the subject have the reputation of doing just that. So, while this instruction could be stimulating if aimed at developing the imagination by parables and comparison with everyday situations, it has generally assumed the same woodenness that chacterizes the teaching of Pancasila morality and history. This routinization makes religion contrast in a poor light with the mass cultural diversions outside the school walls, and is certain not to foster interest in it.

Religious dedication may be better promoted by *pesantrèn*-training, and seems to be on the minds of many rural parents apprehensive about the corruption of national society. Yet it is possibly more than moral anxiety alone that explains the explosive growth in the number of *santri*.[32] As noted in passing, these days the Islamic boarding-schools are also offering the common curriculum of the state schools and so impart the skills necessary in modern life. The upsurge in popularity may therefore be more than a sign of religious enthusiasm, and can be explained by poverty in the countryside. While parents are increasingly aware of the necessity of formal education, not all of them are able to provide for the schooling of their progeny. Besides, the demand may outstrip the capacity of the national school system to offer education to all, apart from the fact that such schooling is more expensive. For many, therefore, the *pesantrèn* is the only way to seek some of the skills needed for one's later advancement in life. In this connexion, it is of interest to note that many of the religious leaders of these schools, *kiai*, are becoming more interested in the secular circumstances of the surrounding *ummat*,[33] getting involved in community development aimed at

32 The people of *Kompas* investigated the impressive expansion of the demand for Moslem education, which they reported in three articles on Sunday 29 March 1992. According to information from the director-general for the development of Islamic infrastructure, the number of *pondok pesantrèn* grew from 6,386 in 1986-87 to 6,795 in 1990-91. In the same period the *santri* almost doubled their numbers, from 829,768 to 1,629,739 throughout Indonesia; they were instructed by 34,659 and 53,181 teachers respectively.

33 Interesting in this respect are the reflections of *kiai* Yusuf Hasyim, Pesantren and national development: role and potential. M. Oepen, W. Karcher (eds), *The Impact of Pesantrèn in Education and Community Development in Indonesia*. Jakarta:P3M-FNS, 1988.

improving material conditions. While conservative quarters resist this opening up to the world, the firm trend seems to be toward some social activism and concern for the problems of modern existence, founded on a changing perception of the world.

The cultural malaise of Indonesia

The Javanese of the sultanates have rightfully been proud of *kejawèn* civilization, a multi-faceted high culture that provided the exemplary reference for the variety of local traditions in the far-flung rural areas surrounding the court. It was not just the palaces that furnished cultural elaboration; in the outlaying districts religious tracts were also written;[34] and encyclopaedic works produced (Anderson, 1990: 274, 290-1). Yet in the second half of the 19th century it became clear that high culture was in decline.

While there are still many vestiges of high *kejawèn*, there are hardly any literati left to keep the arts and Javanese sciences alive, let alone to revive them. They are gradually becoming relics of the past, museum pieces, and even many of the more popular arts, such as the *réyog* dance, once famous for trance and spirit possession, are tamed for the entertainment of tourists, and folklorized as tokens of regional identity. What remains is local traditions, a set of Javanese identities that are worthwhile to *mudik*, to travel up-country for, but that do not encompass the Javanese as a civilization.

Many younger people really do not care about this state of affairs and are indifferent to the nostalgia of some about a living *kraton* and the fullness of ritual, ceremonial, etiquette, and language. They have grown up in a different environment and acquired a distaste for hierarchical relationships and circumspect behaviour, which they experience as anti-democratic and out-of-date. It is that type of Javaneseness they gladly leave behind.

Meanwhile, some of these same youngsters are shocked by what they come up against in Jakarta, at least by its official, 'Javanized' ways,

---

34 This is one of the interesting points in I. Kuntara Wiryamartana's Ph.D. dissertation *Arjunawiwaha*. Yogyakarta: Duta Wacana Press, 1992.

155

such as hierarchy, command, and authoritarianism, the mantras of government, and the hypocrisy of official statements. According to them, instead of finding Indonesia in the capital, they find everything they disliked and thought to have left behind, a new type of Java that is acted out by a class of privileged parvenus who compete with each other for status, prestige, and publicity.

This very vital Javanese-Indonesian mongrel culture has begun a life of it own, feeding on capitalism, Development, technocracy, globalism, and consumer culture, which all make it morally vacuous and void, offering little to identify with, other perhaps than pride in 'modernity' and the idea that Indonesia does not lag behind in its quest for progress and the future. Perhaps this is the first sign of an evolution towards a new great tradition in the third world, but is it correct to think so?

Great traditions, civilizations, have 'universalistic' pretensions. It is not only that they arch over local diversity, but they also have a moral content, such as nationalism, law, or religious commands, that transcends the particular. To them belong exemplary centres, also in the field of ethics, providing guidance and cultural leadership. In these senses, Jakarta is not the centre of a great tradition, but merely another seat of exploitative government whose moral pretensions are no better than empty propaganda. Its very dependence on business and Development, and the ways it relates to them, makes corruption an integral part of the system; it is the oil that greases it.

If the present practices of the capital are taken to represent Indonesia, then the performance, seen from the point of nation-building, has gone awry. Indonesian nationalism, the cement that glued its diversity together, has been replaced by business, a bureaucratic state, and an army. Often people from the Outer Islands will wryly comment that to them Indonesians equate with Javanese;[35] others amazed me by telling the story of their descent, say, part Ambonese, part Javanese, part Betawi, while not identifying as the new breed 'Indonesian', but

35 The higher representatives of the Republic in government and the military are overwelmingly Javanese. By 1980, all 15 territorial military commands were in the hands of officers from Java who, with 89 percent, totally dominate the commanding positions in the army (Drake, 1989:263-4). It should also be born in mind that often Javanese do not make any bones about speaking of their self-styled cultural superiority. The combination of power and ethnic arrogance leads to their being the ones who define what is Indonesian.

rather feeling apprehensive about which ethnicity *(suku)* to identify with. The owners of the state, that very special brand of privileged people, are not greatly worried. In facing the future with their *Pembangunan* and Pancasila mantras, they project a rather self-confident image. Perhaps the talk about the Second National Awakening — I refer to the opening speech of the Minister of Education and Culture at the national Cultural Congress in November 1991 — is a sign of a dawning awareness that not all is well in the realm, but as long as money flows, the president gets re-elected, and Development-planning aims at forming the complete Pancasila man *(manusia Indonesia seutuhnya)*, the Republic is on track, irrespective of Sukarnoist nationalism.

I do not know how important the feeling of national solidarity is in keeping a country together, how crucial it is that people should be able to think of themselves as belonging to one community.[36] Such a belief also has a moral side, concerning obligations, making a personal contribution, self-sacrifice for the common weal. It is from this sense of pride in nation that a civil society may arise with its beliefs in personal responsibility for the common good, of political participation, and of democratic control. But what Jakarta has to offer is morally sterile, undercutting national pride and the possibility of the emergence of a civil society. The potential for the growth of such a society is being stifled by money and mass culture, by education resulting in social indifference and technical competence, by the compulsive striving for conformity and uniformity, with all this making the country appear as a state without a nation.

The absence of enthusiasm for the nation heightens the need for, and strengthens, the bonds with religion and area of origin. These ties are particularistic, referring to primordial groups whose strength is in

---

36 Drake (1989) draws attention to many quantifiable factors other than nationalism that may be indicative of national integration, such as transportation and trading linkages, the national mass media, communication networks, shared language and school education, the uniform system of national administration, government propaganda and development programmes, the banking systems, the spread of official expenditure, etc. In most of these terms, the country's integration is steadily advancing, as was the case with the former Soviet Union, for instance. In the last chapter, she also notes the adverse influence of transregional economic and political factors, such as the conspicuous gap between rich and poor, population pressure, Javanization, and political repression.

concrete, personalized relationships, and may, in the case of Islam, also stretch as far as the world-wide *ummat* that, again, does not bring the nation into focus. It may even be argued that the strengthening of ties to the area of origin — necessary for a meaningful identity — is counterproductive to building Indonesian culture, and signals a trend away from the ideals of 1928 when the formation of the future state was seen as a morally binding commitment.

CHAPTER 9

The dominant image of society

It was no chance occurrence that the 1991 Cultural Congress coincided with the end of the first 25-year period of development planning and the beginning of the second, in which Indonesia is supposed to start flying on the wings of industrialization while leaving its agricultural past behind. In entering the future, a new consciousness is needed — creative, scientific, disciplined — to master sophisticated technology and information systems. And so the transformation of culture becomes a necessity.

The resolutions the mammoth congress formulated are depressingly tame, inspired by reserve in facing an authoritarian government, and it is questionable whether the colossal show will contribute anything at all to the projected Second National Awakening, that is also expected to come about in the second long-range planning period. But the utterances and discussions at the congress itself were not subdued, while pin-pointing the obstacles to cultural growth.

In his summary article about the deliberations, Yudhistira ANM Massardi observed that the feet on which Indonesia was supposed to be walking into the future have gone flabby and even put down roots, causing a cultural inertia that is killing creativity. He identified these growths as bureaucratization, centralization, repression, and 'conglomeratization', or the monopoly-dominated structure of the economy (*Editor* 5/8, 1991). From this analysis, it becomes clear why the congress's formal resolutions were so unsatisfactory, with the conclusions to be read between the lines being nothing less than an indictment of the *Orde Baru*.

In his speech, retired general Soemitro expressed his displeasure at the evolution of Indonesian society in which *priyayi-isme*, or feudalism, thrives. He observed that this is a deviation from the founding ideals of the republic. Indonesia is not a kingdom but a democratic state, but at present it seems to be overgrown by a feudal parasite that strangles democracy, keeps people stupid, and avoids dialogue. In this way, creativity, the spirit of free competition and striving after excellence are smothered, while at the same time parliament and the courts cannot function. Corruption, irresponsibility, and abuse of power are deeply and firmly ensconced in such a state. Altogether, it weakens the development of a citizenry and thus of a strong nation. People grow fearful and cowardly, always intent on pleasing the boss, sapping the quality of the relationship between superiors and inferiors, in which the powerful partner can do no wrong and where bootlicking substitutes for frank exchanges.

When scrutinizing the constitution of 1945 that is the official basis also of the New Order state, it is clear that the founding fathers had something else in mind than what has evolved, but perhaps they were naive or too idealistic. They wanted something very different from their colonial experience, something modelled on the European ideals of a civil society; what they did not take into account were their own cultural roots, and they could not have foreseen the entrepreneurial potential for corruption.

They wanted to build a solidary nation, guided by egalitarianism and a sense of the common welfare, in which political publicity, democratic control, and the rule of law would prevail. In spite of their regional diversity, people would also take pride in, and eagerly identify themselves as, being Indonesians, as the free citizens of a new country in which their voices would be heard, having taken their destiny in their own hands. To check on the extremes of individualism, deliberative institutions should be respected, yet people would be allowed to organize on the basis of their own political priorities and class interests.

What they got was turbulence and turmoil, struggle and strife, deception and discouragement. The ideals of the nation grew vaguer, the state overwhelming. But is that a feudal arrangement? While general Soemitro's observations are correct, the label feudalism may hide more than it reveals. In the former days of noble and colonial rule, people were squeezed to obtain resources for the benefit of the dominant class. Yet they also enjoyed a measure of protection, while the 'state' as it presented itself was neither bureaucratic nor anonymous, but represented by concrete, known persons to whom the subject was connected as a kind of client. It may not have been a very pleasant relationship, but it was accepted as part of the order of existence, and thus a moral element inhered within it, the superior patron also having a stake in not bleeding his subjects dry. And so, there was something like a "moral economy" (Scott, 1976) in place.

Feudal arrangements may make for all the misery the good general depicted, but there are other aspects to it that make the popular word somewhat unfortunate when describing what is going on. While we see patronage and clientage, privilege and moral particularism, monopolistic enterprises and the exploitation of position in the Indonesian state, the ties between government and population are rather anonymous, abstract and bureaucratic. Exchanges are not personal and direct, but mediated by money; wage labour has become the rule in production, with Development meaning the accumulation of capital rather than care for the common welfare.

It is this combination of a strongly centralized and highly hierarchical structure of state, together with the workings of capital, that define the mode of production and the way the country is run. By its concentration of power and privilege at the centre, the state has also grown extremely jealous of its self-styled prerogatives, tolerating no deviation. Not being buoyed up by the nationalist sentiments of its population, it is rigid and violent by nature. Already, in the discussion of the ideas that underlie the exercise of leadership, we have seen that the obsession with unity recognizes the inherent danger of diversity. This leads to an internal colonialism that pushes its way forward irrespective of the interests of citizens or subjects, seeing the country as a kind of private possession. The populace of that territory must be submissive or suffer the consequences.

The weight, the pressure, of this heavy-handedness forces people apart, makes them conform with the position the leadership assigns them: to be an aggregate of individuals, a floating mass that should be controlled from above, and whose inner diversity is not recognized to exist. The state does not enter into dialogue but shoots from the hip, and moral or other protest is a dangerous activity. It is thus better to busy oneself with one's own affairs only, to avoid involvement, and not to ask too many questions.

Basically, it is an amoral order in which political power and big business combine, not involving the people, who each and all follow their own survival-oriented ways. In such a situation, the very idea of public debate and a common weal is out of place, democracy an irrelevant dream, and cultural growth a near-impossibility, other, of course, than in social satire and that caricature of culture, consumerism. It is a mass society in the making, uprooted, ruled by money and force, that does not command loyalty or foster the responsibility of citizenship. By not involving its people, such an entity is destined to be ethically void.

The question to ponder is whether there is a chance that all this will be open to change, whether bureaucratization, centralization, repression, and 'conglomeratization' will give way to an open society brought to life by a creative and responsible citizenry in which the ideals of the generation of 1928 will prevail. Nobody among the *budayawan* is optimistic; the state has grown too dominant and deeply rooted. Its main mechanisms of maintaining itself are its exercise of amoral power, its hold over the economy, and the indifference of its subjects, who browse in flocks on the products of mass culture.

It does not seem probable that anything like a 'civil society' will soon be in the offing, even though the rise of a native class of entrepreneurs has been noted, especially since the mid-1980s. At that time, the state began to lose its near total hold over economic development, while the private sector began to press for a say in policy-making (Macintyre, 1991). This process seems to be accelerating with a greater variety of economic players coming to the fore. Yet, whether their participation in the game for profits and protection is going to establish democratic procedures must be doubted. The political process grows more complicated, in pace with the success of economic diversification and development, but the demands on the centre that are formulated in board rooms or chambers of commerce should not be equated with the opening up of society, and the growth of an articulate public.

Strangely enough, there is continuity and recognizability in this experience. A low measure of individuation has always been the rule; people care for and identify with their families, not with abstractions such as the nation. The exercise of power has always been violent and abusive, also in the *zaman normal*; people never felt themselves to be part of politics but rather were lorded over by white or brown bosses. In a society that is status-oriented, hierarchical positions mean honour and privilege, then as now. Position may also carry the attribute of personal power, a precious possession that enables holders to cash in on opportunity and special rights. If a minor person wanted to be protected by such power, he had to seek its patronage, and if that was not possible, he had better stay clear of it. So, what is new?

The greatest novelty is probably the fading of all ethical pretensions and the rise of an alienating environment, where even culture, the production of meaning, seems to be ebbing away. Dominated by economic considerations, modern life in many third world countries — as in Indonesia — gives birth to a disorderly, untidy mass society where poor millions mill around the shopping malls of the newly rich, and where the gap between them shows blatantly. No cultural congresses are going to prevent this development, that may certainly evoke its own destabilizing counter forces, but also, in the short run, more repression.

APPENDIX A

Communication, 1970

In Javanese society, the individual is supposed to maintain a low profile, not to compete but to share, to be obedient, dependent, and cooperative. His voice may be heard in the *musyawarah*, but he should not press his point to the extent that others will find him an obstacle to decision-making. As long as he knows 'shame' *(isin)*, and conforms to expectations and norms, he will be respected; he should give way to superior power, circumstances, or the will of his community; he should *ngèli*, that is, go with the flow. He should not upset the delicate social balance by his private wishes or ambitions; in short, he should be a loyal part of his relevant groups without causing unrest or stir. Therefore, he should master his personal emotions, maintain a front of politeness, and enjoy the serenity of his community and inner being.

Yet the need to express personal feelings and emotions does exist. At *kethoprak* popular theatre, the movies, *wayang* performances, and in some types of mystical expression, people may show enthusiasm and empathic participation. People may even get violently excited at the experience of gross injustice, in situations of mob action or by insult to religion. Such expressions of emotions are occasional, and the preferred tone of life is subdued and quiet, with most people reacting in a very restrained manner.

For the individual, this means the cultivation of a graceful control over emotions and the acceptance of life as it comes. He may, and should, hide behind formality and politeness, not involving himself unnecessarily. Yet some emotion is often shown, and even minor emotions are never entirely hidden. This may upset other people, and it is embarrassing in view of the Javanese ethos and style. Perhaps I, as an outsider, have experienced more of it than is usual in Java because of the research situation and the emotion-laden object of my research, namely, religion and mysticism. Be that as it may, I have been impressed at how often people vented their indignation or frustration in my company.

Among Javanese, the emotional content of communication is expressed by the circumspection with which people approach their subject, the show of embarrassment itself, or the demonstrations of modesty and deference. The emotional charge generally arises from the difficulty that an individual feels in approaching another person to whom he is not intimately related, which include most people beyond the mother and other immediate kin (such as older sisters, or siblings and friends to whom one feels especially close). Towards strangers and those of higher status, a person feels shame, anxiety, fear, and insecurity that are demonstrated by language, inaction, and mannerisms such as excessive smiling, shying away, and giggling.

Excessive shows of modesty can well be observed at public or semi-public gatherings. In a hierarchical society, everybody is pretty much aware of the honours that he deserves because of his position. For instance, on arriving at a function, one will be directed by the master of ceremonies to one's appropriate place — the best places or those nearest the front being reserved for the highest level persons in attendance. Yet, upon entering, people will often insist on sitting in a place somewhat removed from the places where they should sit. The shows of competition in modesty are intriguing, take up a lot of time and give rise to much giggling, until finally everybody is seated exactly according to rank and expectations.

The higher the persons, the longer the preliminaries. Although it is never good manners to come to the point immediately, I found it most fascinating to see two highly educated *priyayi* enact the longest such ritual that I have witnessed. It took them fully fifty minutes of giggling, smiling, showing modesty, laughing, making excuses, refusing to sit on certain chairs, etc., before finally tea was offered and they could come to the point, which was no more embarrassing than a talk about mysticism in which these two venerable gentlemen knew each other to be interested. It takes a long time before the feeling of intrusion upon the other is overcome; it is a barrier that separates individuals from each other, and individuals from their society.

And yet, sometimes, one may need the sympathy of others and be strongly motivated by the desire to communicate. A person with whom I was fairly well acquainted wanted to convey an important message. He entered my room, giggling and smiling. I invited him to sit, and he accepted the ritual tea that is served soon after a guest arrives. He kept giggling and talking about the weather and other topics that were obviously irrelevant to his message. He excused himself for intruding upon me, and continued to talk about trivial things, yet his excessive smiling and giggling demonstrated that he had something on his mind, and that he was under stress — he was obviously trying to overcome the intimidating barrier that separates man from man in courtly Yogyakarta. Smiling and giggling, he finally came to his point — 'My father has died' — and immediately he made his excuses and wanted to leave. He had overcome the barrier and apologized for having done so. He was embarrassed, and so was I, because his father had died.

The extremely high divorce rate in Java may also be indicative of this failure to achieve personal communication. According to Hildred Geertz, the withholding of emotional commitment is apparently typical of most Javanese marriages (1961:134). The extreme pressures generated by the suppression of individual emotions may sometimes be released by the person who goes berserk *(amuk)*, or may be vented at the communal level when order and quietness have been violated. The level of potential frustration may then be indicated by the ease with which communal demonstrations can be whipped up against outsiders — Chinese, religious converts, 'communists', adulterers, thieves — and against whom physical violence and mob action may then be directed.

APPENDIX B

Lottery prediction, 1970

When I was in Yogyakarta, people were under the spell of the *Nalo* (national lottery). A full ticket consisted of six or seven digits, and could be bought officially, but gambling on the *buntut* (tail), or the last two digits of the outcome, was far more popular. The streets were lined with the small stands of the *bandar* ('underground lottery' ticket vendors) who sold the numbers 00 to 99; they paid seventy times the stake if the outcome of the tail of the national lottery coincided with the number bought. Basically, this was good business, but the risks were considerable. The main danger was arrest at the hands of the police or the army, whose actions were entirely unpredictable. Generally, the authorities tolerated this form of gambling, but sometimes, towards the end of the week, they suddenly had an urge to maintain law and order, and arrested *bandar* almost at random. By that time, the *bandar* had collected a considerable amount of money, so that their seizure meant a good income for the servants of the law; other *bandar* let themselves be detained on Thursday, and shared their income with the police while being unable to reimburse potential winners on Sunday because they had been 'arrested'. The *buntut Nalo*, the gambling on the tail, was big business for the authorities, the *bandar*, the people, and the lottery outcome predictors.

I witnessed how *Pak* Amat became one of the most prominent lottery predictors in Central Java. He was of Christian origin, a graduate of Gadjah Mada University, an important man in his *kampung* (ordinary urban neighbourhood), the leader of a small *kebatinan* group, and an amateur student of Javanese psychology. He became a lottery predictor because his pupils and followers began to ask for numbers, and he himself thought that his contact with supernature was 'sure' and 'pure' enough to warrant a try in that direction. It was a matter of controversy among *kebatinan* leaders in Yogya whether he should provide his followers with numbers, but he began to give predictions anyway. His first predictions were 'sure' numbers, which meant that if he said that the

169

outcome would be 15, he meant 15 indeed. At that time, his predictions were based on simple symbols that he received as *ilham* (inspiration) during meditation. His following, consisting of a few Javanese families and Chinese shopkeepers, lost some money but the matter was not taken too seriously; it was fun — partly serious, partly playful. On a certain day, however, *Pak* Amat received a symbol about which he was particularly sure. It looked like this:

With the participation of his following, he interpreted the symbol to mean 15 or 34. Fifteen, because the symbol could be read as 2+1+2=5, with 1 in the central axis, and 34, because 2-1+2 makes 3, and 4 was considered to be strong because of the two 2s. Everybody was pretty convinced by these interpretations, and all concerned played for very high stakes — the Chinese gambling as much as 100,000 rupiah (us$240) on each of the numbers, the Javanese much less, but still more than they could afford to lose. The outcome was 95, and this spelled a crisis. Somebody in one of the Javanese families was ill, and there was no money left to buy medicine. *Pak* Amat felt miserable. The only solution was to re-establish order and unity by conducting a *slametan* in the house of the family that had been most hurt by the gambling.

The *slametan* was to begin at 9 p.m. Everybody was present with the exception of *Pak* Amat. It was the week before the first Apollo mission to the moon, and all were talking about its possible success or failure, while evaluating its significance for the outcome of the lottery. At that time, I ventured a tongue-in-cheek prediction on the outcome of the next week's lottery by an esoteric interpretation of the word 'Apollo'. Later, I was shocked to find that a few of those present had in fact bought the number that I had predicted.

Pak Amat arrived around 11 p.m., and played it masterfully. Apollo was forgotten and we began the *slametan* proper. During his prayer and his speech, he became very emotional. He confessed to being a sinner, a conceited creature of 'God', who had had the vanity to try to interpret 'His' will by giving sure predictions when his inspiration only constituted a *petunjuk* (indication, hint). He repented, he wept, condemned himself for his vanity, and then, at the end of almost an hour, he admonished his flock, in a sublime counterclimax, that they should not doubt the authenticity of his inspiration. On the contrary, his symbol contained the truth and if people still doubted, they should turn the symbol against the light where, in mirror-writing, they could read 95 indeed:

Everybody present, including myself, was shaken and deeply impressed. It was clear that *Pak* Amat did receive very superior inspiration. Obviously, he had access to high knowledge that was hidden from his followers. As the story spread, his following grew by leaps and bounds, and although he still tried to satisfy his visitors with *kebatinan* speeches, it became increasingly clear that the people who gathered around him were primarily interested in his ability to predict the lottery. Consequently, a few of his more serious Javanese followers became dissatisfied and dropped out.

Within a few weeks, *Pak* Amat became the most influential lottery predictor in Yogya. Hundreds of people visited him every day and at all hours, some coming from places as far away as Semarang or Solo. These visitors appeared to constitute a cross-section of the slightly more well-to-do urban population, representatives of all walks of life, from small traders in the market to Chinese shopkeepers, teachers, civil servants, students and graduates, soldiers and officers, male and female, young and old — and virtually all of them literate.

With so many people to interpret his symbolic predictions, there were always winners who gave credit to *Pak* Amat for their lucky number. His fame thus continued to spread, and soon he had to regulate the flow of visitors. On Sundays, he would interpret the Saturday's outcome of the lottery on the basis of his predictions; later in the week, on Wednesdays and Thursdays, he would speak to the crowds that gathered in his yard, to reveal the symbols that would contain the clues for the draw on Saturday night. At that time, he also began to distribute stencils that contained a drawing, a cluster of ciphers, a text from the bible, and the hour at which all of these had been received in meditation. But the people were primarily interested in his speeches, from which they took notes, and which some even recorded on tapes.

Pak Amat used these speeches to tell his audience about *kebatinan,* about right and wrong behaviour, and often that Jesus saves if the sinner repents. His speeches were fun to listen to; generally, they were in an odd mixture of Javanese, Indonesian, and Dutch. His delivery, as the son of a Protestant minister, was that of a full-blooded preacher. He involved his congregation by asking questions, getting answers and by drawing their laughter.

Pak Amat enjoyed all this very much. He reasoned that his lottery predictions gave him the opportunity to 'save' people by way of moral lectures — much like his father had done in church — that the lottery might relieve the poverty of his public, and that he was doing good work because the government had organized the lottery to obtain funds for its development programmes. Whatever his personal justifications and defence against the severe criticism from the church and the majority of *kebatinan* leaders in Yogya, people gathered around him to get some clue about next week's draw, and were obviously not interested in the other aspects of his message.

These people were particularly interested in the behaviour of *Pak* Amat who, as a guru, was thought to have access to high knowledge and insight, and to be so much in step with supernature that his behaviour was coordinated with higher truth, thus revealing the future. This idea is known as *sasmita alam,* and it was this theory of omens that was believed to be most revealing about the outcome of the lottery. When he was dressed in shorts, people would expect a low number; when he had gone to the movies, they wanted to know the number of the row and his seat, and so on. By reinterpreting his 'symbolic' behaviour, people were led to a number, while *Pak* Amat used the same technique to explain why he was always right. An example of his explanations runs as follows:

> The outcome of the tail last week was 21. Why? Last Thursday, when I delivered my definitive speech about yesterday's outcome, my daughter was selling small tubes of sweets; I admonished you to buy them, because we should practise *gotong-royong* and help each other. It was on and in that tube of sweets that the outcome was revealed. On the tube you could read 'Fruit Drops' and 'Fruit Norton'; I told you not

to use mystical parallel ciphers but the straight numbers while adding and substracting. You should have reasoned as follows: you read 'Fruit Drops'; F means 7 if you read it in mirror-writing; then you have D, making 7D. D is the fourth letter of the alphabet. You add the numbers, which makes 11, which you add again, making 2. 'Fruit Norton' is 76, because F is 7 and 'Norton' is composed of 6 letters. You substract and find 1. The outcome must be 12 or 21, because there is left and right, hand and foot, male and female.

What's more, there were 12 sweets in the tube, again indicating 12 or 21. Besides this, the outcome of the week before was 87 for the 87th round of the national lottery. Last week was the 88th round, which was a clear indication, because 100 minus 88 makes 12. Of course, I do regret that I may not reveal the outcome itself. The army would come to arrest me if I did, I would bankrupt the *bandar*. Besides, it is not within the purposes of our government that I give straight numbers, because our government wants to stimulate its development efforts by way of the lottery. Yet, whoever has ears to hear, let him hear, and whoever has eyes to see, let him see.

The people who gathered around *Pak* Amat would acknowledge his unfathomable wisdom and hope that they would understand, too, whenever 'their time has come'.

Having learned the tricks of the trade, I decided that I would experiment with this thinking and act as a lottery predictor. Ever since I had interpreted the word 'Apollo', people would occasionally ask me for numbers, which I had so far refused. This experience was not unique: Catholic missionaries also complained that they were asked for numbers and that their behaviour was a source of inspiration for lottery prediction. Everything and everybody that is considered high, exalted, odd, peculiar, uncommon, may be regarded as an omen. In these latter senses, I certainly qualified. My credibility as a predictor was further enhanced by a reputation for mysticism and a strange way of life.

I acted on the following assumptions: I was peculiar and therefore revealing; things that were associated with me shared this quality, revealing cosmological co-ordination, or real co-incidence; such things might thus be interpreted as meaningful signs for the outcome of the lottery; because of this, people would be willing to sacrifice to obtain such meaningful signs from me. Subsequently, if asked for a number, I would offer such people a one-rupiah note (on which there is a number) for the sum of one hundred rupiahs. On a modest scale, this indeed appeared to work. After a few weeks, I stopped this practice, being satisfied with having tested a way of thinking.

These ideas of co-ordination, revealing form and the absence of pure chance, reappear in all areas of Javanese life; the careful study of the structure of an event reveals its conditioning elements that are interpreted by way of classification, co-ordination, and intuitive reasoning. For instance, the sacrosanct date of Independence, 17-8-1945, was no chance occurrence but a compelling co-incidence *(kebeneran)*, because it was already written in the geographical co-ordinates of the country, in the way that Sukarno spelled his name, in the structure of Borobudur, and in the old prophecies. Such, at least, was the interpretation of the significance of the holy number 17-8-1945.[1] Similarly, there are the numbers 1 to 9 because there were nine Islamic prophets in Java, and because the human body has nine openings; or, *guru* Sumono's principal disciple is called Herman, because together they are *Hermono*; *her* meaning *air* (water) and *mono* meaning man or 'Life'. *Hermono* thus meaning 'the water of Life', or Life's essence. The fact that *guru* Sumono and *dhalang* Herman met each other cannot be a chance occurrence, but is the result of co-ordination. It was a real co-incidence, and therefore cause and fact.

---

1 B. Setiadidjaja, *Arti Angka-angka Keramat 17-8-1945.* Bandung: Balebat, 1965.

The more it changes, the more it remains the same, 1970

The ideal of *rukun* implies the practice of *gotong-royong*, that is, to share each other's burdens and to make voluntary contributions to those in need. Nowadays, such contributions are often asked for to support the celebrations of organizations that one hardly knows exist, or with which one has no direct relationship at all. Especially when people in uniform invoke the norms of *rukun*, it is advisable to smile and to quietly practise *gotong-royong*. Sometimes, such organizations do not bother to go from door to door, but pre-select their donors from among those who drive along the roads. One day, while travelling through Brebes on the north coast of Central Java, I was stopped by the police who demanded to see my papers. They took them to the other side of the road where the police station was located, and I was invited to follow. Nobody cared to inspect the papers, but instead I was handed a written invitation to make a contribution to the celebration of the national police day. Occasionally, one may be stopped and invited to demonstrate one's patriotism by buying a portrait of the president. The traveller is well advised to make his 'voluntary' contribution, and thus to practise *gotong-royong*.

Early on, I wondered about the quantities that my reliable and honest housekeeper bought in the market. She would buy a pound of meat or a hundred grammes of tea, but generally the quantities she brought home did not match the declarations in the housekeeping account. When I asked her about this, she explained that the people in the market were hard pressed and needed to be helped. These people would put some coins under their scales, so that a hundred grammes became eighty, or half a kilogramme four hundred grammes. This was done because the prices were officially frozen at a low level that had become unrealistic; she explained the practice as *gotong-royong*. In a similar manner, teachers needed to supplement their extremely low salaries (US$5-10 a month). To earn extra income, some of them doubled as *becak* (pedicab) drivers at night, but more commonly they would sell school-books and writing materials at prices slightly above the market value, and insist that their pupils buy from them. They would also charge money for passing grades, admission, examinations, basically illegal practices, but accepted by the community as *gotong-royong*. Similarly, civil servants would charge money for their services — small amounts when they were lowly placed, more when they had high rank. Everywhere, one needed to make contributions, to help each other, and to grease the system. One wondered where the borders lay between mutual help, exploitation of the norm, and extortion.

Rukun and mutual aid were at times grossly overstretched in planned or *ad hoc* development activities. Local military commanders tended to need evidence to show to their superiors that they had accomplished their civic mission. I witnessed how, in the impoverished Gunung Kidul area near Yogyakarta, a big *'gotong-royong'* project was carried out in the name of development. Undernourished villagers had to 'volunteer' to build fifteen kilometres of road, for which they did not receive any payment, not even the food for their daily keep, while a large part of them were visibly suffering from hunger oedema. Such cases of forced labour for the improvement of infrastructure, or the forced deliveries of rice to build a national buffer-stock *(BUUD)*, have made people refer to such *'gotong-royong'* practices as 'the return of Japanese times', and even *'cultuur stelsel'* (the system of forced labour and deliveries under the Dutch in the nineteenth century).

The traditional norms of mutual protection and aid are sometimes avoided by people who, because of education, ideals, or foreign background, hope that 'modern' norms will soon prevail. A Yogyakarta police captain, who was regularly in trouble with his superiors because he wanted to judge cases on their merit and not because of the people involved, was also condemned by the people in his neighbourhood for not exercising his influence to help find his younger brother a job. This brother had graduated from Gadjah Mada University and desired to enter the civil service to have a position and an income. The captain lived up to the family norm of mutual protection by letting his brother eat and sleep in his house, but refused to use his influence in finding him a job. One of his ideas of modernity was: 'You have a diploma and merit; you find yourself a job on the basis of these'. Yet most people thought him in the wrong for not helping his close relative more actively.

Similarly, a friend of mine complained about her brother whom she described as a strange person. Even though her brother held an important job in a big national bank, she thought him to be a disgrace to the family because he went to his office on a bicycle and lived in an ordinary bamboo house in an average *kampung*. She was ashamed of this because his position in the bank should mean a display of status and a bonanza for his relatives. She disclosed that her brother had recently had to evaluate a demand for credit of forty million rupiah, the approval of which would have netted him a commission of two million. Yet the brother deemed the proposal to be a risk; he turned down the request and did not pocket the substantial tea-money. His relatives felt ashamed and thought this to be utterly strange behaviour. Ironically, she remarked that her brother thought himself to be a *pahlawan pembangunan* (hero of development) who did not need to respect the values of status and mutual support; she felt this despite his sharing his monthly 100,000 rupiah (US$240) salary with his kin.

Status needs to be demonstrated and, with the possible exception of the religious and spiritual leadership, patrons *(Bapak)* are expected to display the symbols of their position in order to be credible. Possessions and income are derived from position, but such status also results in social obligations, such as the protection of followers. The demands of status are costly, and the income needed to maintain both 'face' and obligations must be looked for in the nebulous sphere of bureaucratic and political power, of the prebends that go with patrimonial office. Some may call the accompanying practices corruption or exploitation, but they are also necessary to maintain a position of leadership by extending protection. Basically, the norms surrounding the institutions of leadership and patronage are far stronger than the control on sources of income.

Yet leaders should not exaggerate the demonstration of power and wealth; the display should fit the status of a *Bapak*. In this sense, it might be a valid proposition to posit that a one-star general is entitled to one big house, one wife, and one Mercedes car, while the three-star general is entitled to three of each. They will be deemed corrupt and erode their standing with those on whom they depend in turn if they claim more than they are entitled to. In a patrimonial hierarchy, it normally pays to know one's place and to be loyal to one's superiors.

'The rule of law', in the sense of equality before the law, is a modern ideal that is much talked about, but that implies values that are far divorced from the present situation in which the powers of hierarchy and protection undermine the values of *rukun* and mutual security. Sometimes these values meet head-on, as was for instance illustrated in the 'Sum Kuning affair', that has absorbed the attention of people in Yogya for more than three years.[1]

Sum Kuning was a peasant girl; she went every day to the market in town to sell a basket of eggs. Returning to her village one night, she was raped by four youngsters who had taken her for a ride in a car. After she had been abandoned at the side of the road, she went to people with whom she was acquainted and asked for help, telling her sad story. A neighbourhood journalist was also listening. Finally, they called the police who took the girl to a hospital; the journalist wrote the story for a newspaper. The incident was very similar to another recent rape in which similar youngsters, 'sons of important people', had been suspected. The story caused a stir of popular emotion in town; people were shaken and the rapes were the hot topics of the day: society had become nervous.

No complaint was filed by Sum Kuning or her parents, yet the police began to engage in some interesting activities. After a few days, they came to arrest the girl at her home, and soon they issued a handout stating that Sum Kuning had made up her story and that she was a subversive element causing social unrest. For thirty-two days, she remained in custody, often maltreated by the police, who finally released their version of her story: Sum Kuning had had voluntary sexual relations with a soup-seller, the police producing a participant and witnesses. The police story was not believed at all, and the press did its best to uncover the facts; meanwhile, a team of lawyers took it upon themselves to serve as counsel for Sum Kuning.

Society remained restive and interested in the outcome of the affair, while the police were making fools of themselves; when the girl was finally brought to court, her acquittal was hailed as a huge victory of justice for the common man over the police. Subsequently, some police officers were transferred, Sum Kuning went to a hospital for

---

1 Kamadjaja et al., *Sum Kuning*. Yogyakarta: U.P. Indonesia, 1972.

mental and physical treatment, and in 1973, the case was still 'under investigation'. The car of the rapists was known and, with a fair degree of certainty, its occupants — 'sons of important people' in Yogyakarta.

The children of important people are, seemingly, well guarded from danger and may sleep quietly no matter what they do. They enjoy powerful protection while the victories of justice and the common man are few and far between. Hierarchy is protected, and to the ruling class, *rukun* primarily means 'no stir' and the forceful maintenance of order.

The abuse of status privilege and the power of protection among the new elites appear to have become facts of life. In minor affairs, such as a rape or other comparable nuisances, newspapers may freely report, and very annoying journalists may be detained and freed again [which also happened in the 'Sum Kuning affair'], but the culprits are seldom if ever arrested. Moreover, the courts seem afraid, legal security minimal, and the control over society by police and army a threatening experience. All too easily, one is accused of being a 'communist'. By 1973, Yogya seemed to have become a society more subdued than ever, with people unwilling to talk, suspicious and afraid: a society of lost hopes. Suppression and the powerful maintenance of order caused people to withdraw into ever smaller circles of loyalty and trust: hierarchy had grown strong without *rukun*.

The evolution of relationships in Yogyakarta, 1980

The interest of this excerpt lies in the informants' awareness of their changing world. Because of it, most respondents were quite eager to talk about the changes occurring in their social environment, especially about those that characterize family life and relations with their wider community. This is not suprising in view of the importance of the family of origin as the exemplary cluster of Javanese social relationships, since the respondents seem to be very conscious of a break with the past. This rupture in their own life poses questions about the link with their parents, and their relations with their own children.

Relationships with parents

During the flight from Singapore to Jakarta, I made the acquaintance of a high-up civil servant in his mid-forties. Accompanied by his wife, he was on his way back from a conference and seminar tour abroad. Chatting about our journey and travel experiences, he became more interested when I told him that I was on my way to Yogyakarta. Since he had been born and educated there, we were soon talking about mysticism and social change; while talking about the changes in the ethos of family life, he volunteered the following story.

> A few years ago, when my father died, I had to prepare his body for burial. It was then that I realized that it was the first time in my life that I had touched his head and I felt rather shocked because of it. He was a real old-fashioned Javanese father, somewhat aloof and distant from his children. We were in awe of him but also felt deep respect. But now all this has changed; in my family, my wife and I are close to our children; they address us in Indonesian, I play and talk with them, and all of us are really intimate.

He offered me a ride to my destination in Jakarta, because his children would meet him and his wife with a car at the airport. There I witnessed a warm family reunion in which the children displayed a good measure of spontaneous affection for their mother and a relaxed yet respectful attitude to their father. Half an hour later, they dropped me on the doorstep of the friend's house where I was to spend the night.

This friend is a highly educated man who knows the world, a descendant of a well-known *priyayi* family whose father held high positions in colonial days. To him, his father had always been a distant person whom he did not much appreciate. Reflecting on his youth, he observed,

> When I was young, I did not experience much family life. I was brought up to feel myself a member of our widespread extended family, and at the age of five I was given into the care of a Dutch family for the sake of my education. When the war came to Indonesia, I came back 'home', doing my middle school in Surabaya, where we became infused with nationalist ideas. All the time, however, my parents remained staunch supporters of the Dutch and could not see the signs of the times.

In his opinion, the experience of a warm family life was a rare occurrence in the circles of his birth, and it is his ideal to develop more spontaneous and intimate relationships among the members of his family than he ever experienced in his youth. For a long time he remained unmarried, refusing to consider the well-born marriage partners his parents suggested. When he finally decided to settle down, he married a Batak girl, which seemed to highlight the rupture between him and his parents. It was only upon their having children that a measure of normal relationships was re-established. Emotionally, however, he rejects his milieu of origin and has developed an aversion to its cultural manifestations. Even though his mother is still alive, he refuses to visit the grave of his father.

My Jakartan friend contrasts with most acquaintances and informants in Yogyakarta, who seem to reconcile the demands of tradition and modernity more gracefully. Yet I was in for a few surprises, such as when visiting the house of a fellow whom I knew as an exuberant artist. I found that he had left home to settle down with a younger mistress. While his children seemingly resented their father, his former wife, *Ibu* Siti, embodied an almost classical example of the capacity to accept *(nrima)*. Her suffering had drawn the children close to her, while she had recourse to the spiritual guidance of priests. The family's atmosphere was a queer mixture of Catholicism, a thoroughly *kejawèn*-inspired family code, and modern high school and university education. Everybody was faithful in fulfilling religious obligations, traditional in honouring their mother — whom they addressed in High Javanese — and in practising one or another of the Javanese performing arts, such as dancing, classical singing, or playing the *gamelan*. Moreover, all the children appeared to be serious in their studies. Without showing remorse about her former husband's decision, Siti commented,

> As long as my husband was here, he considered himself to be the *batin* of the family, I merely being its *lair*. He was the big man, the artist, perennially getting into trouble with the authorities, while I had to see to it that we could eat. He thought himself to be the sun with us merely being satellites. Now we feel more free, although I have to work very hard; I pray a lot that the Lord may help us. More than anything else I hope that my children will become acceptable *(lumrah)* people, serious in finishing their studies. They help me and respect me; they are also modern and independent while knowing Javanese manners. With all seven of them so close to me, I have no reason to complain.

Ibu Siti's circumstances are rather characteristic of women in her position. As a high school teacher in her early forties, she shoulders the responsibility for the education of her children, and she has to work hard indeed. Her solutions and hopes are exemplary of the Javanese ideal of the middle way, of seeking balance between current struggle and hope for the future of her children.

Pak Suryo was born during the Japanese occupation as the eldest son of a minor civil servant. His father was a member of the Muhammadiyah, deeply interested in Mahabharata mythology, and keenly aware of the value of modern education. When war and revolution were over, he continued his schooling up to the end of high school, while seeing to it that all of his nine children received the best possible education. As a young child, *Pak* Suryo had been given into the care of his grandparents in a traditional Moslem *kampung*, receiving his basic school education at the prayer house in the mornings, modern instruction at the Muhammadiyah school *(madrasah)*[1] in the afternoons, while learning to recite the Koran *(ngaji)* in the early evening. At night, the children were allowed to run around, to play, or watch *wayang* until the small hours. Later on, *Pak* Suryo went to a public high school, though still studying Arabic with a religious teacher. If circumstances permit, he prays five times a day, at the same time that he shares his father's interest in *wayang* and mysticism. Meanwhile, he is also a lecturer at Gadjah Mada University.

> All of us admire my father and respect him; all the children, even the youngest, address him in *kromo*. When I speak to my mother, I also use *kromo*, as do my two eldest younger siblings; the others speak *ngoko* with mother. Personally I do not care; my children speak *ngoko* with me, although they should address their grandparents in *kromo*. Well, things have changed. When I was a small child, formal education in religion was quite important; although we were in school morning, afternoon, and evening, discipline was loose and we were allowed to do a lot of running around, watching *wayang* or gambling in the *kampung* where I lived. These days, there is less emphasis on religion and more on discipline for the children. In the morning, my children go to a normal elementary school; in the late afternoon they practise music, sports, or exercise in a drumband. Now religion is taught in the national schools and schooling is more serious than in my time; everything is more serious, even playing. They have to learn from reading magazines, watching TV, or training for sports; they are not playing around as they please any longer like we did, and they go to bed much earlier. They do not learn Arabic any more, do not go to the *madrasah*, and do not learn to recite, yet they are supposed to learn to understand religion; that is why a religious teacher from the Tunas Melati foundation comes to teach them twice a week. They are supposed to go to the prayer house when there are recital exercises. But the emphasis is on their discipline of schooling, and becoming capable people absorbs most of their time.

---

1 This type of school combines instruction in the modern secular subjects with Islamic catechism. For elaboration, see C. Geertz, Modernization in a Muslim society: the Indonesian case. (R.N. Bellah (ed), *Religion and Progress in Modern Asia*. New York, etc.: The Free Press, 1965: 93-108.

Pak Suryo described the relationship with his children as intimate and relaxed while he, as their father, should be the protector of their welfare and spiritual development.

> Children do not depend on us really; when they are born they carry already a good deal of their fate and fortune *(rejeki)* within themselves. What we, as parents, can do is to stimulate and guide them, preparing them for the time they will leave us. In this way, parents earn the honour of becoming the object of reverence *(pepundhèn)* of their children.

Although *Pak* Suryo is a relatively young man (late thirties), his views and experiences seem to correspond with those of *Ibu* Miryam who is about fifty. She was born in the Moslem quarter *(kauman)* of Yogya, her father being an independent trader in batik cloth and member of the Muhammadiyah. Although she completed a secular university education later in life, her early schooling experiences are very similar to *Pak* Suryo's, with much emphasis on the correct recital of the Koran and great freedom in running around until late at night.

> I must have been a very naughty child, because my father beat me a lot. I was very afraid of him. Basically, we lived in a closed family and a strict environment. My parents never took much trouble to explain things, it was always "You must do this, you must do that". Yet we liked to sneak out and watch *wayang* in a neighbouring *kampung*, or to run around with the children there. When my parents suspected us of such things, we were beaten again.

Now she lives with her husband, a widower with children, in a mixed neighbourhood and she likes to contrast her youth with the experiences of her stepchildren.

> As parents, we are responsible for seeing to it that our children know and respect their religion; if they later turn their back on Islam, it is our sin. But yet, how much things have changed! In my time, we just learned to recite and obey the religious rules, now they have to understand the why's of religious behaviour. Their teacher is a modern product of the Muhammadiyah school for religious teachers; he makes the children sing songs and practise dancing to the accompaniment of the *gamelan*, an instrument that was totally taboo in my days. Moreover, they even practise *kethoprak*

popular theatre and watch *wayang* that is staged by a *dhalang* from the IAIN. The present atmosphere has certainly opened up and the serious Muslims are far less defensive and isolated. Yet it remains very important that the children know their religion; it is their guide in becoming moral adults and helps them to develop a purposeful character, a strong *batin*. Especially in these confused times, with all kinds of western influences and relaxed association with people of various religious persuasions, they should know how to distinguish between right and sinful behaviour, and they should be obedient to their parents which, after all, is also a Koranic rule.

At home our relationship with the children is very different from my relationship with my parents; we are closer together, more open, and far less authoritarian. We never hit the children, but try to develop mutual trust and get them to use their own initiative. They address their father in *ngoko*, but since I am their stepmother, they address me in polite language. In the mixed neighbourhood where we live, our children associate with Catholics, and they even took part in their Christmas stage play. We have certainly grown much more tolerant over the years, yet that influence of other religions is very confusing.

At forty, *Ibu* Sri is a leading civil servant of high *priyayi* origin. Of an independent cast of mind, she subscribes to the *kejawèn* ideas about self-development, but she is paternalistic in her attitude toward those who are less refined and educated; therefore she is quite enthusiastic about the government's programme of moral education, *P4*. With her husband seldom at home, she acquiesces *(nrima)* in her role of sole educator of her children and agrees with the official position that religion is conducive to good citizenship. Since the schools in her neighbourhood only offer instruction on Islam, she sees to it that her children pray at the appropriate times while taking them to the mosque on Fridays. She tries to be close to her children, and because of it, she is probably a little too tolerant in giving in to their whims and wishes. But what can she do in a household lacking an authoritarian father at the same time that she must spend much of her time at her office? All she can hope for is that her *kejawèn* wisdom, her strong religious orientation, and the affection she shows them will stimulate her children along the right path and bring her the reward of their reverence.

The above cases reflect some trends in the awareness of educated parents about their changed relationships with their children. Most of them are quite explicit in recognizing the value of religious education, and aware of the fact that they can do little more than stimulate their children 'from behind' in making their moral choices. The idea that they should be deserving of the respect of their children because of their efforts was stated several times. As modern people, they are less convinced that the honour that is due to parents comes automatically, at the same time that they often want to bridge the hierarchical gap between themselves and their children by using intimate language (*ngoko* or Indonesian) instead of traditional High Javanese.

Communal relationships

Ibu Juniar lives in the *kauman*, a very densely populated area of town intersected by narrow lanes that do not allow for motorized traffic. There the faithful Muslims live together in very close proximity to each other, most houses sharing walls in common with neighbours. In that area, everybody is related, or at least acquainted, and ties of community and religion are fairly compelling. Yet she explained to me that shared proximity also led to the tendency to clearly stake out the borders of one's privacy.

> These days, when I want to have a job done, I do not ask a favour of a neighbour or junior relative; that really is too involving, while placing me under the obligation to return the favour at a later date. Since I can pay for it, I would rather seek an outsider to do the job for money. In that way no obligation *(utang budi)* arises, and I remain free to do as I like. This holds for most who are in a slightly better-off position. While it was customary to ask for favours, which were of course expected to be returned at some time, now things are borrowed and loaned, mutual contracts becoming more businesslike, at the same time that people appreciate a measure of individual freedom. When one of my colleagues [she is a civil servant] invites me or a group of us for lunch, I feel better if I am allowed to pay for myself; sometimes that is not possible, for instance, when the office manager invites us; yet I try to avoid such situations; they carry too strong an obligation.

At the same time that *Ibu* Juniar enjoys her independence and cuts neighbourly obligations back to a minimum, she is also heavily involved in modern organizational activities that take her further from home. As an active member of the Muhammadiyah's women's branch, 'Aisyah, she devotes much of her time to general welfare and educational activities that are more satisfactory to her than intense participation in the life of the immediate neighbourhood.[2]

Contrarily, *Bapak* and *Ibu* Santoso deplore the absence of involvement with their neighbours. Living in the Bulaksumur university area, where houses tend to stand apart in compounds of their own, they complain about the demands of modern life. He teaches at Gadjah Mada University and she is a civil servant; professionally both have to involve themselves in many activities that take them away from home. As a result, they feel they have too little time to enjoy their family life and say that they have hardly any to associate with their neighbours.

> Formerly, when a neighbour dropped in, we were expected to make time for a chat and a cup of tea; we enjoyed that situation, it was cosy and leisurely. But these days, what can we do? We have so many obligations. It is really bad manners, but often we have to excuse ourselves, because we have to go to a meeting or on a visit away from home; there is simply no time left for chit-chat and elaborate politeness. What's more, it has become very expensive to maintain the good forms. When we gave a *ruwatan* ceremony for our two sons, we did it secretly, not inviting neighbours and relatives who would expect food and refreshments served in a formal way. It is a pity, though; formerly all of us were much closer together and felt free to stop by at the house of a neighbour. These days we are growing apart, every family living its own life.

Pak Agus is a university lecturer of some means who appreciated his independence; as a long time bachelor he lived in a sparsely populated area in town amidst dormitories, school and office buildings with only a few neighbours around. When he finally married, he decided that he should live in more sociable surroundings, finding himself a house in a village some ten kilometres from town. In the beginning, he and his wife were quite happy to entertain intensive relationships with their neighbours, engaging themselves in the reciprocal demands of village life. But he likes his books and his privacy, and after some two years he

2 In 1992, the family had moved to a new suburban neighbourhood on the fringe of town where she took pleasure in the newly-won privacy.

reduced his involvement in community affairs. Now, six years after moving there, he comments,

> In the beginning, I found it quite interesting and it was good for my wife to have so much companionship. When we had our first child, all the neighbours visited and did their best to offer help. Naturally, we were expected to return the interest shown, and for a while we shared in the whole round of mutual obligations. Yet it took up so much of our time and energy, people dropping by at any moment, seeking advice or just for a chat, while expecting us to do the same. That was all fine, but we began to feel it as a burden after our second child was born. Now, with three children I want to have a family life of my own, to have time for ourselves, and for reading. Besides, I am tired when I come home from town. Our neighbours do not appreciate our present behaviour. Of course, we remain friendly and send a contribution to their occasions, yet keep ourselves at a certain distance, establishing ourselves as outsiders of a sort. Now they make us feel that we do not really belong to the village; they find us odd and expect more interest from our side.

In most neighbourhoods in town, community life is not that demanding and, as long as one does not publicly behave like an odd man out, one can enjoy the privacy of one's family life. *Pak* Trisno clearly enjoyed his freedom in a crowded yet not much integrated area. "As long as I show my face when someone has died and provided I make a small contribution to the most important celebrations, everybody is congenial, while leaving me in peace."

Pak Suryo, a serious Muslim, observed, "It is not so much the neighbourhood that counts, but one's immediate neighbours. To be *slamet* one has to be on good terms with them; one should not try to go it alone but associate with others. When my neighbour gives a *slametan*, I go there and participate. That is the very symbol of good relationships, of unity among ourselves. It makes us feel safe and expresses our good neighbourliness."

Pak Suryo expressed a very well grounded opinion. The wider neighbourhood celebrations, or other expressions of communality, have become much less frequent these days, the major communal manifestations now concentrating on Independence Day. During the days preceding the seventeenth of August, the neighbourhood is cleaned up in a communal effort, walls and fences are whitewashed, and on the day itself many activities are organized for children, while in the evening *kethoprak* or other stage plays may be performed.

This simplification of community celebrations and ritual was clearly brought to the fore by the present practice in the suburban village of Miliran. As little as ten years ago, various *slametan* were still celebrated in tune with the agricultural cycle. Nowadays, however, Miliran has become a real suburb with only three families engaged in agriculture on village land, the rest of the district having become a built-up area. Now only one communal *slametan* is celebrated, namely, the yearly *bersih-désa*[3] ceremony that has been made to coincide with the national day festivities.

In town, living together is gradually becoming a less compelling experience, with the horizons of many extending well beyond the borders of their neighbourhoods, which no longer set the limits of a person's references and activities. One's role is no longer circumscribed by communal expectations, and it is accepted that the demands of material existence have grown to dominate life. In the words of *Pak* Amat,

> When I came to live here, I was an outsider, but people were quick to recognize the value of my higher education. They know me as a jovial and informal person, so soon people came to me with their problems and I have always tried to help them. After a few years I was elected head of the RK (*Rukun Kampung*, neighbourhood association),[4] which I have been now for many years. Yet, as a high school teacher, people expect me to have *priyayi* manners. These days I have begun to make cement breeze blocks, because in a few years I will be pensioned off and I need some additional income. I hope to expand this activity and to give opportunity to some of the released political prisoners *(tahanan politik)* here to earn a living. The people here do not seem to accept this; they do not talk about my involvement with the ex-*tapol* but they say, "All of us can see you working with your hands; next time around we won't elect you again to be head of our RK." Well, I do not care; I have to see to the welfare of my family first of all.

---

3 *Bersih-désa*, annual village festival accompanied by certain purification rites.

4 In cities, RK is now called RW, *Rukun Warga*; RK is reserved for the administrative organization below the village level. See Sullivan, 1992.

Similar independence was demonstrated by *Pak* Saryo, a retired official of the *patihan* (sultan's local government), whose wife ran a boarding-house for students. Within the house, his wife was in full control of financial matters and he would never discuss rental or other monetary problems. Yet he was happy to do the ironing, and also had fun in repairing his decrepit car in full view of the neighbours, his self-confidence obviously not being shattered by doing handiwork. After all, he could demonstrate his status by owning a car and, more importantly, by staging a marriage ceremony for his daughter at which five hundred guests turned up and were well entertained.

Of course, to cultivate good neighbourly relations is important and pleasant, and, for those who care, it may even be a means of status validation. Yet for most people who work in the modern sector, and who enjoy reasonable salaries and upward mobility, communal relationships become less compelling and may even lose their relevance in comparison with the newer, more businesslike patterns of association with fellow workers, colleagues, or remoter others. And thus, naturally, they seek to free themselves to some extent from the imposition of communal obligations. They would not be Javanese, however, if they were not also aware of the importance of being together in life and of the virtue of mutual assistance, but its expression is now found in a wider environment, such as in membership of religious groups, civic clubs, social action-oriented non-governmental organizations, old boy networks, and circles of friendship that are no longer defined by communal ties. So far, this appears mainly an urban phenomenon that may be indicative of the possible spread of new types of association and corporate organization as a substitute for older forms of mutual assistance, the recent emergence of organized groupings of relatives being an example.

This new form of association involves the formal establishment of descent groups *(trah)*. These existed of old among the nobility and *priyayi*, who prided themselves on their pedigree. In the seventies, however, commoners also began to organize themselves in formal *trah* associations, with governing boards and statutory regulations. The direct members are those who trace descent from one apical ancestor, while their spouses are also co-opted as members. While surely giving shape to the Javanese ideal of 'uniting the separated bones' *(ngumpulaké balung pisah)*, that is, of closing ranks with people who belong together because of family ties, I suspect that these formal *trah* are especially organized among those families who are better-off, upwardly mobile, and who have economic and/or status interests to defend. Whether they will develop into some sort of corporate family groupings is too early to tell; information is still scanty on this new form of association that was first reported by Sairin (1982).

The integration of community and neighbourhood is giving way to other, more particularistic and professional, forms of association. For a long time, communal ties were maintained 'naturally' in a situation of greater socio-economic equality that was further characterized by rather stringent social control in which one feared the eyes and ears, and the opinions, of others. In town, the younger generation is less impressed by the demands of community life, *Pak* Suryo observing,

> In villages, people may still feel controlled by the opinion of others, but for sure, my children feel free and are not *isin* in the presence of others. Of course, they maintain a minimum of good manners, and will certainly dress and behave properly, but they are practical and pragmatic, seeking their own ways. The social compulsion that was characteristic is declining rapidly in town, and people are less afraid to show their true selves, their personality. At the same time that they are less conformist in their behaviour, they are also developing a deeper interest in expressing their individuality. On the one hand, there is an upsurge of personal anniversary celebrations that underline one's unique character and, on the other, of a renewed interest among the young in expressing themselves in new and traditional *kejawèn* practices, such as fasting, retiring from society, the study of secret knowledge, and the practice of *silat* [a discipline of self-defence that requires meditational preparation]; in short, they seek to strengthen their individuality, their *batin*

According to my informants, this latter interest among the young appears to be a fairly general phenomenon in Yogyakarta. It has also been reported by Guinness, who found much interest in esoterism and *silat* practice, especially among the half-educated and underprivileged *kampung* youths who are left behind by the development of the wider urban society (1986:115,125). Interestingly, an upsurge of *kebatinan* practices has also been noted among the rank and file of the army; the officer who reported this saw these practices as a reaction against the discipline of army life in which expression of individuality is suppressed.

Whatever the causes of this quest for individual expression, such as the weakening of communal identity and ties, unemployment and feelings of being left behind, or traditional self-fulfilment in a situation characterized by strong social control, it is clear that communal ties, and the corresponding imposition of a style of life, have considerably weakened. On the one hand, this seems to lead to greater individual freedom and, on the other, to an orientation to other forms of organization and association in which colleagues, friends, and relatives acquire a new importance.

Vertical relationships

When I visited *Radèn* Sunarko, who is currently a professor of mathematics at Gadjah Mada University, our conversation was interrupted by a tricycle driver knocking on the door. When my host opened up, the man, who was rather agitated, inquired whether it had been Sunarko's son who had just collided with his *becak* and then driven off without stopping to see what damage he had caused. Well, it could not possibly have been *Radèn* Sunarko's son, because he had none, but when he was seated again, he observed, "That was a courageous type!"

R. Sunarko, who is a gentle yet enterprising person of impeccable *priyayi* origin, was obviously rather impressed by this incident, because a few days later he was still talking about it. Referring to the period of his youth, before the war, he observed that it would have been inconceivable at that time for a common man of such minor status to have walked in upon a person of rank and position to disturb him bluntly with his personal affairs, but these days all that had changed. The most shocking experience of his life had occurred in 1978, when the army moved onto the university campus to quell student protest. While walking back from his office on his way home, he had been stopped by an army man who had pointed a gun at his head, as if he, gentle and diminutive of stature, yet every inch an aristocrat, could possibly have been mistaken for a student protestor.

It was not that *R*. Sunarko admired the ways of student protest, but he was at least understanding and tolerant of their need to vent their frustrations,

After all, they are still students, immature adults. Of course, they should not take to
the streets and shout and yell, even if they are right in their protest. Such manners
are unjavanese and distasteful. We Javanese are people of the middle way (*ngono ya
ngono, ning aja ngono*; yes, you are right, yet do not do it). The main problem, however, is with our new leadership. That army action was sheer intimidation. Those
people only understand power (*wewenang*) and how to inspire fear. What they lack
is natural authority and the wisdom to guide (*kawibawan*). They imagine themselves
to be parents of the people, and the people, the children, have to submit (*tunduk*) to
them, but they lack the qualities that make people accept their leadership spontaneously. They think that they can rule because of their power, but what they inspire
is fear rather than respect. After all, who are they? Mere upstarts, gross (*kasar*) and
petty minded (*kerdil* (I)).

Perhaps they will mature, becoming refined (*alus*) as good leaders should be. Then
students will not take to the streets nor will it be necessary to intimidate them with
tanks and guns.

Whatever the value of his musings, they were obviously not
shared by Colonel Sumantri who originated from a similar background.
In his middle forties, he had made his way into the military through a
university education, and is a staunch defender of the army's self-proclaimed role in developing the country. In commenting about the recent
spate of student unrest, he initially took the same line as *R.* Sunarko.

It is a problem of our youth that they are so free now, yet they should not forget that
they are still immature. If they want to make a contribution to the development of
our country, they had better know their place and study. Of course, not everything is
well and there is a lot of corruption; the fault is not so much with the army; the soldiers are dedicated, but many problems originate in the civil service. If our students
think they have reasons for criticism, they should put forward their points in open
discussion. We are a democracy and all voices may be heard. But taking to the streets
is bad manners and unindonesian.

When I observed that there are few practical alternatives and a lot
of coercion is involved, the colonel did not disagree.

Isn't that normal? Wherever people live together, there are always rules and norms to
stick to and there is always a measure of compulsion. We have a task to fulfil in this

country. The security and well-being *(slamet)* of the people is a higher goal than individual rights. What can we buy with 'basic human rights'? Besides, their protests were insincere and improper; what we need is development and stability.

Talking about social changes in Yogya, a journalist showed me a picture of the deputy ruler, *Sri* Paku Alam, shaking hands with village headmen.

This is a sensational change. Imagine this only a few years ago! Then these headmen would have had to pay obeisance *(sembah)*, yet now *Sri* Paku Alam shakes hands with them! Or take the sultan himself; he participated in election rallies for Golkar, showing himself to the people as a democratic leader. Once the Dutch thought to make a Hollander of him, but what they got was an Indonesian. The old aristocracy is not all that exalted any longer; they have stepped down and come closer to the people.

The enthusiasm for what the journalist called 'democratization' of relationships was certainly not shared by *Pak* Sayono who, as a buyer of tobacco, has a clear picture of village life in the area surrounding Yogya. According to his observations, the situation of the rural poor was deteriorating all the time, with landed property becoming concentrated in the hands of a few.

Musyawarah, village solidarity, *gotong-royong*[5] — all that crap! Those who have land get more, and those who have little are losing whatever they have. *Pak Lurah* (headman) and a few others get richer and richer and do not need to listen to the others. When there is a *gotong-royong* project, the poor just have to do the work. Now they have even made the *lurah* a civil servant, giving him more power still by backing him up as a representative of government. The rich class in the villages send their children to school in town and even to the university; the poor, they have to beg to eat and if they want to go to town they may even have to borrow a pair of pants!

Pak Sayono is known as a temperamental person, and at his office he is the unquestioned boss, yet there is a point in his moral indigna-

---

5 These terms were popularized and became official ideology during the Sukarno period. They were thought to reflect a certain village egalitarianism and its democratic style. Since neither egalitarianism nor democracy are marked Javanese traits, the words remained mere slogans.

tion about the emergence of a powerful class of haves, in the villages as well, versus the pauperization of many. Those who have become better-off and more influential are becoming leaders because of affluence and power and not because they are generally accepted or have charisma.

> We have always been an exploited people, suffering from oppression, but these days things are getting worse. Who told you about democratization? They should rather tell you about the deepening of suffering, and for all those who suffer there is no way out. These days corruption is legal; to protest against it is not.

Summarizing, we may note the opening up of certain, formerly status-dominated, hierarchical relationships, such as those with parents, titled nobility, and others whom one meets casually. Communal relationships also appear to have become more relaxed, losing their rigidity of form at the same time that they are showing a tendency to become more businesslike and less prone to generating obligations. We noted that hierarchical relationships tend to be defined by power more than by status, which may result in a low degree of social solidarity.

The rise of the new power-holders has led to 'neo-feudalistic' lifestyles coming into being, with many trying to translate their newly aquired means into status and prestige, while lacking the refined accomplishment or the charisma of those who were formerly held in esteem. Overall, it often appears that power has become more important than the ability to give guidance, that possessions are becoming more important than wisdom, and that justice is subservient to political and executive expediency.

The vertical organization of society appears as clearly established as ever, though at the same time it does not dominate culture any longer. This is because the value content of hierarchy has changed, having become an order of power and command while losing legitimation and spontaneous acceptance. The present system of power relationships does not represent a moral order in which there is satisfaction in the fulfilment of one's social and cosmic place; it is now an environment in which one strives for survival rather than fulfilment. The subsequent social relationships allow for new interpretations and experiences that open the way for novel cultural developments and, eventually, the growth of a technocratic and businesslike society.

Yogyakarta's transition, 1980

Cultural responses

With the ending of the Java War in 1830, the Javanese nobility definitely lost its original ruling and military functions. Literally domesticated, they developed into a dependent class of administrators. Protected against more adventurous exploits by the power of the colonial ruler, the original warriors became courtiers, developing a highly intricate *kraton*-centred culture. The nineteenth century did produce a number of great literary works that are sometimes spoken of as the Surakarta renaissance,[1] but the basic trend of its cultural development was one of refinement for its own sake, that has more aptly been described as a process of involution. In this elaboration, court culture was largely devoid of innovation, consequently developing a self-suffocating refinement, overspecialized like a dinosaur and thus ultimately doomed to extinction.

According to Sutherland, who expressly excludes the South-Central Javanese principalities from her analysis of the making of a bureaucratic elite, the former fully, or quasi, independent, class of rulers was transformed into a class of subordinate allies of an alien ruler, gradually developing into an uprooted elite, "whose refined and overelaborated cultural life was probably more the result of impotence than of specific Javanese traits" (1979:viii). Not being knowledgeable about 'specific Javanese traits' other than cultural characteristics, I feel it is worth noting that this culture of refinement developed to its greatest height in the relatively independent court centres of Yogyakarta and Surakarta, where it set the cultural standards and enjoyed a deeply felt prestige that lingers on, among some, in nostalgia for the old days.

However suffocating and futureless the cultural development at the courts may have been, we should also note the vital role of the

---

1 The best known examples are the *Serat Centhini* (±1820), Mangkunagara IV's *Wedhatama* (±1860), and the works of 'the last of the great court poets', *R.Ng.* Ronggawarsita (1802-73). See Ricklefs (1981):120, 285.

principalities in producing new ideas to interpret the changing times. From the turn of this century onward, modern western, and middle-eastern, ideas began to exert their influence and gave rise to a new cultural elite that was peripheral, or even in open opposition to court culture. In 1908, young, progressive members of the *priyayi* class formed the Budi Utomo; in 1912, the Muhammadiyah was also founded in Yogyakarta. In that year, the Sarekat Islam started up in Surakarta, while *Ki* Hadjar Dewantara's Taman Siswa educational ideas were first given shape, again, in Yogya (1922).[2] These first modern associations were clear reactions to changing times and the colonial experience. At the same time, we may also take note of the early development of the popular *kethoprak* theatre, and the new interpretations of Javanese wisdom, such as those taught by the princely ascetic *Ki* Ageng Suryomentaram. The sultan of Yogyakarta also set interesting examples, as in opening a section of his palace to his subjects, and entrusting his sons to the care of Dutch families in order to foster their modern education.

When the Japanese were defeated and the Dutch attempted their ill-considered comeback, Yogya naturally became the revolutionary capital of the then fledgling Republic of Indonesia, with the sultan granting a part of his palace to accommodate the first university of the country. Then, when the revolution had run its course, Yogya was drained of its human resources and potential. Many of its most capable citizens settled in Jakarta, and the town became a backwater, where the impulses of modernity seemingly did not penetrate. Although Gadjah Mada University still attracted many students from all over the archipelago, it soon ceded prominence to the Universitas Indonesia in Jakarta. For a while, therefore, Yogyakarta seemed to lapse into an isolation that belied its erstwhile vitality.

During that time, it seemed as if *priyayi* culture was reasserting itself. With its orientation toward the past and its dominant ideology of well-ordered relationships, it seemed to shield Yogya society from the processes of change going on in Jakarta and the nation. The same period saw the remarkable development of organized *kebatinan* mysticism, in Yogya and all over Java. Although an undeniable orientation to the

2 The history and development of these movements and associations has been well documented; see Ricklefs (1981) chapter 14 and p. 287.

past inspired this revitalization of the mystical practice, its widespread popularity and congregational form are clear indicators that it should also be seen as a quest to seek new meaning in the foundations of Javanese culture in the face of modernity. This notwithstanding, *kejawèn* mystical expression does, of course, belong to a certain style and form of life that was embodied in the social organization of the sultanate.

Changing society

The patrimonial bureaucracy of the sultanate reflected the ideals of social life. It was a 'sacred' order legitimizing obligation to hierarchical position and giving meaning to an individual-centred ethic of social place. The ideal of well-ordered, hierarchical relationships focused on the position of the ruler, who was thought to represent the inmost nucleus of an examplary, basically unchanging system of morally unequal relationships. The reference to the king gave reason to all other aspects of behaviour and a static conception of society. Whatever happened, the status quo ante would at some time restore itself, a concept which, in its turn, gave reason to a remarkable orientation to the past and a cyclical conception of history.

The concept and experience of this order were self-containing; one belonged as a matter of course, and although it was not in reality all that 'unchanging', it could be understood within the limits of *kejawèn* thinking. As a system of relationships, it was expressed in language, and an elaborated etiquette in which persons were assigned their rightful place. And now, rather 'suddenly', it appears that the pillars of order have been eroding, and that the props upon which court-centred culture rested have decayed.

Apparently, Indonesia and the world outside have invaded the wholesome arrangements of yester-years, and Yogya is not a selfcontained universe any longer. Whether awareness has changed because of modern school education, the increase in literacy, the diffusion of nationalist and political ideas, or the loss of *kejawèn* culture per se, the fact remains that the old conceptions of a stable and 'unchanging' order have been undermined by a new opportunity structure, social mobility, and a rapidly expanding middle class, all of which seem to have contributed to the dissolution of the ethic of social place and the hierarchy of the sultanate.

Patrimonially organized hierarchy, with its expectations of benevolence, protection, and moral guidance, is no longer part of the experience of the vast majority of the unorganized masses in village or town. While the old forms continue to protect those who are members of certain well established organizations, such as the army, the civil service, universities, cultural and political associations, or big national companies, most people already experience real problems in finding remunerative work, let alone patronage and protection.

Generally, hierarchy now means the experience of the power of the state or bosses, with whom people have no relationship at all. The privileged and better-off persons who are known to them also appear to have become choosy in their extension of patronage, while accumulating the money they need in order to partake in the life of a modern society; they seek to safeguard their own newly won status and position while becoming less concerned for all those who are left behind.

These tendencies that make for a loosening of vertical integration have not been balanced by the creation of horizontal bonds among the underprivileged. While they initially found some form of organization in joining the progressive political parties, all forms of class-based association are now discouraged. What one witnesses these days is a survival orientation, as a result of which moral horizons are contracting and solidarity is declining. *Rukun* and mutual help remain ideals that are becoming gradually more difficult to maintain, while many other, older norms and customs are also losing their validity.

This is especially clear in what is reported from village society. Developmental activities and new agricultural methods bring benefits to those who are better-off, at the same time that they rationalize their operations at the expense of the old opportunity structure that guaranteed at least subsistence for the village poor. The former appear to have lost their interest in village solidarity, and now orient themselves to urban life styles and advanced education for their children. As a result, the forms of patron-client integration have simply disappeared, and the basic class structure of village life has become blatantly obvious (Hüsken, 1996).

The same is true in town, where *kampung* life is increasingly experienced along class lines. This is clear from the work of Sullivan (1992), and although Guinness (1986) did not draw this conclusion from the data he gathered in Yogyakarta, his material substantiates it. It also surfaced in my interviews: the more well-to-do people do not want to be burdened by obligations to others. Although they do appreciate good form and congeniality, they prefer to mind their own business, irrespective of the needs of others, especially if these latter threaten to become a burden on their resources.

Neo-feudalism

In the seventies, Yogya's uniqueness had been breached. At that time, we note the emergence of new middle classes and general mobility while the old structures of vertical integration were giving way. The government of the sultanate had virtually ceased to function, the then ruling sultan living in Jakarta and his *kraton* having been transformed into an attraction for foreign tourists. In the absence of this cultural and social leadership, the pretensions of *priyayi* culture became meaningless. In short, the former vertical orientation of life in Yogyakarta did not make sense any longer, having lost its compelling dimensions.

It has been replaced by a new, national order that lacks the natural integration of a patrimonial society. So, while formerly the leadership of the high and mighty was taken as a matter of course, the new leaders do not enjoy *kejawèn* cultural legitimation. Whoever is high these days is high because mighty, and the crude fact of power has become more important than refinement or cultural leadership. Of course, leadership has always been from the top down, in spite of the modern nationalist ideology of *musyawarah*, *mufakat* and *gotong-royong*, or the current emphasis on democratic rituals. The difference lies in the credibility of the present leadership: at a time when parents are trying to come closer to their children, the powerful are tending to grow further apart from the people they rule. And where parents have a natural link with their offspring, the present class of leaders merely has a line of command that sets them apart from the ordinary citizen, while the weight of power tends to fracture society rather than to integrate it.

At Independence, there were hardly any very rich or very powerful Indonesians, and the positions of many revolutionary leaders were
legitimized by the trust that the people placed in them. Meanwhile,
however, political, administrative, and economic leadership has evolved
into a self-serving establishment that is distant from the ordinary people. They have become special and economically powerful while no
longer depending on trust and spontaneous following. Having power
and resources, they have become independent of popular acceptance,
and in spite of their rhetoric about national solidarity and an ethical
Pancasila way of life, they have also changed their style. So, while people believed in the sacredness of sultans and the display of cultural
refinement, the more upwardly mobile new style leaders need to assert
their positions by the display of goods and riches.

The latter tend to identify with status, while investing much of
their psychological energy in its presentation. They appear to be outwardly directed, growing dependent on the acknowledgement of their
status, the outer world's perceptions of them touching them directly in
their inner being, as it were. These very traits characterize the 'neo-feudalism' of many members of the ruling class, who pattern their style
after the old *priyayi* example while lacking the links to refinement and
mastery of the inner self. Their 'neo-feudalism' is essentially a nouveau
riche imitation of an outdated style of life.

Reference to *priyayi* styles is not their exclusive privilege, its characteristic orientation to rank and honourable white collar employment
still dominating the perspectives of many who are somewhat mobile,
even in the villages. Those parents who can afford it will often invest
heavily in their children. The national school education, however, is
directed to future urban employment, preparing for the university or a
civil servant's existence. Often, reaching the sixth grade of elementary
school leads to those so educated thereafter looking down on agricultural work and coming to expect 'honourable' employment in town, that
is only rarely available. In this way, schooling often contributes to
unemployment and idleness among the educated village youth, at the
same time that the less educated and poor cannot afford to remain
unemployed for any length of time.

As long as *'priyayi* style' merely leads to neo-feudalism, imitation,
and joblessness, it is culturally sterile. It is the hybrid offspring of the

court-cultural dinosaur, and a lowly commoner, that feeds on power and capitalist development, expressing itself in self-indulgence and sycophancy. Coming into being as a caricature of what it tries to imitate, it cannot be expected that this stream of culture will be self-sustaining. In the same way that a new, more open-minded middle class took over the development of thought and culture at the beginning of this century, it may now be expected that the impulses for a future cultural renewal will also come from other classes than the self-styled elite.

Individual and society in Yogyakarta, 1980

A persistent theme running through the interview material collected in Yogyakarta is the evaluation of action and situations in terms of *slamet-tentrem*. Things are good, or can be lived with, because they are not upsetting, because they guarantee quiet continuity, and as such they are always judged in terms of subjective experience. It is important to be well regarded, to be economically self-sufficient, and not to be subject to gossip, because it frees one to be at ease with oneself. Why does one master oneself? In order to feel quiet. Why does one conform to the stream of social life? In order not to be disturbed. Why does one help others? In order to be helped when need arises. Why does one supplicate the souls of one's parents? In order to experience blessed continuity. Why does one avoid conflict? In order to be at peace. By not involving oneself unnecessarily, one maximizes one's chances of living a satisfactory life: a withdrawn existence appears to be wise. To this an East Javanese informant living in Yogya commented,

> In East Java, we like to have many friends and to associate with many people. Soon we are familiar, addressing each other in *ngoko*. We do not try to cultivate self-mastery for its own sake, and we are quite spontaneous in showing our emotions. Here the people are different. The people of Yogya seem to enjoy a certain individualism, avoid disturbing each other, with everybody going his own way while pursuing his own purposes. When they grow older, say, over forty, they seem to be capable of accepting any situation, while being patient and at peace with their existence.

Whether this strong contrast holds is difficult to judge, but it is certain that a measure of imperturbability is shown, and cultivated, as an ideal of social life in Yogyakarta. Yet virtually no local informant would define his situation as being quiet and undisturbed in a life independent of his social and material circumstances. His social life even appears to be rather central to his preoccupation with a peaceful existence. Although he does not evaluate his experiences in terms of intimacy and deep friendship, his social standing and acceptance appear to score high among his conditions for a satisfactory existence. When questioned, people would refer to their social dependence in achieving their goals and, in their opinion, only fools tried to go it alone. To be alone, to fight one's own battles and to establish one's independence apart from one's fellows, was never seen as desirable, and certainly was no way to a peaceful existence. One feels at peace "because we mutually entertain good relationships".

> We need the others if we want to feel protected in life; we have to support each other, feeling safe in being together. Who would I be if I were alone? I would not have any position. It is pleasant to be together, to feel at home *(krasan)* with those who are close to us. Yet this does not mean that we are deeply loyal to each other where economic issues are concerned. We are not like the Chinese[1] who really stick together in their family life. We talk about homage *(ngabekti)* to our parents, but they really practise it. Look at us; as soon as there is an inheritance, we divide it up, everybody pursuing his own material interests. We have difficulty in trusting each other in economic matters, and such relationships among ourselves are weak. Yes, we are close *(deket)* to each other, we practise *rukun* and compromise, but we are not really intimate. I may be intimate with a friend who does not live under the same roof, and with whom I can discuss my problems whenever I feel depressed because of the frustrations of family life.
>
> I should show honour to my parents and maintain good relationships with those who are close, but what I strive for is to be independent of them, to care for myself, to have enough and to stand on my own feet. That is why *kebatinan* fits *(cocog)* with our character, seeking one's own way and finding power in a private relationship with 'God'; it makes us feel important as individuals.

A well-known critic of Javanese society developed an interesting complementary theory of why the self, or the individual feeling *(rasa)*, has become the true measure of all things. In his view, the objective, outside world is experienced as hard to deal with, not being susceptible to direct control and mastery. In order to explain this, he took a historical perspective in which he noted the long history of set-backs and reverses that Javanese society experienced, and which consequently

---

1 Several informants spontaneously compared this aspect of Javanese with Chinese family life.

became a part of the self-experience of the people of South-Central Java.

This historical experience was one of being a loser *(kalah)*, first of all against the penetration of Islam, then the VOC (Dutch East India Company), and finally, the colonial government. Yet these losses against the forces from the outside were never acknowledged. Instead, a tendency built up to retreat into a world of fantasy *(khayalan)* that denied these facts and that, as a defence mechanism, glorified Javanese spiritual superiority and the refinement of culture. Subsequently, retreat into a self-centred world of make-believe replaced the confrontation with the unyielding world outside.

For the individual, this world of make-believe focused on the achievement of status and prestige. With status becoming the only real thing in the world, one identified with it, and the satisfaction of one's self, of one's *rasa*, became dependent on status recognition. In the process, all moral problems became subordinated to the satisfaction of one's self. The worst threat to that self would be to lose, that is, to be shamed and suffer insult, because "it is better to die than to be shamed", and "it is worse to lose status than to lose money". As a result, the upholding of status for its own sake blinded people to its 'objective' consequences and led to a certain narrow-mindedness and obstinacy, in which status satisfaction assumed greater importance than the more mundane material conditions of life.

In his view, the basic cultural theme that has crystallized is "to win or to lose", in life in general, and certainly in the confrontation with others. In questions of status, the Javanese are unforgiving, not given to compromise or tolerance. "It is like the *wayang*, one wins or dies. To ask for forgiveness is to give in and lose." Because of this, he often found people to be stubborn in trying to protect their status by all means. It is therefore reasonable to please the boss and to create a world of half-truths that is satisfactory to all. "In protecting one's status, every action is permissible and every lie reasonable. Let the boss have it as he wants it, I am not concerned. To tell a lie or write a false report are unimportant. If that protects me, it is good."

Everyday life is characterized by the experience of losing. Most people are powerless and have to follow orders, or they suffer from the effects of natural causes, poverty, inflation, injustice and hopelessness.

In other words, the confrontation with the outside world is not a source of happiness, so why not deny it and build oneself a dream? Life outside should be pushed aside while creating a personal truth that acknowledges the superior value of one's self.

It is our subjective valuation that is important. Of course, in life we experience setbacks and powerlessness, but there need not be any contradiction between what is experienced externally and the feelings one experiences. The trick is to compartmentalize, to separate the one from the other, to conform outwardly while living another existence inside. The very struggle for survival, and the technocratic, impersonal style of development, have destroyed our social life. Leadership has become merely compulsion and former loyalties have become vague, because now relationships are measured in money only. The living community of village or neighbourhood is disintegrating, and everybody experiences the necessity of trying to care for himself and his family irrespective of others. The wise man deals with this bad experience by retreating into himself while constructing his own truth inside. The separation of our outside from our inside experiences is of great survival value, and guarantees our continuity.

Our critic also applied his theory about the avoidance of confrontation with the concrete, objective world, and the importance of fantasy and self-deceit, to the practice of development. In his view, the slogans of development and moral education were another instance of a self-made truth in which elements of show, false reporting, wishful thinking and shaky statistics contrasted sharply with the real conditions of the people and concrete achievements. Certainly, schools were built, but the question of the quality of education was not asked; people attended at family-planning sessions, because they were forced to do so, but the results were negligible; impressive statistics were duly produced, but what was their real value? Wherever he looked, he noted a discrepancy between what was said and what actually existed, in line with what he saw as the basic Javanese orientation towards the objective world. The material world is illusory, a *wayangan* that derives its meaning from the subjective ideas that bring it to life; even in this technocratic age, this world is not mastered in terms of its own laws, but by the inspired formulas and make-believe that appear to have a greater value.

Whatever the worth of these musings on development, our critic's complementary interpretation of the relationship between individual and society makes sense. One's subjective feeling is the most precious of possessions that one should protect against the depressing experiences that are beyond individual volition and control. By creating a fantasy world of status, or by seeking retreat into the deep self, one can deny the frustrations that are caused by the confrontation with the outside, objective world.

Outward presentation primarily serves to protect inner experience from disturbance, and thus one is willing to go with the flow, to tolerate others, to submit to power where it cannot be avoided, to break off relationships that are unsatisfactory and that do not agree with one's feelings, to cultivate the right contacts vital to survival, and to keep a certain distance by not involving oneself in the affairs of others. It is not harmony *(rukun)* for harmony's sake that is important; it is important to remain undisturbed. Basically, every man is his own saviour and should seek his own way. In keeping the deep self out of sight, one remains morally and ethically an island to oneself. As soon as a person allows that self to surface in the social process, "he would split society". Consequently, it is wise to be closed off, to attempt not to let the outside world penetrate into one's self-experience.

It does not seem that the rapid opening up of life in Yogyakarta has caused a different kind of valuation of experience, although many people have more trouble in compartmentalizing their experiences at present. While some of them are socially mobile and relish their newly won status, others are left behind in poverty and frustration. Yet, because of the vanishing of the old and the absence of a new, meaningful social arrangement, all seem to be thrown back on their own resources. In this way, inner life comes closer to the surface and its separation from outside experiences becomes less profound, so people become more vulnerable. While this may strengthen their conviction about the wisdom of reserving the inner self for oneself, and of denying the setbacks that they experience, it may also lead to a gross individualism rather than the inward-directed personality, which knew how to strike a balance between the outer and the inner aspects of life.

We have noted that the resources of Javanese wisdom are increasingly out of reach, especially for the younger generation that seems to respond with eagerness and spontaneity to the opening up of society. Yet their joining in the life of the vast, hegemonic Indonesian nation-state offers them hardly any possibilities for meaningful participation and civic responsibility, and it thus remains politic not to seek involvement where it can only lead to frustration. For the present, the best channel for social participation appears to be to turn to the 'modern' monotheistic religions, such as Islam, that offer a righteous conviction, congregational life, and modern organized activities.

Whether Islam, as it presents itself in Yogya, has much to offer in terms of building a new society is still too early to say. According to Nakamura's analysis of Muhammadiyah's ideology, it is a doctrine for individual conduct based on Islam, that, as an ethical theory for individuals, lacks specific programmes for social reform, or political strategies to implement them. The picture of an ideal society is one in which everybody is a good Moslim, and behaves as such (1983:176-77). This ethical theory is fully congruent with the *kejawèn* ethic that good order and prosperity will follow from the sincere practice of *kebatinan (mamayu hayuning buwana!)*, and corresponds with the tenets of Pancasila moral education, which emphasize that a good society results from the inner discipline of the individuals who compose it.

If this analysis is correct, we should not expect that a basically different relationship between individual and society will result from the current process of Islamicization in Yogyakarta. People will possibly be made more conscious about questions of ethics and personal choice, but the solution to these questions will remain as individual-centred as ever. I therefore agree with Nakamura's conclusion that the thinking that underlies Muhammadiyah's ideology expresses the view that society is a mere aggregate of individuals, and demonstrates an absence of sociological conceptualization. This thinking has deep cultural roots and places the wholesomeness of society in the individual fulfilment of obligations and task. It seems that this view will give meaning to individual experience for quite some time to come.

Islamicization, 1980

Most students of Javanese society are familiar with the dichotomy between faithfully practising and nominal Muslims (*santri* versus *abangan*). As a formulation claimed to describe social reality, it still guides the thinking of many scholars, as if life in Java were static and not subject to change. Nowadays, there are good reasons to doubt the heuristic value of the *santri-abangan* cleavage. This fission, elaborated in Geertz's *The Religion of Java*, can now be seen to have belonged to a former structure of society, that has vanished rapidly over the past twenty years. At present, at least as it appears at the level of the urban educated middle classes, the two mainstreams in Javanese culture seem to be converging. Moreover, and this is often insufficiently appreciated, all Javanese, whatever their degree of Islamicization, share in Javanese culture. That culture is not necessarily religiously expressed, but contains a common vision of man, society, and the ethical conduct of life.

At first sight, an observer is struck by the vast differences between *kejawèn* and orthodox Middle-Eastern religious conceptualization. In the latter thinking, the centre of the universe is God, and the course of history is His Volition; man is a mere creature who should live attuned and subjected to the will of God, since if not, he is damned and incapable of a just life. In other words, a transcendent God is the measure of all things, and man a mere servant who derives satisfaction and legitimation from following the rules and religious obligations set by God. In this creed, therefore, man wants to discover and know God's will: hence the importance of the Koran, the hadith, the shari'a, and the religious scholars *(ulama; kiai)*, who interpret and hand down the rules to go by.

Yet a second look is warranted. As in any place where a high, or universal, religion reaches new converts, it undergoes a process of localization. So, also, Islam in Java was moulded into a Javanese image. Furthermore, the Islam that reached Java had travelled a long way, and en route taken on the mystical and esoteric traits of Sufism, which fitted

Javanese thinking and religiosity. Then again, a basically syncretist and tolerant mentality provides fertile ground for new religious inputs. Thus, step by step, Islam was able to establish itself even at the *kejawèn* courts of the Javanese rulers, who appropriated some of its titles and symbols, until nowadays almost all Javanese will acknowledge themselves as Muslims, while blending Islamic thought and practice with older Javanese elements.

In recent history, a typical cultural conflict emerged, first as an inner Islamic struggle, then gradually also along the line of *abangan* versus pious *putihan ('santri')* Islam, finally culminating in the political power struggle that marked the period from the preparation for independence to the fall of Sukarno (roughly 1945-1966). The origins of this cultural conflict date back to the late 19th century, when the influence of orthodox and reformist Islam first made itself felt in Indonesia. This influence roused and stimulated conscienticization and emancipation movements among Javanese Muslims. In other words, a (religious) 'way of life' began to be questioned, and conscious choices needed to be made to establish a self-assured identity. In that conscienticization process, debate developed about a Javanese versus an Arabian way of doing things, a traditional *(kolot)* versus a modern practice, Moslem reformism versus traditionalism, secular (colonial or national) state versus a Moslem society, and finally about the lifestyles and practices of committed versus non-committed Muslims.

This quest for identity also led to a split between those who practise their religion faithfully and those who are not interested in the formal practice of religion. This cultural cleavage became aggravated when it acquired political dimensions, giving rise to disparate cultural communities, intolerance, and intense ideological struggle. It was at that time that Clifford Geertz did his research.

For many years now, the New Order government has been trying to defuse the conflict, first, by a rather effective policy of depoliticization of the religious issue while supporting (national) policies of interreligious tolerance, and further, by making religious (Islamic) education compulsory in all schools, by building religious infrastructure (institutes for higher Islamic education, mosques, prayer houses), and by fostering a unifying national Pancasila ideology that transcends the religious diversity. These policies seem to have been remarkably successful.

At the same time, the divergent Islamic communities have entered the modern world. If self-proclaimed righteousness once legitimized their isolation (and reputation for backwardness), now they have become emancipated in terms of modern education, leaving the *kolot* image behind, while opening themselves up to the life of the nation — rather than orienting themselves almost exclusively toward Mecca — and by developing an openness towards and tolerance for others.

The combination of government policy and emancipation is resulting in a rapid acceptance of Islam by people who would not willingly have identified with it some fifteen or twenty years ago, when the *santri-abangan* conflict was still in the open as an emotional issue. Especially among members of the new middle classes, acceptance of Islam is spreading rapidly now; first of all, because it no longer implies a political choice; then secondly, due to the emancipation of large segments of the Islamic community; and thirdly, as a result of the religious instruction their children receive in school.

Among these people, there is a trend away from Javanism, especially from its hierarchical orientation, from its rituals and esotericism, and the practice of mysticism. To them, the congregational religions (principally Islam, but also Catholicism and Protestantism) seem timely and attractive in providing an identity and a mental grasp on life. By contrast to the practice of mysticism as an individual endeavour that is time-consuming and self-centred, the congregational Middle-Eastern religions seem to offer a truth that is independent of the self, a book as revelation, and a theology that is reasoned and systematic, all of which is very similar to university learning, and eminently modern. In their contemporary lives, there is less room for mystical speculation and more interest in organized religion.

On the whole, a weakening of both the *kejawèn* tradition and Islamic isolationism may be expected, and thus a weakening of the opposed cultural identities. Both ways of life essentially belong to a past period, namely, the order of the sultanates with its dominant *kejawèn* tradition. That order was of a politically stratified (two) class society, in which commoners (and Muslims) were expected to accept the social hierarchy and their lowly place in it. This has now vanished. These days, education has emancipated the commoners, while giving rise to a mixed, educated middle class that is giving shape to a new

Javanese-Indonesian culture. Consequently, the *abangan-putihan* oppo-sition will no longer be the stress line along which conflicts are expressed, which is as it should be. After all, *abangan* and *putihan*, although contrasting, belong together, as in the *sang Merah Putih*, that is, the noble Red and White Indonesian flag.[1]

---

1 The root *abang* means red, *putih* white.

Pramoedya's tetralogy, 1988

After years of imprisonment on the island of Buru, Pramoedya was finally heard from again in 1980 with the publication of the first two volumes of his prison-conceived, great historical novel. In *This Earth of Mankind* (*Bumi Manusia*, 1980), and *Child of all Nations* (*Anak semua Bangsa*, 1980), the reader is introduced to the colonial environment around the turn of the twentieth century through the novel's main character, Minke.

When we first meet him, he is one of the very few Indonesian pupils at a Dutch secondary school in Surabaya. This important intellectual experience in an alien environment sets him free from the fetters of his high-born Javanese background. While absorbing advanced European ideas, he also discovers through bitter experience that he is a second class citizen in his own country. This stimulates him to excel in his mastery of Dutch, which he demonstrates by writing for a Dutch-language newspaper. Upon travelling into the interior of Java, he is confronted with the truth of colonial exploitation and the injustice that is perpetrated against the suffering peasant masses. Indignant about what he has seen and heard, he writes a series of articles for his newspaper that is not accepted by its editors. Slowly, it dawns upon him that the newspaper is owned by the almighty sugar interests, and that all the time he has been working for one of the tools of colonial exploitation. More importantly than that, he slowly begins to realize that he himself is culturally colonized, that he has become a little Dutchman, and that his freeing himself from 'feudal' Javanese thinking has only led him to fetter himself to another style of perception that is equally inadequate to understand what is going on in his country.

When he is goaded into becoming aware that he does not know his own people, and that he is even unable to write for a Malay-language newspaper, the foundation has been laid to develop the story of his further emancipation and the discovery of nationalist ideas. This theme is further elaborated in *Footsteps* (*Jejak Langkah*, 1985), when

Minke becomes fully aware of the colonial predicament at the time that the first modern native associations are organized. Actively propagating the emancipation of the colonized, his writings increasingly get him into trouble with the Dutch authorities, however sympathetic a few of them may be to the highly accomplished Javanese.

The last volume, *Glass House* (*Rumah Kaca*, 1988), tells about the efforts of the colonial government to control the population, its budding nationalism and political aspirations. These efforts make the country like a house of glass in which the authorities can monitor and manipulate any movement among the population. At the hand of an indigenous intellectual who works for the Dutch in suppressing the national wakening, we are further made aware of the perfidy of colonialism in its ability to subvert the minds of the people as one of its instruments of control.[1]

These four volumes span the period from 1890 to 1918, and are inspired by the biography of *R.M.* Tirto Adhi Suryo, an influential journalist who played an important role in the early period of national awakening. Their great interest lies in the clarity with which a new view of the human condition is developed. Even though the characters are naturally conditioned by their past experiences, they are no longer willless victims of times and circumstances but develop an awareness of their conditioning, and can thus develop hopes, future perspectives, and political ideas. While the structural argument of the exploitation of a people under the yoke of colonialism is clearly developed, the main emphasis is on the consequences of this for the subjugation of the spirit. These works expose the realities of society, and are a great step forward from the escapism and self-centredness that characterizes most Javanese-authored Indonesian fiction. In the words of *Kompas*'s critic Parakitri,

> With this novel Pramoedya breaks through the stagnation of recent Indonesian literature that was merely obsessed by technical innovation while wandering in confusion and psychological emptiness, isolating individuals from social issues, or that was merely reduced to the cheap entertainment of "pop" novels. This novel digs down to the roots: (Javanese) culture itself.

1 Pramoedya's quaternary novel has been translated by Max Lane and is published by Penguin (Australia) Ltd.

Pramoedya's historical novel makes one think of the comparable works of José Rizal in the Philippines at the end of the nineteenth century. With *The Social Cancer* (*Noli Me Tangere*, 1887), and *The Reign of Greed* (*El Filibusterismo*, 1891), he published a convincing indictment of the colonial situation at the end of the Spanish reign, aimed at awakening the readers to their oppression and mental subjugation. In this, Rizal was remarkably successful and he is now recognized as a hero because of it, the father of the national awakening. Pramoedya's penetrating historical-sociological analysis also has the potential for awakening people to their situation. So, after wavering for almost one year, during which the first two volumes were printed in unprecedented editions, the authorities concluded that the works were 'Marxist analysis' and should be banned.

Basic human rights, 1992

The 'diplomacy' of the Netherlands' Minister of Development Cooperation, Jan Pronk, caused the abrogation of all aid-related ties between that country and Indonesia (March 1992). It also stimulated the sagging spirit of nationalism and a renewed discussion about human rights and democracy. The two translated newspaper clippings that comprise this appendix, are self-explanatory while relating to a variety of issues that have been discussed in the previous chapters.

From *Kompas*, 30 March 1992

Indonesia should pay more attention to basic human rights

Indonesia's rejection of Dutch aid will bring back the idea of the nation, strengthen self-confidence, and prop up Indonesia as leader of the Non-Aligned Movement (NAM). On the other side, however, it is also a challenge to the country to pay more attention to the problems of basic human rights and democracy.

"Nowadays, basic human rights and democracy have become a kind of world 'religion'. This connects basic rights and democracy with aid, making one a precondition for the other. So, in order that foreign aid keeps streaming in, we have to satisfy that precondition," said the Head of the Muhammadiyah University Malang, A. Malik Fadjar to *Kompas* on Saturday 28-3.

According to him, the Inter-Governmental Group on Indonesia (IGGI) was born out of a pragmatic decision, remote from political and ideological considerations. After 25 years, negative effects were becoming more and more felt, such as a weakening of self-confidence as a free and sovereign nation. This became very clear when Pronk used the cover of IGGI to put pressure on the government.

On the one hand, this pressure is a means to check whether the government is going to be more careful in handling the problems of basic rights and democracy, but on the other hand a disregard for our feelings of nationalism. Pronk merely believed that, by using the issues of basic rights and democracy, he could directly rally the support of the majority of the Indonesian population. He did not foresee that the force of nationalism, such as is reflected in the saying *right or wrong, my country* is still stronger than the demand for basic rights and democracy.

It became clear, when the government rejected Dutch aid, that there were almost no groups that opposed this policy decision, including the NGOs that on other occasions had caused Pronk to change his opinion and to be less outspoken as a partner in the contest [with the Indonesian government].

Bung Karno

Further on, Malik remarked that the rejection of aid will bring back nationalism, bringing together [again] the people as a free and sovereign nation. Besides this, it will also give new legitimacy to the leadership of the New Order. Of course, this is good for internal political interests. In facing this period of take off, we need to prop up a new nationalism, he said, while acknowledging that nationalism has been fading among several circles of society. This is clear from the monopolizing of business opportunities, the hoarding of capital, and capital flight. "Without being inclined to prejudice, I see that nationalism is very weak precisely in the upper circles of society. Mark my words, it is those who own the money who can leave the country or buy themselves foreign citizenship."

"Khomeini was necessary to rebuild Iran's nationalism after the country was pawned by the Shah to America, and thus it had to confront the States. We can also see Iraq and Libya that, although they have to court danger, are going this way. In order to promote national reconciliation, the Philippines had to drive out the American military bases at Subic and Clark, with the risk of losing money. That does not matter, nationalism is dear indeed."

Seen within the dimension of foreign policy, the rejection of aid came at the right moment and will strengthen Indonesia's credibility as the leader of the NAM, so Malik said. It is clear that he sees President Soeharto's current actions as being like those of *Bung* Karno at the time of his political manoeuvring of *the new emerging forces*. In essence, these are the same, namely, to get rid of the dependence on developed countries, and to demonstrate dignity and prestige as a free and sovereign nation.

"Then *the new emerging forces* gave birth to the Bandung Declaration [1955], and it may now be hoped that the post-IGGI period will produce a new *credo* for the NAM countries. After the cold war era, the developing countries are in need of a new political arrangement," explained Malik.

For instance, the considerations behind Japanese aid are economical and political: such as, is there export potential for Japanese goods?; does it bring profit on investment?; while it also fits the idea of war reparations. Now [however, there also arise] many local groups, including members of parliament, who demand that aid be related with basic rights and democracy.

Moreover, Indonesia felt the influence of the universal commitment [to human rights] in the case of the tragedy in Dili on 12 November. The international world brought it sharply into focus and Indonesia was thrown into confusion. This did not happen when the massacres of Tanjungpriok and the Lampongs took place [although] the apparent number of victims was higher. At the time of the Tanjungpriok and Lampong cases, the problems of basic rights and democracy had not yet become the central and universal commitment of the world.

Handling these problems all at once can best be done as a preventive measure to restrain the possibility of negative effects from the rejection of Netherlands' aid. According to Malik, it is not impossible that the disappointed Dutch will exploit the problem of basic rights and democracy with the aim of inciting other donor countries to put pressure on Indonesia. These donor countries will certainly investigate whether the Dutch allegations are true. If it is clear that the Dutch assumptions are wrong, Indonesia can further strengthen its credibility in the eyes of the donor countries.

Budiawan, in *Bernas* of 8 April 1992

Harmony and basic human rights

When 'basic rights' are used as an instrument of intimidation that infringes upon self-respect, then it can be understood that it gives rise to a reasoned defence: "The problem of basic rights is our problem. According to the national Indonesian concept, basic rights touch upon the harmony between individual and societal interests. This concept is thus different from that of western countries that only emphasizes the basic rights of the individual".

This type of excuse clearly explains that basic rights are relative. This means that every state or nation has the right to formulate its own conception while deciding its own scale of values. In the Indonesian conception, basic rights are (supposedly) to be found in 'harmony'. And so harmony is stressed. This means that harmony is the value that is held in high esteem.

Indeed, harmony is a word that sounds mellifluous to the ears, but it is not necessarily always really beautiful before the eyes. This is because basically harmony is a concept about an 'ideal state' in which individuals will mutually adapt to each other in order to reach a goal about which all of them are agreed.

This implies the presupposition of the free will of the person to renounce (part) of his private interests in order to shape the common interest. In this way, the key word in the conception of harmony becomes 'togetherness', without causing anybody to feel that he has been victimized.

How beautiful if such a condition could (always) be created. How mature people would be under such circumstance. Yet the problem is whether such an ideal condition can really come about when interpersonal relationships are (always) coloured by dominance and subordination. In other words, is it possible to give rise to a state of pure harmony?

This question directly touches upon the claim that basic rights are relative. This claim has to be questioned, because making things relative can easily let them be side-tracked into vagueness. When the gist or essence of the idea of human rights has been blurred, then, however mellifluous the sound of the formula of the reason given, we are basically concerned with ideology. This means that framing the reason with geographical, historical, and cultural arguments that accentuate Indonesia's 'special qualities' is possibly no better than a mask to cover the denial of basic rights.

Apart from what we consider as 'their [Dutch] arrogance' — a way of putting it that reminds us of the Period of the National Crusade — we have to acknowledge that the idea of basic rights historically originates from western society. It is therefore logical that the framework or format of the idea of basic rights is not free from the distortions of social, historical, and cultural struggles in the West. Be that as it may, we must also recognize that the gist or essence of basic rights is universal and absolute, meaning that they are valid for every man because he is human, and not because of one or another sectoral or regional quality.

It appears that the gist of the idea of basic human rights lies in the awareness that society or the human community can only be worthy of respect when every human individual, without discrimination and without exception, is honoured in his totality. This wording, with stress on 'every human individual', is often misunderstood as a reflection of individualism (and liberalism) that we then reject because our cultural roots are in togetherness and the sharing of burdens.

There is one thing that we fail to see when we reject or doubt the idea of those basic rights that we find individualistic, namely, that there are basic duties behind the basic rights. To put it simply, what is meant by basic duties here is the principle of respecting the basic rights of others. We can demonstrate this as follows:

I am a smoker. It is my right to smoke or not to. When I want to smoke, but there is somebody else near me, then I should not just easily use my 'right' to smoke, because I have the 'duty' to respect the right of others to air that has not been polluted by burning cigarettes. Therefore, if I want to use my right to smoke, then, at the very least, I should ask permission from the other people near me.

This situation can change when we found our perspective about basic rights on the principle of harmony.

I am a smoker. Near me is somebody who I have never met before. I smoke, and then try to acquaint myself with that person by offering him a cigarette. He declines because he does not smoke. Moreover, he is allergic to smoke, which I realize because he covers his nose with a handkerchief. But apparently he is reluctant *(sungkan)* to say so. Perhaps he is worried that I'll feel annoyed when he broaches the subject. And that would mean that the friendly intention of getting acquainted would be destroyed.

Thus, in order to maintain harmony, that person is forfeiting his right to unpolluted air. This means that I profit from my right, but by way of forcefully depriving another person of his. Yet, 'harmony' is maintained, because we continue to be engrossed in our conversation as if there is no problem between the two of us.

The first situation demonstrated that 'openness' is a kind of a necessity. Because, by way of openness, an attempt can be made to bridge differences of interest, whereas in the second case openness appears as something that is costly, because its price is the possibility of destroying harmony.

Inherent in both the principles of honouring basic rights and of creating harmony is the possibility of causing infractions to basic rights. Yet the mechanisms to prevent these are very different. According to the first principle, possible infractions are always under the control of the other party, and such control is guaranteed by the rules relating to positive law. In the second case, however, the controlling mechanism depends on the 'sensitivity' or the 'ability to empathize' of each individual with the other individuals in his community.

Because the degree of sensitivity is different among people, while it can also easily be manipulated, this latter mechanism is really very person-centred and contains many weaknesses. Infractions of basic rights occur very easily under the principle of 'harmony', because it is often, though not necessarily, grounded in those 'who enjoy harmony most'.

The possibility of manipulating the creation of harmony is aggravated when interpersonal relationships are coloured by the pattern of domination and subordination. The partners in the lower position are most often vulnerable, so that, 'in the name of harmony', they will *tepo-seliro*,[1] not interfere in the actions of the dominant partner, who already truly infringes upon the basic rights of his underlings. In other words,

---

1 This euphemistic use of *tepa-slira* transforms its meaning into its reverse and is an interesting example of the pollution of language and ethics in modern Indonesia.

we may observe that the inferiors have no choice but to let their rights be sapped by those who are more powerful.

At the point that the limits of tolerance have been exceeded, they may perhaps take the courage to express themselves. And instead of demanding the sapped rights they have lost, they will merely appeal for justice. With this appeal, they demonstrate that they have really been conditioned not to be aware of what are their true basic rights. When this awareness of basic rights is further reduced, they should no longer be considered as *insiders* but as *outsiders within the community.* In other words, they have been alienated. And this is the costliest price of making an ideology of harmony. So, now we can see that the assumption that harmony by itself contains basic rights is an idea that puts these basic rights themselves at stake.

Of course, harmony is an ideal condition that we should strive after. But when this is used as an ideology with which to beat those who demand their basic rights, then the seeds of disharmony have really been sown. Because in a genuine harmony there is neither a partner who hits nor one who is hit, or who is forced to hit himself. Genuine harmony is grounded in a pure conscience. But, once again, this is an ideal condition.

We have indeed the right to defend ourselves when our self-respect is wounded. But when our self-defence becomes too much of an apology that seeks to protect itself behind so-called nativism, then it reflects the reluctance to grow up. And isn't adulthood, or the desire to grow up, also characterized by openness and the readiness to be introspective?

Bibliography

Akhmadi, Heri, *Breaking the chains of oppression of the Indonesian people: defense statement at his trial on charges of insulting the head of state.* Ithaca, N.Y.: Cornell University Southeast Asia Programme, CMIP, 1981.

Anderson, Benedict R., *Language and power: exploring political cultures in Indonesia.* Ithaca (etc): Cornell University Press, 1990.

Atkinson, Jane M., Shelly Errington (eds), *Power and difference. Gender in Island Southeast Asia.* Stanford, Cal.: Stanford University Press, 1990.

Bahan Penataran P4. Jakarta: BP-7 Pusat, 1990.

Booth, Anne, *Agricultural development in Indonesia.* Sydney (etc): Allen and Unwin, 1988.

Bourchier, David, *Dynamics of dissent in Indonesia: Sawito and the phantom coup.* Ithaca: Cornell Modern Indonesia Project, 1984.

Breman, Jan C., *The shattered image: construction and deconstruction of the village in colonial Asia.* Dordrecht: Foris, 1988.

Budiman, Arief (ed), *State and civil society in Indonesia.* Clayton, Vic.: Centre of Southeast Asian Studies, Monash University, 1990.

Dipojono, Bonokamsi, Mental health and current Javanese native medicine. *Djiwa: Madjalah Psikiatri* 2/3 (1969).

Dipojono, Bonokamsi, Javanese mystical groups. W.P. Lebra (ed), *Transcultural research in mental health.* Honolulu: University of Hawaii Press, 1972.

Drake, Christine, *National integration in Indonesia: patterns and policies.* Honolulu: University of Hawaii Press, 1989.

Echols, John M., Hassan Shadily, *Kamus Indonesia-Inggris*. Jakarta: Gramedia, 1989.

Emmerson, Donald K., *Indonesia's elite: political culture and cultural politics*. Ithaca (etc): Cornell University Press, 1976.

Errington, Shelly, Recasting sex, gender, and power: a theoretical and regional overview. Atkinson *op.cit.*:1-58.

Geertz, Clifford, *The religion of Java*. London: Collier-MacMillan, The Free Press of Glencoe, 1960.

Geertz, Hildred, *The Javanese family: a study of kinship and socialization*. London: Collier-MacMillan, The Free Press of Glencoe, 1961.

Guinness, Patrick, *Harmony and hierarchy in a Javanese kampung*. Singapore (etc): Oxford University Press, 1986.

Hatley, Barbara, *Kethoprak: performance and social meaning in a Javanese theatre form*. Sydney: Department of Indonesian and Malayan Studies, University of Sydney, 1985.

Hatley, Barbara, Theatrical imagery and gender ideology in Java. Atkinson *op.cit.*: 177-207.

Hüsken, Frans, *A village on Java*. Leiden: Royal Institute of Linguistics and Anthropology, 1996.

Keeler, Ward, *Javanese shadow plays, Javanese selves*. Princeton, N.J.: Princeton University Press, 1987.

Keeler, Ward, *Speaking of gender in Java*. Atkinson *op.cit.*:127-52.

Lombard, Denys, *Le carrefour javanais: essai d'histoire globale* I, II, III. Paris: École des hautes études en sciences sociales, 1990.

Macintyre, Andrew, *Business and politics in Indonesia*. North Sydney: Allen & Unwin, for Asian Studies Association of Australia, 1991.

Mulder, Niels, *Mysticism and everyday life in contemporary Java*. Singapore: Singapore University Press, 1980 (2nd rev. ed.).

Mulder, Niels, *Individual and society in Java. A cultural analysis*. Yogyakarta: Gadjah Mada University Press, 1989 (2nd rev. ed. 1992).

Mulder, Niels, *Inside Southeast Asia. Religion, everyday life, cultural change*. Amsterdam (etc): The Pepin Press, 1996 (2nd rev. ed.).

Nakamura, Mitsuo, *The crescent arises over the banyan tree; a study of the Muhammadiyah movement in a Central Javanese town*. Yogyakarta: Gadjah Mada University Press, 1983.

Paget, Roger K. (ed), *Indonesia accuses: Soekarno's defence oration in the political trial of 1930*. Kuala Lumpur (etc): Oxford University Press, 1975.

PMP I, II, III. Departemen Pendidikan dan Kebudayaan, *Pendidikan Moral Pancasila*, SMP kelas 1, 2, 3. Jakarta: Balai Pustaka, 1990.

Reid, Anthony, *Southeast Asia in the age of commerce, 1450-1680*. New Haven (etc): Yale University Press, 1988.

Ricklefs, Merle C., *A history of modern Indonesia, c. 1300 to the present*. London: The Macmillan Press, 1981.

Sairin, Sjafri, *Javanese trah: kin-based social organization*. Yogyakarta: Gadjah Mada University Press, 1982.

Scott, James C., *The moral economy of the peasant: rebellion and subsistence in Southeast Asia*. New Haven (etc): Yale University Press, 1976.

Siegel, James T., *Solo in the New Order; language and hierarchy in an Indonesian city*. Princeton: Princeton University Press, 1986.

Soeharto, Ramadhan K.H., G. Dwipayana, *Soeharto: sebuah autobiografi*. Jakarta: P.T. Citra Lamtoro Gung Persada, 1989.

Sularto, St. (ed), *Menuju masyarakat baru Indonesia*. Jakarta: Kompas/ Gramedia, 1990.

Sullivan, John, *Local government and community in Java. An urban case study*. Melbourne: Oxford University Press, 1992.

Suryakusuma, Julia I., The state and sexuality in the Indonesian New Order. *Paper*. Conference on Gender Perspectives in Indonesia. Seattle, University of Washington, 1991.

Sutherland, Heather, *The making of a bureaucratic elite: the colonial transformation of the Javanese priyayi*. Singapore: Heinemann Educational Books, 1979.

Index of names

Subject index

Glossary of terms of address

Bapak	father, patron, thus Mr., Sir
Bu	abbreviated form of *Ibu*
Bung	brother, thus also fellow
H.	*haji*
Ibu	mother, matron, thus Mrs., Lady, Miss
K.H.	*kiai haji*
Ki	title of respect for learned spiritual leaders
Kiai	title for venerated Islamic scholars/teachers
Mas	term of address among friends/aquaintances; in public usage it indicates a person of rank
Pak	abbreviated form of *Bapak*
R.	abbreviation of *Radèn*
Radèn	great-great grandson of sultan/king; lowest rank of nobility
Radèn Mas	great grandson of sultan/king
R.M.	abbreviation of *Radèn Mas*
Sang	honorific epithet
Sri	honorific (royal) title